Best Outdoor Adventures
Colorado Front Range

Help Us Keep This Guide Up to Date

Every effort has been made by the author and editors to make this guide as accurate and useful as possible. However, many things can change after a guide is published—trails are rerouted, regulations change, techniques evolve, facilities come under new management, etc.

We appreciate hearing from you concerning your experiences with this guide and how you feel it could be improved and kept up to date. While we may not be able to respond to all comments and suggestions, we'll take them to heart and we'll also make certain to share them with the author. Please send your comments and suggestions to the following address:

Globe Pequot Press
Reader Response/Editorial Department
246 Goose Lane, Suite 200
Guilford, CT 06437

Thanks for your input, and happy trails!

Best Outdoor Adventures
COLORADO
FRONT RANGE

A Guide to the Region's Greatest Hiking,
Climbing, Cycling, and Paddling

CHRIS MEEHAN

GUILFORD, CONNECTICUT

FALCONGUIDES®

An imprint of The Rowman & Littlefield Publishing Group, Inc.
4501 Forbes Blvd., Ste. 200
Lanham, MD 20706
www.rowman.com
Falcon and FalconGuides are registered trademarks and Make Adventure Your Story is a trademark of The Rowman & Littlefield Publishing Group, Inc.

Distributed by NATIONAL BOOK NETWORK

Photos by Chris Meehan
Maps by Melissa Baker

British Library Cataloguing in Publication Information available

Library of Congress Control Number: 2020953010

ISBN 978-1-4930-4542-6 (paper : alk. paper)
ISBN 978-1-4930-4543-3 (electronic)

∞™ The paper used in this publication meets the minimum requirements of American National Standard for Information Sciences—Permanence of Paper for Printed Library Materials, ANSI/NISO Z39.48-1992.

Contents

Overview

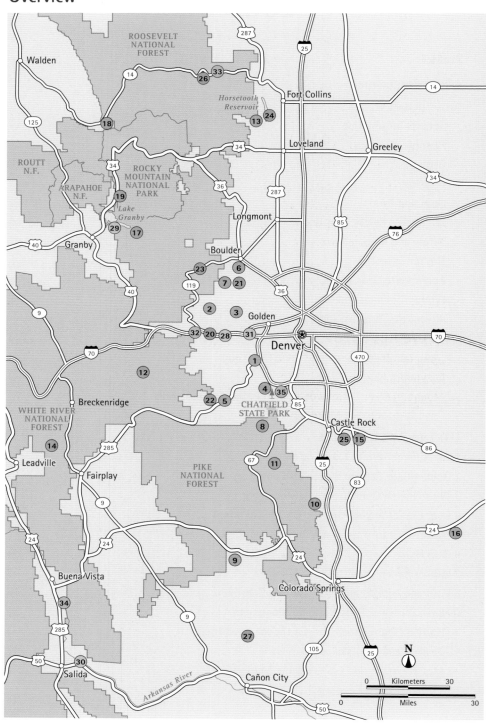

Climbing Adventures. 117

Cycling Adventures 165

Paddling Adventures. 190

Preface

Colorado is a mecca for adventure, loved by residents and drawing well over 80 million visitors every year, many for recreation. It's known for its rugged mountains, pristine rivers, fossil discoveries, eons of native history, and Wild West and homesteading past. The Front Range spans more than 120 miles, from Fort Collins and Boulder to the north to Denver and south to Colorado Springs. The Dakota Hogback, which runs from New Mexico to Wyoming just west of most of these cities, is essentially a long-running gateway to the Rockies, behind which most of the adventures in this book are found. A few are located east of this area but still showcase Colorado's rich geologic and natural and human history and wonders. We wanted to make it easy to find the type of adventure you're looking for, so the book is organized by adventure type—hiking, climbing, bicycling, and paddling. It is also organized by proximity to Denver, which is home to the state's largest population base and transportation corridors. Adventures are evaluated for difficulty. While some are extreme, others are family friendly, which is noted. These adventures represent the best of the best—things you won't find anywhere else—and showcase some of Colorado's lesser known natural wonders.

Acknowledgments

Exploring Colorado in an increasing variety of ways is one of the great pleasures of my life. Learning its history—natural and human—is fascinating. Going that extra mile into the woods, reaching the top of the peak, finding the eddy after a powerful chain of rapids or reaching the anchor on the climbing route, finding myself and my companions surrounded by this majestic place, these are the things that keep my blood pumping, my heart happy, and my mind looking for the next adventure.

As always, there are too many people, organizations, and things to thank—from the land itself and time, which has formed this land as we all get to experience it today; to the state and its people, which are actively supporting outdoor recreation in all its forms; and to the organizations and people that are actively protecting wildlife and creating and developing sustainable trails and climbing routes. And of course to my family and cadre of adventure buddies.

In particular I want to thank my folks, Hugh and Martha, my brother, Colin, and his wife, Analiese (you will be missed), all of whom I dragged out on some awesome adventures around Salida. Thanks, too, for dealing with me for all these years.

I've explored Colorado with so many wonderful friends over the years too. From John Lunsford, who I've known since we were 4 years old, to newer buddies like Kern Heron. There's also a core of buddies I've gone on adventures with regularly, including Rebecca Slyder, Aron Roberts, Clay Perry, Chris Seaver, Becca Frager, and Lee Mauney—I came across some of your research when I was researching this book. There are a ton more than this of course, but these people come first and foremost to mind. Thanks to the incidental adventure buddies, all the people you share a unique space with for a moment in time, catching an eagle flying overhead or being buzzed by a hummingbird—those are special moments.

Thanks to Kevin Capps, owner of Denver Mountain Guiding; Sarah Hammer and her husband, Mark, who own The Adventure Company; and Alan Baldo, owner of Liquid Descent. Each of them offered advice for this book.

Of course I need to thank FalconGuides and my editors, Jess d'Arbonne—we'll climb more and get out for other adventures soon!—and Dave Legere. Thanks for giving me additional time with this project. I'd also like to thank Joe Novosad, who helped me realize there really wasn't a book like this for Colorado.

Special thanks to all the amazing volunteers who selflessly give time for search-and-rescue operations and for those who help build and maintain trails and climbing places, the advocates pushing to preserve wild places and public lands. These people give thousands of hours of their time to make all of this possible, reducing the monies that state and federal government would otherwise have to invest for maintenance. Please consider supporting them—there's a list at the end of the book. Thanks to the sportspeople—hunters, anglers, and others who help support wildlands through fees, licenses, and tags.

Skeet Glatterer and Dale Atkins contributed safety information for *Climbing Colorado's Fourteeners*, and I'm reusing some of that here. Their input was invaluable.

Thanks to the National Park Service and the Bureau of Land Management for allowing access to the scores of roads and trails that wend deep into the heart of the mountains. Colorado Parks & Wildlife, county parks, and open space divisions are doing an incredible job creating local trails and adventure activities, and they deserve thanks as well.

Finally, special thanks to the pioneers we'll never meet, from Native Americans who trapped eagles on the top of fourteeners and used local earth for their pottery. And thanks to the homesteaders, early miners, and pioneering climbers of the late 1800s and early 1900s—men and women alike.

Introduction

"Go West, young man, go West!" These are words from Horace Greeley—namesake of Greeley, Colorado—words that all on Colorado's Front Range take to heart as they look west to the oft-snowcapped, granite peaks of the Rockies. It's home to innumerable adventures, from world-class skiing and snowboarding, to whitewater, to trails that touch the sky, to rock and ice-climbing routes.

Elk, moose, pika, eagle, hawks, hummingbird ptarmigan, and hundreds of other animals call the mountains home. Wildflowers abound at all elevations, from the elephanthead, lupine, and columbine that crowd streambeds to alpine forget-me-not, saxifrage, and sandwort that find purchase in the unlikeliest of alpine crags over 14,000 feet high.

The geology is a complex mix of rocks thrown up in ancient uprisings, melted and molded by extreme pressures, and then carved away by water and wind. Rocks 1.2 billion years old are sometimes found next to rocks that are just 25 million years old. Mountain valleys, cirques, and peaks were carved as recently as 1 million years ago; mountain streams, creeks, and rivers continue carving canyons today.

All this resulted in a wild, untamed playground for adventure-seekers, and that adventure starts in the backyard of the Front Range's Dakota Hogback. Within a 30-minute drive of Front Range metropolises, you can encounter myriad adventures, from family-friendly nature trips and fossil parks to extreme rock climbing, mountain biking, and whitewater—it's magical. This book will help readers find the best of each of these adventures based on my personal experience and from the perspective of experienced outdoors adventurers, athletes, and leading guides.

In writing this book, I often found myself overwhelmed by the awesomeness of Colorado. Sounds silly, right? The absolute hardest thing was figuring out what *not* to include in this book. I'm not complaining; it's an embarrassment of riches worthy of a lifetime of exploration.

There are easily more than 2,000 trails in the Front Range encompassing 6,000 miles, well over 12,000 named climbing routes, hundreds of miles of whitewater, and even more flatwater—all within 3 hours of Colorado's Front Range. I haven't done all of that yet.

In choosing adventures for this book, I tried to select ones that uniquely showcase aspects of these natural riches—places that show unique geological features, like the Paint Mines and fossil beds; places that challenge the toughest of climbers, boaters, and bikers. But I also made a conscious decision not to include some of Colorado's most famous attractions, like Rocky Mountain National Park. Don't get me wrong, I love it up there! But there's so much more of the state to see.

Colorado's residents are active outdoors people, and undoubtedly this guidebook will not include some of their favorite adventures or places. I'll face criticism for what I did and did not include, and that's OK; I welcome it. Perhaps I'll include that one place you found that you love to share in a later edition of this book; I'd love to hear about it. I'm also sensitive to the idea that some places are sacred to those who love them, and I would never out someone's secret fishing hole, so to speak. There are places I love that I haven't included in this book for that very reason. To get me to share them with you, I guess you'd just have to find me in the wild or shoot me an e-mail. There are plenty of amazing adventures I didn't include, such as hiking and snowshoeing St. Mary's Glacier or climbing at the Garden of the Gods or North Table Mountain. Great Sand Dunes National was a little too far away to justify as a day trip, but check it out!

Hopefully, for Coloradans there are adventures in this book they've never experienced and it will encourage them to seek them out. It offers close-in hikes and climbs as well as adventures a little farther from home, but still within a day's reach. For visitors, recreational or otherwise, this book offers a smattering of what Colorado has to offer and truly showcases the best of Front Range adventures.

Some of the areas in the book overlap, like climbing and rafting in Clear Creek Canyon or hiking and climbing in Staunton State Park; that's partly by design. These playgrounds offer multiple types of adventures, and one of the fun things friends and I did in envisioning this book was concocting how we'd undertake multi-adventure days. Our record is currently three, but I can easily see ways to do four or more if you put your mind to it.

Now, go. Have fun; take friends and family. Enjoy the cerulean skies and the trail crunching underfoot, the waves walloping the boat, the precarious precipice of a vertical rock wall with fingers and toes clinging. Go forth and adventure!

Adventure is what you set out for. Adventure is what you get. But the two are often not the same. After all, it wouldn't be much of an adventure if they were!

General Information

For general information on Colorado, visit the official website of Colorado travel: colorado.com. The site contains a wealth of vacation information.

Visitors to the state can find vacation information, free state maps and brochures, and clean restrooms at Colorado's welcome centers, which are located near most of the major highways as they enter the state. For more information, visit colorado.com/WelcomeCenters.aspx.

Area Codes

Colorado has four area codes: The Denver/Boulder metro area (extending out to Longmont, Idaho Springs, and Castle Rock) uses 303 and 720. The 719 area code serves the greater south-central and southeastern part of the state, including Colorado Springs, Pueblo, Buena Vista, Leadville, Alamosa, and Del Norte. The 970 area code covers the northern Front Range, Eastern Plains, and West Slope, extending east from Craig to Sterling and south from Craig to Durango and Cortez.

Wildland and Park Contacts

The majority of the adventures in this book are on public lands. You can learn more about these spaces at the following sites:

Bureau of Land Management: blm.gov/colorado

Colorado Parks & Wildlife: cpw.state.co.us

National Park Service: nps.gov/state/co/index.htm

USDA Forest Service—Rocky Mountain Region: fs.usda.gov/r2/

US Fish & Wildlife Service—Mountain-Prairie Region: fws.gov/mountain -prairie/co.html

Getting Around

If you're hiking, climbing, biking, or paddling you're going to have to get there. If you're taking a tour or a guided hike, climb, or whitewater adventure, your transportation needs will likely be limited to getting to a parking lot. If you're going out on your own, you'll need reliable transportation. It's really hard to hail a taxi

20 miles from nowhere with no cell reception. All of the start points for these adventures can be accessed by car, but some are on dirt roads.

Many Colorado backcountry roads are closed in winter. Respect these closures. Getting stuck on a high alpine road in temperatures below freezing is not fun, and whoever comes to get you out will not be happy about it. Some of Colorado's paved roads also are closed in winter. To learn more about what roads are closed, check the Colorado Department of Transportation (CDOT) website (cotrip.org). Or call them at (877) 315-7623; 511 on your cell phone (Colorado only).

History

Colorado's popular—and true—history is full of cowboys and miners and Native Americans. But the land that is Colorado today saw its first humans long before modern Native Americans. Relics at the Lindenmeier Site near Fort Collins in northern Colorado place members of the Clovis culture in Colorado as early as 11,000 years ago. The cliff dwellings in Mesa Verde National Park were built sometime in the 1190s. It's possible that people of the Clovis culture were the first to climb some of Colorado's fourteeners, and some of these peaks are still regarded as sacred places by Native Americans.

The first Europeans to reach Colorado were Spaniards who came via the southeast, naming places like Culebra Peak and Pueblo—heck, "Colorado" is a Spanish word for red! After the Spaniards came trappers and traders, like those who overwintered in Poudre Canyon. The first known European-American to come to Colorado was James Pursley. He wintered with the Ute Nation near South Park in 1805 and found gold flakes in a stream there.

In 1806 President Thomas Jefferson sent Lt. Zebulon Montgomery Pike to survey what is now the southwestern United States, including southern Colorado. They named a fourteener for him. You might have heard of it.

The gold rush of 1859 brought settlers hoping to find their fortune in the plains and on the mountains. These settlers and prospectors panned the rivers and streams and were the first to ascend some of Colorado's fifty-three fourteeners; they definitely named some of these mountains, such as Handies Peak.

Following the Civil War the federal government began a more earnest effort to understand Colorado and the West. Two federal surveys in the 1870s really explored Colorado's high country: the Hayden Survey, led by Dr. Ferdinand

Vandeveer Hayden, and the survey led by Lt. George Montague Wheeler. They made many of the first known ascents of fourteeners and explored deeply into the mountains.

Geology

Some of the rock that makes up Colorado's fourteeners today is more than 1 billion years old; these Ancestral Rockies are long gone, eroded to rubble. Rocks in Kansas trace back to those extinct monoliths, borne on the backs of glaciers.

Today's Rockies are a complex mix of time. Longs Peak, the northernmost fourteener in the state and on the Front Range, is composed of 1.4-billion-year-old silver plume granite. Pikes Peak, the southernmost Front Range fourteener, is also composed of 1.2-billion-year-old granite but was exposed just 50 million years ago during the Laramide orogeny, an intense period of mountain-building in the state. The Eocene epoch, about 34 million years ago, created the rocky tombs of ancient plants and animals found at Florissant Fossil Beds National Monument; the conglomerate rock at Castlewood Canyon was also formed around this time.

The mountains were and are being carved by erosion—all those scree fields are clear evidence of that. Glaciers—most now melted—also played a huge part in sculpting the bowls, basins, and moraines of Colorado's Front Range.

The same conditions that created the Rockies in Colorado also deposited countless minerals and ores there, which Native Americans have used in their jewelry for centuries.

Word of gold in 1859 brought people from far and wide to Colorado's vast high country. The mountains have been exploited for minerals ever since. Uranium to gypsum, gold to copper to lead—it's all in the Rockies. This section could go on for quite some time but will end before getting into a discussion of Precambrian deposits and the Laramide orogeny. There are other books about that!

Weather

Regardless of difficulty, one of the biggest factors to consider in undertaking any of the adventures in this book is weather.

Although Colorado is known for experiencing 300 sunny days a year, the weather is way more complicated. There's a well-known adage in Colorado: "If you don't like the weather, wait 10 minutes." At altitude and above tree line, it's more of an inverse. If the weather looks bad, it's probably going to get worse. A blue sky can swarm with clouds in mere minutes. In lower elevations you're not quite as exposed to the elements, but lightning and winds—even tornados—can suddenly arise.

It's largely because the Rockies are the first major breaker that clouds encounter between the West Coast and the Midwest. Their water-heavy bellies scrape against the peaks and disgorge rain, sleet, snow, thunder and lightning, wind—sometimes all at once. The rain and sleet can turn solid dirt and rock into slick surfaces in minutes. Snow can turn into whiteout conditions at higher elevations. These extreme conditions are rare along the Front Range, which usually experiences fantastic, mild temperatures in summer and winter, but adverse weather is more likely as seasons change.

Thunder and lightning are nerve-wracking and—at best—can impair decision making as you scramble to get out of the most dangerous situations, whether roped into a rock face, floating on a river, or hiking high above tree line. At worst they're potentially deadly.

In June 2015 fifteen people and a dog were struck by a lightning bolt on Mount Bierstadt. The people were lucky; all survived. The dog did not. And in July 2015 a newlywed couple was struck by lightning on Mount Yale. It took other climbers 45 minutes to reach a location where they could get cell reception to call 911. It took more than 2 hours for rescuers to reach the couple. (In a more remote area, everything could have taken a lot longer!) The 31-year-old bride died.

The worst storms generally roll into Colorado during the afternoon in late spring and summer, striking the high mountains first then heading east toward the plains. But lightning can happen at any time up there—even during sleet and snow. To learn more about how to deal with lightning, check out the "Safety" section, where search-and-rescue experts offer advice.

Most of the time Colorado's weather is spectacular, and visibility can stretch for 100 miles or more on sunny days. Afternoon storms offer a welcome respite on hot summer days and roll out quickly—and Colorado has plentiful rainbows.

As this book deals with adventures ranging in elevation from 6,000 feet to over 14,000 feet, it's important to think about the impact of elevation on temperature. For every 1,000 feet of elevation gain, the temperature drops about 4°. On a sunny summer day when it's 90° in Denver, it could still be in the 50s on top of a fourteener. So even in the heat of summer, always bring rain/wind wear and an insulating layer.

Despite the cooler temperatures, you're more at risk of sunburn at altitude. The sun's rays are 26 percent stronger at 14,400 feet than at Denver's famous 5,280 feet. Sun protection is a must. Places you might not think about protecting as much need attention too. That means the underside of your forearms, under your chin, your nostrils, and your earlobes. Sunlight reflecting off bright rocks, snow, and water can burn the inside of your nose. It's quite uncomfortable!

This guide primarily covers spring, summer, and fall adventures—of course wintertime whitewater adventures in Colorado are highly unlikely. Winters in Colorado close alpine roads. It's awesome to rock climb outdoors in January and February, but that isn't likely in most of Colorado—Shelf Road is a glorious exception!

Still, more people are venturing into the mountains in winter now than ever before to snowshoe, ski, or snowboard, and winter hikes can be just as fun as summer adventures. Just be prepared for the colder weather.

If venturing out in winter, remember that snow and ice pose unique dangers, such as slips and falls as well as avalanches and moats close to rocks and trees. Winter adventures also require more gear, and more weight. Road closures mean longer treks into the backcountry, and you have to remember that winter days are shorter. All together that means it takes more time and more effort to take on these adventures in the winter months. Times and mileages given for the adventures in this guide are for spring through fall, assuming normal conditions.

Flora and Fauna

Colorado's biodiversity is incredible. In Castlewood Canyon alone there are four separate microclimates—grasslands, montane forests, Fontaine scrublands, and riparian habitats—even though the changes in elevation only range a little over 100 feet. While each of these microclimates has different vegetation habitats, the more than 200 birds in the area and other animals often roam freely between the different habitats.

Similarly, when climbing a mountain, whether small or over 14,000 feet, you'll pass through multiple climate zones, from montane to alpine. You're likely to travel through forests of ponderosa pine and Douglas fir before reaching lodge-pole pine and aspen and then spruce, fir, and limber and bristlecone pine—all this interspersed with mountain meadows, willow marshes and wetlands, and alpine lakes and streams. Finally you'll reach the alpine tundra, where stubby plants like club moss and moss campion are merely inches tall but decades old. These plants are weather hardy but not boot hardy, so please stay on-trail to minimize impact. Walking on rocks instead of plants is even better!

Wide swaths of evergreen forests have been decimated in the past twenty years, owing largely to drought and climate change. Pine and spruce beetles are at the heart of this epidemic and have killed more trees than forest fires. While pine and spruce are healthy in much of the state, you will come across some of these de-vegetated lands. Thus far, land managers haven't been able to remedy the problem; shorter, warmer winters have exacerbated the problem by allowing the beetles to reproduce at record rates.

Massive avalanches in 2019's huge snow season also wiped out large swaths of trees. Similarly forest fires have had their impact, as noted in the Colorado Trail segment adventure.In 2020 Colorado also saw an unprecedented fire season. Three forest fires surpassed the record for the state's largest wildfire, which had occurred in 2002. The largest, the Cameron Peak Fire, was nearly twice as large as the previous record holder.

Colorado also is famous for its quaking aspens. Aspen groves are some of the largest living organisms on earth and reproduce chiefly by root sprouts—every tree in an aspen grove is likely a clone. They're usually found in moist, protected areas; they spread aggressively and live at elevations of up to 12,000 feet. However, they're more commonly found at somewhat lower elevations. Trunks of aspens are often scarred by elk, bear, and other animals, which also eat aspen bark and shoots in winter.

Speaking of elk, these lumbering quadrupeds are found in alpine meadows throughout Colorado. White River National Forest has the largest elk herd in the world, numbering nearly 40,000 by some estimates, so it should be no surprise that the Maroon Bells and other mountains in the forest are called the Elk Range.

Other mountain wildlife includes moose, found in places like Colorado State Forest, mule deer, black bears (there are currently no known grizzlies in Colorado), and mountain lions.

Mountain lions are elusive and much more likely to spot you than you are to spot them. If you notice an area with a lot of bones, particularly bones with some signs of recent predation, you may be near a mountain lion. Toward the end of 2019 it was confirmed that some wolves have been spotted in Colorado as well. However, neither predator is likely to attack humans, especially if they're in a group.

Mountain goats and bighorn sheep graze at high elevations and are likely to be the biggest mammal you'll see high up on a fourteener. The animals you're most likely to see—or hear—at higher elevations are marmots and pikas. The best way to spot them is by letting your ears guide your eyes. Listen; then look.

Marmots, which look like a mix between beavers and groundhogs, are larger and easier to see. They like to sun on rocks. Pikas blend in with the rocks and often scamper underfoot on more-remote trails.

Please don't feed the wildlife—no matter how cute! Don't leave your stuff around. If camping, hang your food and anything else with an odor—toothpaste, lotion, etc.—in bear bags at least 10 feet off the ground and preferably suspended between two trees. Certain parts of Colorado now require the use of bear canisters for overnight stays.

It's not just bears you have to worry about. Chipmunks, squirrels, and mice can gnaw through that nice new $400 tent to get at your tasty treats. Marmots love rubber, and many people who leave their trekking poles behind to climb a rocky summit come back to find the rubber chewed off their grips. Don't throw food away. Pack out what you don't consume. The more handouts and trash animals get from humans, the more likely they are to chew through tents in search of food, or eat wrappers or other trash and get sick.

Colorado is a birder's paradise. Crows, magpies, blue Steller's jays with their black crowns, and pesky Clark's nutcrackers and gray jays (nicknamed "camp robbers") are found throughout Colorado. Hummingbirds whir near flowers and alpine water sources. Ptarmigans are masters of disguise on snow or rock and gravel and often surprise unsuspecting hikers and snowshoers. Eagles were caught and trained by Native Americans on Longs Peak, and today you'll occasionally see birds of prey at the state's highest altitudes.

Alpine lakes and creeks are amazing spots for cutthroat trout. Anglers can also find stocked sport fish such as rainbow and brown trout in much of the state.

Wilderness Restrictions and Regulations

Colorado is a wild place! The state has two national grasslands, eight national wildlife refuges, twelve national forests, forty-three wilderness areas (not counting wilderness study areas), and a growing number of national parks and monuments; Browns Canyon National Monument was established in 2015. The state manages an additional forty-two parks and 346 state wildlife areas. Counties manage even more. The majority of activities in this book are on public lands; however, occasionally they abut private lands, as on rivers and creeks or trails that track through private lands.

Regardless of land ownership, please respect laws, regulations, and requirements. That means practice Leave No Trace ethics. Don't camp too close to water sources, pack your trash out, don't take alpine souvenirs, and make campfires only where allowed. Leash your dogs as required. While most places have information about local requirements and closures—some rock climbing areas are off-limits from February to July to allow raptors to breed, for instance—check out the landowner or manager listed for each adventure to learn about local requirements and regulations before heading out. It's up to us to protect these lands.

Sign trail registers and, if offered, use wilderness tags. These could be required in the future, and fines could be assessed for not using them. Both help land managers understand how many people are accessing Colorado's mountains and backcountry and help government entities allocate funds. In the event of a lost adventurer, they also help search-and-rescue teams get a better idea of where you're at.

Leave No Trace and Adventure Etiquette

Leave No Trace ethics help protect wild places. These principles ask users of the backcountry to leave things as they've found them, to not scar the land with fires or trash, to travel on known or established trails, and to camp at least 200 feet from streams, lakes, and trails. Learn more about Leave No Trace ethics at LNT.org.

In addition, I like to carry a plastic bag with me on the trail. If you find wrappers or waste on the trail, please pick them up and carry them out. If hiking with children, you can gamify it a bit by calling the trash "trail treasures"; you can pick up dirtier items yourself.

Peak Celebrations and Respecting Wilderness

You just accomplished something awesome and now want to celebrate. Do it; you've earned it! Celebrations come in many forms. Show the world; do it with style and your own unique flair. One group did keg stands on top of Mount Princeton. Some people do headstands, yoga poses, or bring a stuffed animal or some other personal item with them.

Probably the most common celebration selfie for climbing a fourteener, for instance, is a photograph that includes a sheet of paper with the elevation and peak name written on it—kind of boring; you can do better! There's also a problem with those signs: A lot of people leave them up there. A fourteener is not a trash can. You pack it up, you pack it out. With minimal effort you can make sure the peak is in as good or better shape for everyone who comes after you. Scores of responsible, albeit bitter, climbers carry out trail trash all the time, including those thin, lightweight, compaction-friendly signs. Woodsy Owl never made it to 14,000 feet, but his message holds true: "Give a hoot, don't pollute!"

When celebrating any wilderness achievement, don't spend the whole time bragging about it on your cell phone. If you must call someone, keep it short and as quiet as possible. No one else wants to hear you yapping on the phone in the wilderness.

Along the same lines, leave those Bluetooth speakers at home or in your vehicle. "Flight of the Valkyries" is an amazing piece of music; it's inspiring, it's victorious, but no one wants to hear it or the latest Taylor Swift song blasting away when they're hiking. When you play music in the mountains, you're not hearing birdsong or marmot and pika chirps—and you lessen your and everyone else's chance of seeing wildlife.

Please be respectful of wildlife; you're a visitor in their home. And be respectful of nature's other guests—your fellow adventurers.

Hiking with Dogs

Some people take their dogs on adventures. They're welcome on almost all of the hiking and climbing adventures—but please keep them on a leash. Dogs are not allowed on a few of these adventures, such as the Florissant Fossil Beds. That information is offered in the at-a-glance section at the beginning of each chapter under "Canine compatibility." If you're climbing a crag, please keep your pet tied up while you're climbing. I wouldn't recommend bringing a dog on any whitewater adventure.

Dogs can make almost every trek in this book. I'd be wary of taking them on the Sawtooth, though. Your pup may not be able to climb across an exposed ridge or rock face, and trying to carry your pal over these hazards could put both of you in danger. Please check with the landowner or manager to learn more about specific dog regulations.

Safety and Preparedness

Being safe at altitude is much different than normal hiking. FalconGuides reached out to search-and-rescue experts for their advice in the hopes of helping reduce accidents, and here's what they had to say. These tips are primarily geared toward climbing mountains but are applicable to rock climbing and whitewater adventures as well.

People get into trouble because they underestimate weather, terrain, and/or their ability to navigate and overestimate their ability to get out of trouble when trouble happens.

Prepare

- Do all the research you can to ensure safe travel in the mountains.
- Try to climb with people who have more experience than you, and learn from them.
- Understand your skill and risk levels, and choose routes you're comfortable with climbing.
- Map out travel plans ahead of time, and familiarize yourself with your planned route.
- Start early. Be reasonable and conservative in your estimate of how much time you need to complete a climb.
- If traveling with a group, which is always preferable, stay together, have a leader, be aware of peer pressure, and know when to turn back.

Don't underestimate the adventure. Keep in mind that climbing means vertical gain. High altitudes with thinner air means reduced exercise capacity. Give yourself time to acclimate to altitude. Be aware of the symptoms of acute mountain sickness (altitude sickness) at altitudes as low as 9,000 feet. Training will help you have enough physical reserve to handle emergency issues like weather, medical problems, and route finding.

Share

Always let someone responsible know your itinerary. This could be family member or a responsible friend. Other people who hike or climb are more likely to be accountable because they know what's at stake. Make a list explaining:

- Where you are going and how you're getting there.
- Vehicle description and license plate number.
- What you plan to climb and which route you're taking, as well as any alternative trips or side trips.
- The colors of your jacket, pack, helmet, and, if camping, tent.
- Your planned return time. This includes a reasonable estimate of return to the trailhead and when help should be contacted. Remember that in the backcountry and even in small towns, cell reception might be limited or unavailable. It may take longer than expected to let your contacts know you're OK if you can't ring them from the trailhead itself.
- Emergency contact information. Each adventure lists the number for local land managers, but sheriffs' offices will contact search and rescue when needed.
- Appropriate skills. Take a mountaineering course to get a good foundation for climbing difficult fourteeners. Take a class in rock climbing to familiarize yourself with proper rope and safety techniques or a class in whitewater navigation to learn important skills like escaping a kayak and barrel rolling. Then start adventuring with those who have more experience and learn from them.
- Appropriate gear. Acquiring all the gear you will eventually need or want can be a long process. Be sure to have at least the Ten Essentials (see page xxvii).

Check the Weather and Adjust Plans as Necessary

In the days before you plan to head out, check the weather where you plan to adventure and make any necessary changes to your trip—including rescheduling. Also check the weather the day or morning you leave. A great site for general forecasts is weather.gov.

Lightning

During summer, lightning is a main hazard in Colorado, particularly atop mountains above tree level. It's also dangerous on the water and while climbing, as many rock faces in Colorado have high concentrations of iron and other metal.

Lightning and thunderstorms are most common in the late morning and through the afternoon, but lightning can strike any time of day or night.

Sage and oft-repeated advice is: Climb early, and turn back if a thunderstorm is brewing. To minimize risk of being caught in a storm, study weather forecasts where you plan to adventure before setting out. Learning to read the clouds for signs of danger is also important.

Turning back early is the biggest key to avoid being in the wrong place at the wrong time, but turning back or descending from high points as a storm is looming does not guarantee safety. Lightning can strike anywhere, even objects—like you—that are much shorter than close-by objects such as trees, ridges, even summits.

A lightning strike can start miles away. It's not seeking a target from the start but is attracted to an object within the last 50 to 150 feet of its range. This is why a dog can be struck while walking next to a human.

Most climbers are concerned about a direct lightning strike, but most injuries and deaths are due to ground currents and side flashes, not direct strikes. That's because lightning can hit a tree or boulder and then spread along the ground.

To minimize the risk of lightning strikes, keep at least 6 miles and preferably at least 8 miles from a storm. The "Flash-to-Bang" method of estimating the distance of lighting is the best way to get an idea of how far away lightning is. A delay of 5 seconds between a lightning flash and the sound of thunder is equal to about 1 mile. A delay of 40 seconds means lightning is about 8 miles away. At best, thunder can be heard about 10 miles away, but even a slight breeze can muffle the sound.

Hikers and climbers move much slower than thunderstorms. Even a slow-moving thunderstorm can travel 8 miles in the time it takes a hiker to cover 1 mile. Fast-moving storms can cross that distance in much less time. So if a thunderhead is moving in your direction, especially if you can see lightning and hear thunder, it's time to get moving.

Lightning Safety
- Pay attention to towering and building clouds. They may quickly develop into storms capable of producing lightning.
- Hailstorms often produce lightning at altitude.
- The best clues of lightning danger are visible flashes and audible thunder. Remember: If you can hear thunder, you're already in danger.
- There are no obvious clues to the immediate threat of lightning danger until the first flash occurs.

- Just because a storm has just passed, do not assume safety. According to the National Oceanic and Atmospheric Administration (NOAA), 50 percent of lightning deaths occur after a storm has passed.
- Turn around early. It's better to turn around early and not be faced with lightning danger than to be faced with lightning danger and wish you had turned around.

If Caught in a Lightning Storm
- Immediately get off elevated areas such as hills, mountain ridges, or peaks.
- Move down the mountain—and keep walking.
- Never lie flat on the ground.
- Never shelter under an isolated tree.
- Never use a cliff or rocky overhang for shelter.
- Immediately get away from ponds and lakes.
- Stay away from objects that conduct electricity, such as barbed-wire fences, power lines, and windmills.
- If in a group, spread out so that you increase the chances for survivors who could come to the aid of any victims of a lightning strike.
- Wait at least 30 minutes after you hear the last sound of thunder before heading toward a summit.

Don't let summit fever overcome good judgment. One of the hardest things to do is turn around, especially when in sight of your goal. But many lightning accidents have occurred because climbers did not turn around. Dedicating yourself to reach a summit, no matter what, may appear admirable but can lead to deadly decisions. When in doubt, turn around; the mountain will always be there.

The Ten Essentials

When adventuring, you should always carry necessary gear on you. This includes at a bare minimum the ten essentials for hiking and mountaineering. If hiking in a group, certain items on this list can be spread out among the members:

1. Navigation and communication. Map and compass are still essential despite electronics—batteries go dead, devices get wet, things break. Maps should be waterproof or kept in a bag. Global Positioning System (GPS) units and

smartphones are great, but they're no fail-safe replacement for the old stand-bys. You can also bring a SEND (satellite emergency notification device). Note that cell phone reception is limited in Colorado's backcountry.

2. Proper clothing. A rain jacket is a must, as is a layer of insulation—even in July and August. Jeans are not proper climbing/hiking clothing; most jeans are cotton, and they suck to hike in when they get wet. They stay heavy, cold, and wet, which is at best an inconvenience and at worst can lead to hypothermia. Colorado whitewater is fed by snowmelt in the mountains. This makes the water much colder than in most places. Wet or dry suits are required early and late in the season. They're even nice to wear in the hottest months.

3. Sun protection. Sunglasses, sunscreen, hats, and clothes. Clothing can serve as sun protection, hence some outdoor companies publish the SPF levels of clothing on their tags. Remember, the sun is stronger at altitude.

4. Illumination. Headlamps are inexpensive, lightweight, and great illuminators. Flashlights are good; a smartphone flashlight doesn't count.

5. First aid. Bring supplies appropriate for the trip. It doesn't have to be a big kit. You won't need antivenin on top of the mountain, for instance. It's wise to take a first-aid class and know how and when to administer care and when to make an emergency contact.

6. Fire starter. Make sure you have a fire starter capable of defeating the elements. Your Bic won't flick in a monsoon!

7. Repair kit and tools. This includes things like patches for tents or bicycle tires, knives, and battery backups or chargers for your devices.

8. Extra food. Hopefully you won't need it, but a few extra bars or some gorp may save the day for you or another climber.

9. Water. Bring extra water and/or water treatment. Modern filtration systems like the Sawyer Mini fit on disposable water bottles, weigh ounces, and are extremely simple to use. However, if there are no water sources nearby, you're out of luck. Carrying extra water is always a good idea.

10. Emergency shelter. A small, ultralight piece of protection—like a tarp, bivy sack, trash bag, or emergency blanket—can serve as a makeshift shelter or signal for search-and-rescue personnel.

Appropriate Gear

Wear a helmet for all rock climbing, cycling, and paddling adventures in this book. These are extremely fun but potentially dangerous sports. Head protection is necessary, and brain buckets work wonders. A helmet is recommended for the more difficult hikes, like the Sawtooth, as well.

Clothing

Jeans are not appropriate clothing for long days of adventure with varying weather conditions. They soak through quickly and get heavy, dry slowly, and chafe uncomfortably. Probably the best pants for long hikes or climbs are synthetic pants or shorts, which offer a combination of durability, breathability, water resistance, and wind resistance.

Wool or synthetic base layers are excellent insulators for early and long days, particularly in spring and late fall. Many people wear or bring such layers in summer as well, since temperatures can vary dramatically throughout the day, particularly if you're going into the high country. Whatever you choose to wear, be ready to sweat for any of the mountain hikes, bikes, or climbs. Good gear "breathes." You can purchase inexpensive synthetic clothing at Target or Walmart that will do in a pinch; however, outdoor specialty shops have a great selection of clothing designed specifically for the outdoors that are meant to last.

Footwear

Don't purchase some super-heavy, super-thick boots and expect to be comfortable hiking on a hot August day. Your feet will be stuck in a soup of sweat and sock. Your feet will blister. If you're hiking in winter or mountaineering, that's the boot you'll likely need; otherwise, consider light hikers or trail runners.

Waterproof is nice, but waterproof footwear doesn't always breathe that well, so your feet might get wet from sweating. And unless you're wearing good, high gaiters, if you step into a stream higher than your footwear's cuff, they're still going to get wet on the inside. I have a penchant for hiking and climbing in my modified Chacos, which might not be a popular choice, but they work for me. Such sandals allow wearers to kick pebbles loose between foot soles, while shoe beds and feet dry quickly; on the downside, wearers can scrape their feet up much more, and the ankle protection is minimal. A good breathable shoe, or a light hiker if you need the ankle support, is likely the best solution for hiking. It offers a combination of grip, breathability, and comfort. Whatever style of footwear you choose, keeping your feet happy means you'll be a lot happier too.

Rock climbing shoes are required for rock climbing. For boating, sandals like Chacos or Tevas are recommended, as are water shoes or neoprene booties, particularly in spring or fall, when the water is colder.

Winter Climbing and Mountaineering

This book is aimed toward warmer adventures. The wilderness is open year-round, and more people are taking advantage of the backcountry in winter. But winter poses additional dangers like avalanches, turning some trails that are perfectly fine in summer into veritable death traps in winter.

Ice climbing and couloir climbs are fun winter activities. In the Rockies, avalanches are winter's version of lightning—deadly and surprising. Learn more about avalanches and how to avoid such dangers by educating yourself or taking classes. At the very least, check the Colorado Avalanche Information Center (avalanche .state.co.us) for current conditions and basic safety information.

If a road is closed by a snow berm, respect that closure. Many, many feet of snow can pile up in winter, and even if a road looks relatively clear, don't trust it. It's closed for a reason. Enjoy more time adventuring with your snow gear, and plan for longer hiking, snowshoeing, or cross-country skiing times.

Avalanches

Most climbers consider avalanches a winter problem; however, on Colorado's fourteeners and other high peaks (those above 12,000 feet), deadly avalanche accidents happen year-round. Since 1990 avalanches have killed twelve climbers, and half those deaths occurred in June, July, and October. As the popularity of climbing fourteeners in winter grows, so too, sadly, will avalanche accidents. Compounding the problem is that popular summertime routes are not always safe routes in winter and spring.

Avoiding avalanche danger requires learning to recognize where and when avalanches can occur so that you can avoid dangerous slopes. Learning where and when avalanches occur is a blend of art and science that takes time and experience. Fortunately, it's not rocket science.

Slope angle is critical as to whether terrain can produce an avalanche. Most avalanches occur on slopes between 30 and 45 degrees—slopes that are also perfect for climbing, skiing, and glissading.

Complicating matters is that avalanches can be triggered from shallow slopes at the bottom of steep slopes. With so much to know, the best way to learn about avalanches is to take an avalanche course and travel with those who are experienced with avalanches. Keep in mind, however, that while education teaches the rules, nature teaches the exceptions.

The American Avalanche Association (avalanche.org) is the best source for high-quality local instruction.

Mountain Rescue

There will always be risk associated with outdoor activities, but this information will help decrease the dangers engendered by these issues. Nevertheless, anyone can have a "bad day in the mountains." When that time comes, it is better to call for help sooner rather than later. Your situation, and the weather, is likely to get worse.

Mountain search-and-rescue activities in Colorado are performed by volunteers whose services are free of charge. However, if you require medical transport (ambulance or helicopter), you will be billed for those services. When you do need help, it's important to let rescuers know about any medical conditions you have and what issues you're having if they're not readily visible.

CORSAR Card

When you're hiking or climbing in Colorado, purchase a Colorado Outdoor Recreation Search and Rescue card. They're pretty cheap, and your purchase directly contributes to the state's Search and Rescue Fund. It is not insurance. The fund helps reimburse rescue teams and sheriffs for costs incurred in your search and rescue. Funds remaining at the end of the year are used to help pay for training and equipment for these teams. You can buy a CORSAR card from many outdoor recreation shops or online at colorado.gov/sar.

Information contributed by:
Skeet Glatterer, MD, FAWM, Alpine Rescue Team, Evergreen, Colorado (co-medical director); chairman, Mountain Rescue Association (MRA) Medical Committee; US

delegate (alternate) International Commission for Alpine Rescue (ICAR) Medical Committee

Dale Atkins, Alpine Rescue Team, Evergreen, Colorado; past chairman, Search and Rescue Committee, American Avalanche Association; past president, American Avalanche Association; past vice president, Avalanche Rescue Commission, International Commission for Alpine Rescue

Adventure Classifications

Hiking

Hikes in this guide use widely accepted climbing classifications set by the Yosemite Decimal System (YDS): Classes 1–5, with Class 5 being the most difficult and requiring at least some form of protection. Class 5 is considered rock climbing, and those terms will be defined in that section.

Class 1: The easiest level of climbing; basically walking on a trail or path.

Class 2: More-difficult hiking on or through terrain that can require bushwhacking or scrambling on scree. With the exception of pushing branches away, Class 2 hiking rarely requires using your hands.

Class 3: Climbing gets quadrupedal. You may need to use hands to climb up over rocks or up into chimneys that have very little exposure. You're relatively safe on Class 3 hikes, although some may require helmets.

Class 4: Things start to get dangerous. Class 4 hikes and climbs involve significant exposure, and a fall could cause significant injury; loose scree on a very steep slope could fall on your head. This is semitechnical climbing, and you're using your whole body to climb up or down.

Class 5: This is technical climbing. At Class 5 you should definitely be wearing a helmet and should be on-rope.

Climbing

The YDS system also accounts for rock climbing classifications. With anything over Class 4 hiking and climbing, protection should be used. Even falls on "easy" Class 5 climbs can result in serious injury or death. At the very minimum, a helmet should be used. In addition, climbers should use harnesses, ropes, and belay equipment on Class 5 climbs. They should know how to tie proper knots and belay other climbers and know rappel techniques. After Class 5, climbs are graded with more difficulty, starting with 5.0. Between 5.0 and 5.9, each grade increases by a decimal point. Harder climbs—those 5.10 and above—carry additional designations of difficulty from "a" to "d." So you could have a 5.10c or a 5.14a climb. Here's rough guide of those ranges:

5.0–5.5	Easy	Generally a steep section of a hike or climb with large handholds and footholds as well as a decent amount of protection. Beginners can usually climb these.
5.6–5.8	Intermediate	These climbs generally have smaller, but still good, placements for feet and hands. The rock face ranges from near vertical to vertical. Beginners may be OK, but intermediate climbing skills are helpful.
5.9–5.10d	Hard	Holds are smaller; the rock face is vertical and may be overhung. Rock climbing skills are essential here.
5.11a–5.12d	Advanced	A vertical, if not overhung face with small holds for hands and feet. Significant rock climbing skill is needed, as are grace and hutzpah.
5.13a–5.15d	Elite	Expert-level, extremely technical climbing. Climbers at this level generally have years if not decades of experience and are dedicated to the sport as almost an art.

Note: There are no 5.14d or 5.15+ climbs in this book. In fact, there are only a few climbs in the state rated in that range.

Whitewater

Whitewater classifications are adopted from the Class I–VI scale developed and promoted by American Whitewater. *Note:* A river run is classified by its hardest rapids, and many named rapids carry their own classification.

Class I: Easy. Water moves quickly with riffles and small waves. It's easy to avoid obstructions.

Class II: Novice. Rapids are obvious, as are channels to avoid or take them on. Most obstacles are easily avoided by trained paddlers.

Class III: Intermediate rapids. These are generally moderate waves where it becomes more difficult to avoid obstacles. Paddlers must be confident in their skills to navigate tight passages and obstacles, including strainers, ledges, and holes. Scouting is advisable for inexperienced paddlers and rafters. May be too challenging for flatwater canoes. Self-rescue is generally easy.

Class IV: Advanced rapids. These are larger, tough, but usually predictable rapids. Paddlers must be able to navigate a boat precisely. Rapids can include waves, holes, or constricted passages that demand fast maneuvers, including "must" moves above dangerous hazards. Scouting is helpful for most. Risk of injury to swimmers is increased, and self-rescue may be difficult. A good barrel, or "Eskimo," roll is required at this level.

Class V: Expert. These are long, violent rapids with dangerous obstacles and added risk. There may be big drops and unavoidable waves and holes. Chutes can be very narrow, with little room for error. Swims are more dangerous, and self-rescue is often difficult—even for extremely advanced experts.

Class VI: Exploratory or Extreme. Most haven't been attempted because of difficulty, unpredictability, and/or danger.

Note: This guide doesn't include any Class VI rapids.

How to Use This Guide

This guidebook has four sections: Hiking Adventures, Climbing Adventures, Cycling Adventures, and Paddling Adventures. Some of the areas overlap. For instance, there's awesome whitewater and rock climbing in Clear Creek Canyon—some fun hiking and biking as well. So you have plenty of options to up your adventure by combining multiple adventures in the same area.

Each adventure description begins with a short overview, including the difficulty of the activity and where the adventure is located.

Next you'll find the quick and dirty information, including start location, and closest town with services. For hiking, cycling, and paddling adventures, each section includes the distance, average trip time, difficulty, type of terrain, best adventure seasons, schedule, whether camping is available or any fees or permits are required, maps, driving directions, and other relevant information. This section also includes basic information about land ownership/management as well as their contact information. "Finding the trailhead" provides turn-by-turn directions to the trailhead/starting point from the nearest major highway. For climbing adventures, "Finding the crag" then gets you from the trailhead/parking area to where you'll start your climb. Directions to the put-in and takeout are provided for all paddling adventures.

The Hike/Climb/Ride/Paddle section provides an accurate description of each route and adventure, including significant milestones. The meat of the chapter, this is a detailed and honest, carefully researched impression of the route. It often includes area history, both natural and human. For hiking and cycling adventures, the mileage cues in "Miles and Directions" identify all turns and trail or road name changes, as well as points of interest along the given route. Paddling entries use criteria relevant to those adventures. Whitewater adventures, for instance, note milemarkers on the road as a navigation tool for significant milestones like rapids. Climbing areas and routes also note whether a climb is sport or traditional route, the number of pitches on a climb and the climbing gear you'll need as well as hardware you'll encounter on the crag.

Note: All figures are best estimates using actual measurements from GPS units, satellite imaging, and other methods. Elevation gain, distance, and trailhead elevation are all best estimates using actual measurements from GPS units, mapping software, and maps. Commercial GPS units are only accurate within a number of yards, and elevation information in these devices is affected by barometric changes. A host of unavoidable issues limit the ability to offer precise mileage and elevation figures, from the height of the trekker to how closely or loosely switchbacks are followed or how fast the river is flowing and how strong a paddler is. Trip times are calculated very generously. Hopefully you'll be done quicker than the estimate, but don't count on it.

Using the Maps

Maps are provided for each route. Given the distance, elevation changes, and difficulty of some of the adventures in this book, these maps should be considered reference material only.

A more-detailed topo map is strongly recommended for most of these adventures. Detail can mean the difference between enjoying a fantastic day and ending up at an impassible cliff or a steep, exceedingly dangerous patch of scree. Before you head out, study the map and transfer routes to them with a waterproof pen, if needed.

National Geographic Trails Illustrated maps show most of the hiking routes described in this book, but not all. They show rivers too. But unless it's a boating-specific map, it won't have rapids and classes listed. If you're using a GPS device or your smartphone, sites like 14ers.com, mountainproject.com, alltrails.com, and hikingproject.com often have GPX files of the routes that you can load onto your device.

Ranking the Adventures

In ranking the difficulty of the adventures, we used some commonsense and other methodologies and practices established by outdoor adventurers, athletes, and guides. Hikes and climbs are ranked from Class 1 (easy) to Class 5+, which requires protection including ropes, helmets, and harnesses. Hiking times were calculated from personal experiences and supplemented using hiking time calculators, such as the one offered at TrailsNH.com.

Rock climbing routes in this book are rated using the Yosemite Decimal System (YDS), which is common in the United States, although not internationally. Routes are graded from 5.0 to 5.9 for easy to intermediate routes; from 5.10 to 5.15 each number carries an additional "a" to "d" gradient marking additional levels of difficulty.

In rock climbing the grade is established by the person or persons who made the first recorded ascent and established the route. The YDS is the same whether it's a traditional route (meaning protected by gear the lead climber places) or a sport route, where lead climbers clip quickdraw into established bolts in the route. Some climbs are reevaluated over time by community consensus, but generally the initial rating stands. The difficulty levels are further explained in the "Climbing Adventures" section of the book.

Whitewater runs are evaluated based on the International Scale of River Difficulty created by American Whitewater, which ranks rapids from Class I to Class VI. Class I rapids are easiest; think flatwater with a ripple or two or a rock sticking out of it. Class V rapids need a strong set of well-earned skills to navigate. Class VI rapids are those that even many expert rafters and kayakers should consider avoiding or portaging around. This guide doesn't recommend any Class VI rapids and only some Class V rapids, which usually occur during high-water events.

These measures are highly subjective, but they're the best possible way to evaluate each type of adventure. Hiking paths may be drastically altered by an avalanche, rockfall, mudslide, or even a single treefall, adding difficulty. Unlike gyms, outdoor rock climbing routes don't have well-marked paths; a climber has to find the foot- and handholds—it's one of the beautiful things about the sport. The holds you ultimately use may be widely different from those envisioned by the route setter, changing the difficulty for you—not them. Similarly, any whitewater sportsperson will tell you that you have to evaluate the rapids. Stream flows drastically change some rapids. A low flow rate can turn a Class IV rapid into a Class II rapid; a high flow rate can transform that same rapid into a Class V+ crusher, slamming a boat into a rock face or potentially sucking it into a hole—both of which could have dangerous, even fatal, consequences.

That said, a 3-mile, Class 1 hike like the Paint Mines has minimal risk of harm and should be appropriate for almost everyone, from tykes to older folk, or those who simply aren't as spry as the used to be.

Map Legend

Municipal

- ═〔70〕═ Interstate Highway
- ═〔6〕═ US Highway
- ═〔105〕═ State Road
- ═〔57〕═ County/Local Road
- ═══ Featured Local Road
- ═ ═ ═ Featured Unpaved Road
- = = = = Unpaved Road
- ├──┼──┤ Railroad

Trails

- ██████ Featured Trail
- ██████ Featured Climbing Trail
- ██████ Featured Cycle Route
- ------ Featured Paddle Route
- ------ Trail

Water Features

- Body of Water
- River/Creek
- Intermittent Stream
- Waterfall
- Rapid

Symbols

- ① Trailhead (hiking adventure)
- ⑳ Trailhead (climbing adventure)
- ㉘ Trailhead (cycling adventure)
- ㉜ Start (paddling adventure)
- ❓ Visitor/Information Center
- Overlook/Viewpoint
- ■ Building/Point of Interest
- ⏝ Bridge
- ⛺ Campground
- † Cemetery
- Fire Tower
- Put-in/Takeout
- *1* Mileage
- ▲ Peak
- 🅿 Parking
- Picnic Area
- Restroom/Toilet
- Water

Land Management

- National Park
- State/County/City Park or Forest
- Wilderness/National Monument

HIKING
ADVENTURES

There are thousands if not tens of thousands of miles of trails along Colorado's Front Range. This collection of hikes highlight some of the most awesome and unique trails the region has to offer while not focusing on the most famous places like Rocky Mountain National Park. From challenging, epic mountain climbs to family-friendly hikes to amazing places, these are among the most incredible hiking adventures along Colorado's Front Range.

Most trailheads of the Colorado Trail are well marked.

Hike 1 The Summer White House on Mount Falcon

This is the closest adventure to Denver in this book. With fantastic views of the Rockies, Denver, and of course the world-famous Red Rocks Amphitheatre, Mount Falcon is ideal to whet your appetite for more adventures. The trail also is home to a unique feature, the Summer White House, the remains of which make the whole trek worth it. The well-established trail has great signage and is easy to follow. With about 1,500 feet of elevation gain spread over 3.1 miles, it's a bit of a heart thumper, but it's still easy enough for most families. Those who wish to can up the challenge with a trail run or on a mountain bike.

Start: Castle Trail at the Mount Falcon Morrison Trailhead

Distance: 6.2-mile upside-down lollipop

Hiking time: About 3.5 hours

Difficulty: Easy to intermediate; wide, well-marked trails

Elevation gain: Roughly 1,500 feet from trailhead to peak

Trail surface: Dirt, interspersed with some rockier sections

Best seasons: Year-round; mud season likely the most challenging

Other trail users: Cyclists, trail runners, equestrians

Canine compatibility: Leashed dogs permitted

Land status: Jefferson County Open Space

Camping, fees, and permits: Free parking

Schedule: Open one hour before and after sunset

Maps: USGS Morrison; National Geographic Trails Illustrated #100: Boulder/Golden

Nearest town: Morrison

Trail contact: Jefferson County Open Space; (303) 271-5925; jeffco.us/open-space

Finding the trailhead: From the intersection of CO 8 and CO 74 in Morrison, head south on CO 8 for 0.9 mile. Turn right onto Forest Avenue. At 0.2 mile turn right onto Vine Street and continue until you reach the parking lot (3852 Vine St.). There are 52 spots in the parking lot, which fills up quickly on nice evenings and weekend days. When the lot fills, people had parked along Vine Street in the past, but a new lot was opened in November 2020 to help alleviate overflow. GPS: N39.64685° / W105.19654°

The Hike

What makes Mount Falcon and the Summer White House great is the ease of access to the trail, as well as the trail network that allows you to extend or shorten the adventure to suit your needs and abilities, making it an ideal adventure for families or those not used to hiking in Colorado. Completing just the first part of the Castle Trail and returning on the Turkey Trot Trail makes an easy 3.0-mile loop.

The best of the area includes hiking the well-trod Castle Trail to the Walker's Dream Trail and the Summer White House. An area where trekkers easily access incredible 360-degree views of the whole region, with Denver and Golden to the east, world-famous Red Rocks Amphitheatre just a few miles north, and the stately, often snowcapped Rockies to the west. This is the adventure to whet your appetite for the endless adventures that Colorado offers.

The Summer White House was John Brisben Walker's attempt to create a summer vacation spot for the president in Colorado's foothills in the early 1900s (see sidebar). Walker wanted to build the vacation spot near his home, Walker Castle, which conveniently would have been a stone's throw from the president's

A faint rainbow looking east from Turkey Trot Trail.

JOHN BRISBEN WALKER, PIONEERING ENTREPRENEUR

If someone were to tell you one person once ran *Cosmopolitan* magazine, cofounded a railroad company, developed one of the world's most iconic and famous music venues, developed a theme park, sponsored the United States' first car race, inspired a mountain park system, and more, you'd think Elon Musk or Richard Branson must have stepped back in time. But that's the legacy of John Brisben Walker, a fascinating renaissance man who had a lasting impact on Colorado and the Front Range.

Don't get John Brisben Walker confused with Scot John "Johnnie" Walker, namesake of the famous scotch. Though the two were both sons of the 1800s and entrepreneurs, their lives were separated by the Atlantic Ocean. John Brisben Walker was born three decades later, in 1847, near Pittsburgh, Pennsylvania.

Walker, a graduate of West Point, won and lost many fortunes over his lifetime. By the time he was 26, he'd already served as a general in the Chinese Army and had lost a fortune in the Panic of 1873. Walker's first venture into Colorado came around 1879 when the US government asked him to explore agriculture in the West. He bought the 1,600-acre Berkeley Farm in northern Denver and introduced alfalfa as a cash crop. He then bought land near Union Station in Denver and created the first amusement park in the region, River Front Park.

His interests expanded beyond Denver, and he began purchasing land in the foothills around Golden and Morrison, Colorado. He donated some land from the Berkeley Farm in Denver to what has become Regis University.

He bought *Cosmopolitan* magazine when it was faltering in 1889 and turned it around, publishing works from authors including Sir Author Conan Doyle and Mark Twain. He returned to the East Coast and New York to run the magazine and pursue other interests, including buying early plans for the Stanley Steamer automobiles designed by the Stanley twins.

As Walker prepared to move back to Colorado with his second wife, Ethel Richmond Walker, he sold *Cosmopolitan* to William Randolph Hearst in 1905. Upon their return to Colorado, Walker began promoting and developing more of the foothills, including Mount Falcon and Red Rocks. He purchased that land on May 31, 1905, and named it "Garden of the Titans." In 1909 they built the Walker Castle atop Mount Falcon.

The natural amphitheater was deemed "acoustically perfect" in 1911 by internationally renowned opera singer Mary Garden. She was accompanied by Walker's wife, Ethel, on the violin.

In developing the region for entertainment and relaxation, Walker also built a road to the area, hiking trails, and more. He built a cog railway from the park to the top of Mount Morrison behind it, making it the longest cog railway in the world at the time. This was also the same period when he started promoting the idea of the Summer White House and started developing the concepts that would become the Denver Mountain Parks system.

The city of Denver was swayed into purchasing Red Rocks in 1927, a few years before Walker passed on in 1931 at age 83. Already legendary, the venue was built and rebuilt over time. Most of today's Red Rocks Amphitheatre was built by the Civilian Conservation Corps (CCC) between 1936 and 1941.

In its more than a century of use as an amphitheater, everyone from Ray Charles to John Denver, Radiohead, The Flaming Lips, and The Beatles have played there. Led Zeppelin played their first US show there, and U2 filmed the video for "Sunday Bloody Sunday" at the venue.

Walker, however, led a rocky life. He sold Red Rocks for $54,133, and though he had raised many fortunes throughout his days, he died poor. Mount Falcon, which still bears visible remnants of Walker's ambitious life, was created in 1974. It pays tribute to him with signage, as does nearby Red Rocks.

John Lunsford takes in the remains of the Walker Castle.

Sunset over Mount Falcon.

summer mansion. However, only the cornerstone and a corner foundation of the project were completed in 1911, and Walker's mansion burnt down in 1918, presumably struck by lightning. The remains of the castle are still there, visible from the Summer White House. If you want to extend your hike a bit, it's an easy, relatively flat jaunt to the remains of the castle.

The hike begins on relatively flat, scrubby meadow surrounded by tall grasses, yucca, and more. It travels through bands of scrub oak, mountain mahogany, and other deciduous trees and bushes at lower elevations. As the trail wends up the mountain, you'll wander through bands of evergreens including Douglas fir, ponderosa pine, and junipers. On a quiet day it's possible to see deer, Abert's squirrel, and even falcons along the hike. While there are potentially some bears and mountain lions in the area, you're not likely to encounter them.

Much of Castle Trail is exposed to the sunlight, which makes it great for jaunts on cool days. On hot days, however, there aren't many places to find shade until you're a little higher on the trail. A great spot to rest and cool down on a hot day is close to the Turkey Trot Trail junction, about halfway up the trail, in terms of both elevation and distance. The trail mellows out as it approaches the picnic pavilion near the Walker's Dream Trail junction.

A multiuse trail, Castle Trail is also used by bikers, trail runners, and equestrians. Please be aware of others on the trail and be prepared for mountain bikers, particularly around sharp turns in the trail. Turkey Trot Trail is for hikers only, and generally has less traffic than Castle Trail.

Miles and Directions

0.0 Start at the trailhead at the southwest corner of the parking lot by the toilets, near the park tables and benches.

0.1 Stay left and continue on Castle Trail at the junction with the Turkey Trot Trail, heading southwest.

0.6 After passing modern houses to the left, encounter some long, easy switchbacks.

0.9 The trail makes a sharp left and continues on a southwest trajectory as it continues to climb.

1.1 The trail makes an arcing right and heads north.

1.4 Just after a horseshoe turn, the Turkey Trot Trail rejoins the Castle Trail on the right, making it easy to head back and shorten the hike if needed. Continue on the Castle Trail to keep climbing.

1.7 Take an elbow in the trail to head primarily west as the trail gets a little more rocky in an open stretch.

2.3 After a relatively straight section of trail, come to another elbow as the trail enters a small patch of pine trees.

2.5 Come to another sharp elbow in the trail and head toward the gazebo.

2.6 Just after the gazebo take the Walker's Dream Trail to your right to reach the Summer White House.

3.0 Reach the end of the trail at the signage and cornerstone of the structure. Return to Castle Trail.

3.4 Rejoin the Castle Trail. Turn left to return toward the trailhead. (Option: Head right to the ruins of John Walker's castle, extending the hike by 1.0 mile, total.)

4.4 Turn left at the signed upper junction of the Turkey Trot Trail to form a loop. (Option: Continue down the Castle Trail to return to the trailhead.)

The Summer White House on Mount Falcon

4.6 Continue to the right at a sharp elbow in the trail.

5.3 There's a good overlook of Golden and Denver just left of the trail.

5.7 Start encountering some loose rock on the trail as it enters lower meadows.

6.0 Turn left at the junction, rejoining the Castle Trail.

6.2 Arrive back at the trailhead.

Adventure Information

Mount Falcon. www.jeffco.us/1332/Mount-Falcon-Park

Parking lot (webcam). mtfalconcam.jeffco.us/video.cgi?resolution=CIF&camera=1

Outfitters

Bentgate Mountaineering. 1313 Washington Ave., Golden; (303) 271-9382; bentgate.com. Open Sun–Fri; closed Sat.

Wilderness Exchange. 2401 15th St., Ste 100, Denver; (303) 964-0708; wildernessx.com

Vital Outdoors. 1224 Washington Ave., Golden; (303) 215-1644; vitaloutdoors.com

REI Denver Flagship. 1416 Platte St., Denver; (303) 756-3100; rei.com

Great Pre- or Post-Adventure Spots

Woody's Wood Fired Pizza. 1305 Washington Ave., Golden; (303) 277-0443; woodysgolden .com

Barrels & Bottles Brewery. 600 12th St., Unit 180, Golden; (720) 328-3643; barrelsbottles .com

Tributary Food Hall & Drinkery. 701 12th St., Golden; (303) 856-7225; tributarygolden.com

Hike 2 Golden Gate Canyon State Park Loop

Magnificent meadows, aspens and conifers, views of the often snowcapped Continental Divide, a network of more than 40 miles of trails with stunning views of mountains and more, as well as its proximity to Denver, all make Golden Gate Canyon State Park a fantastic place for an adventurous day. This fun, challenging loop takes you through flowery meadows, forests, and settlers' artifacts and around the western parameters of the park. Options to shorten the trek significantly while still maintaining a loop hike make it ideal for families and those who want to test themselves on whether they're ready for longer hikes.

Start: Ralston Roost Trailhead

Distance: 12.0-mile loop

Hiking time: About 6 hours

Difficulty: Intermediate

Elevation gain/loss: 2,150 feet of elevation gain, spread throughout

Trail surface: Primarily dirt; some rocky sections

Best seasons: Year-round

Other trail users: Mountain bikers, campers, equestrians, rock climbers, anglers

Canine compatibility: Leashed dogs permitted (leash 6 feet long or less)

Land status: State park

Camping, fees, and permits: Daily park fee, paid at the Golden Gate Canyon State Park Visitor Center; additional fees for camping

Schedule: Open year-round, 5 a.m.–10 p.m.; visitor center open Tues–Sun, 9 a.m.–4 p.m.

Maps: USGS Black Hawk; National Geographic Trails Illustrated #100: Boulder/Golden

Nearest town: Golden

Trail contact: Golden Gate Canyon State Park; (303) 582-3707; cpw.state.co.us/placestogo/parks/GoldenGateCanyon/Pages/default.aspx

Finding the trailhead: From the intersection of CO 93 and Golden Gate Canyon Road, head west on Golden Gate Canyon Road; continue for 12.8 miles. Turn right onto Crawford Gulch Road. Parking for the trailhead is in 0.2 mile, on both sides of the road (92 Crawford Gulch Rd.). *Note:* The visitor center (restrooms) is on the right side of the road, about 0.1 mile from the turn onto Crawford Gulch Road. The parking areas are small, but there is additional parking at the

Aspens in fall splendor along the trail in Golden Gate Canyon State Park.

Horseshoe trailhead, another 0.3 mile down the road, or at the nearby visitor center. GPS: N39.83301° / W105.40847°

The Hike

The history of Golden Gate Canyon Sate Park stretches back to at least the 1850s, when Lewis Ralston found gold flakes in his pan near Arvada in the creek that now bears his name. It's the same creek that courses past the visitor center and across the road from the trailhead.

This hike begins at the Ralston Roost trailhead and celebrates even more of the park's heritage and history, winding through meadows cleared by John Frazer, who settled in the area in 1869, and Charles Greenfield and his family, who settled a 320-acre homestead in the area in 1920.

Frazer had tried mining gold at Black Hawk but found that supplying miners and other homesteaders in the area could be profitable as well. He cleared a road to a flat area for a hayfield, built a cabin and a barn, and planted a small vegetable garden. Frazer accomplished all this with a bum leg. He worked with Samuel Parker, an African-American settler. Frazer's brother Rufus, who followed John out west, also homesteaded in the area. Today the remains of Frazer's barn and a mower are still in the meadow, about 2.0 miles into the hike. But they are far from the only attractions on this trek through the park.

The park teams with wildlife, including mule deer, elk, moose, and bighorn sheep. Smaller animals abound as well, including beavers, bobcats, martens, foxes, and more. Mountain lions and black bears live in the area as well. Birds seen in the area include bald and golden eagles, blue grouse, ptarmigan, Steller's and gray jays, rosy finch, and others.

Much of the area is dominated by conifers, including ponderosa pine and Rocky Mountain juniper, as well as Douglas fir. But the park is also one of the closest places to Denver to see aspen groves glow gold in the fall.

The hike begins with some quick elevation gain as it climbs toward the meadows through aspen groves and conifers on the remnants of old dirt roads. The climb mellows out as it comes to Greenfield Meadow, a lovely place to look for wildflowers in summer. There are some backcountry campsites along the trail.

At the northern end of the meadow, the remains of Frazer's cabin and Frazer Meadow are visible; you can learn more about him thanks to some signage. It's a fantastic area for views to the south, with aspens and snowcapped mountains in the background. This is also where you can shorten the hike by taking the Mule Deer Trail back to the parking lot. Continuing on, the Mule Deer Trail skirts the east side of Tremont Mountain. Though it's relatively flat, there are some slightly rocky, technical areas here.

Shortly after crossing Gap Road, come across Panorama Point, one of the gems of this hike. A patio offers views of a 100-mile stretch of the Continental Divide, from Grays and Torreys Peaks to the south to Longs Peak to the north.

As the trail comes back around the western side of the park, flanking the western side of Tremont Mountain and heading south, it often parallels Mountain Base Road to its east, offering fantastic views to the west as well as easy access to a number of picnic and rest areas as it makes a gradual decent.

As the trail leaves this area and heads back into the forest, it begins a final ascent for the day as it climbs Ralston Roost on the Black Bear Trail, gaining more than 700 feet of elevation over 1.7 miles. From here the trail quickly descends another 1.5 miles, snaking through the forest on mostly dirt terrain with some rockier areas. The Black Bear Trail ends at the Ralston Roost lot.

Miles and Directions

0.0 Start at the Ralston Roost Trailhead parking lot or the Horseshoe Trailhead/Frazer Meadow parking lot, about 1,500 feet farther northwest on CR 57.

0.1 Take the Horseshoe Trail to the right.

0.4 As the trail turns northwest, begin a gradual ascent. The trail gains about 450 feet over 0.9 mile.

1.2 Stay right at the trail branch as the elevation lessens into Greenfield Meadow and camping areas (both sides meet with the Mule Deer Trail).

1.9 Turn left, followed by a right in about 200 feet at the junction with the Coyote and Mule Deer Trails. (Option: Continuing straight on the Mule Deer Trail leads to the Black Bear Trail and back to the parking lot.)

2.2 Go right at the junction of the Mule Deer and Coyote Trails and begin a short ascent. (Bailout: Turn left onto the Coyote Trail to reconnect with the Mule Deer Trail on the west side of the park, shortening the hike to 8.8 miles.)

3.9 Pass a short connecting trail that leads to parking and the Harmsen Ranch Guest House (reservations required).

4.2 Cross Gap Road.

5.0 Continue on the Mule Deer Trail as the Raccoon Trail joins.

5.2 Pass Panorama Point (a great area for pictures).

5.3 Continue west on the Mule Deer–Raccoon Trail as smaller spurs rejoin the larger trail.

5.4 Reach the Panorama Point parking area. There are toilets, picnic tables, and a viewing platform nearby. Continue on the combined Mule Deer–Raccoon Trail.

6.0 Stay left (west) at the junction where the Mule Deer and Raccoon Trails split.

6.3 Cross Mountain Base Road (CR 2). For the next 2.0 miles the trail stays close to Mountain Base Road, offering numerous places to rest with some picnic tables and parking areas.

7.0 Pass Bootleg Bottom parking and picnic area to the east.

7.1 Continue south on the Mule Deer Trail at the junction with the Coyote Trail.

8.1 Reach the Ole Barn Knoll parking and picnic area (toilets); continue on the Lower Mule Deer Trail.

Golden Gate Canyon State Park Loop

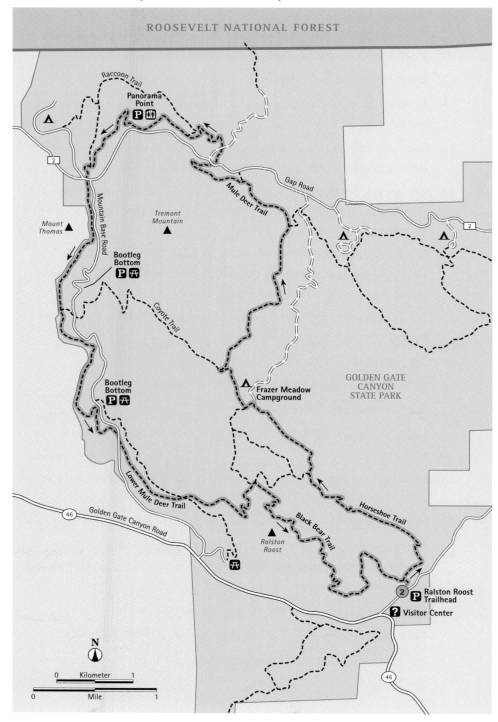

ROOSEVELT NATIONAL FOREST

Raccoon Trail

Panorama Point

Mule Deer Trail

Gap Road

Mountain Base Road

Tremont Mountain

Mount Thomas

Bootleg Bottom

Coyote Trail

Bootleg Bottom

Frazer Meadow Campground

GOLDEN GATE CANYON STATE PARK

Lower Mule Deer Trail

Horseshoe Trail

Golden Gate Canyon Road

Black Bear Trail

Ralston Roost

Ralston Roost Trailhead

Visitor Center

N

Kilometer

Mile

8.4   Cross Mountain Base Road.

8.9   Stay left on the Mule Deer Trail at the junction with the Blue Grouse Trail. Begin your final ascent for the day as the trail heads east and climbs 700 feet over the next 1.1 miles.

9.5   Begin some short switchbacks as the trail climbs about 200 feet.

9.7   At the junction of the Horseshoe and Black Bear Trails, take a right to head southeast on the Black Bear Trail. Continue on the Black Bear Trail as it zigzags up.

10.2   Reach your second high point of the day at 9,300 feet; begin the descent to the trailhead.

11.0   Encounter small switchbacks on the final descent.

12.0   Arrive back at the trailhead.

Adventure Information

Organizations

Colorado Parks Foundation. Denver; (303) 8128-8078; coloradoparksfoundation.org

Outfitters

Bentgate Mountaineering. 1313 Washington Ave., Golden; (303) 271-9382; bentgate.com. Open Sun–Fri; closed Sat.

Wilderness Exchange. 2401 15th St., Ste. 100, Denver; (303) 964-0708; wildernessx.com

REI Denver Flagship. 1416 Platte St., Denver; (303) 756-3100; rei.com

Great Pre- or Post-Adventure Spots

Woody's Wood Fired Pizza. 1305 Washington Ave., Golden; (303) 277-0443; woodysgolden .com

Barrels & Bottles Brewery. 600 12th St., Unit 180, Golden; (720) 328-3643

Tributary Food Hall & Drinkery. 701 12th St., Golden; (303) 856-7225; tributarygolden.com

Hike 3 White Ranch Open Space: Rawhide Loop

This gorgeous, easy hike across flowery meadows offers views of rolling hills, the plains, and a glimpse into Colorado's ranching past. Complete with intact buildings and old ranching equipment, the Rawhide Loop is a fantastic adventure close to Denver. With a network of more than 20 miles of trails on easy terrain, this open-space park is a family-friendly wildlife haven with a herd of happy mule deer.

Start: White Ranch Park West Trailhead

Distance: 5.0-mile loop

Hiking time: About 2.5 hours

Difficulty: Easy

Elevation gain: 760 feet

Trail surface: Dirt road, natural surface

Best seasons: Year-round; fantastic flora and fauna with wildflowers in spring; decent foliage in fall

Other trail users: Equestrians, mountain bikers

Canine compatibility: Leashed dogs permitted

Land status: Jefferson County Open Space

Camping, fees, and permits: Camping permits required (fee); check with Jefferson County Open Space

Schedule: Open year-round, 1 hour before sunrise to 1 hour after sunset

Maps: USGS Ralston Buttes; National Geographic Trails Illustrated #100: Boulder/Golden

Nearest town: Golden

Trail contact: Jefferson County Open Space; (303) 271-5925; jeffco.us/open-space

Finding the trailhead: From the intersection of CO 93 and Golden Gate Canyon Road, head west on Golden Gate Canyon Road. At 3.9 miles turn right onto Crawford Gulch Road and continue another 3.9 miles. Turn right onto Belcher Hill Road; continue 1.8 miles and turn left into the lot (25373 Belcher Hill Rd.). GPS: N39.81901° / W105.28631°

The Hike

No matter the time of year, this former ranch is a stunner. It's the largest park in the Jeffco Open Space and has a network of trails suitable to users of all ages and needs. In spring and summer it offers wonderful wildflowers; in winter it's a great, easy place to snowshoe or cross-country ski.

First used by Native Americans, but likely first settled by George Belcher in the 1860s, the land was owned by a series of interesting characters, including former coal miner James Bond of County Devon, England, who bought the land in the 1880s. We don't know if he liked his martinis shaken or stirred.

The park takes its name from Paul Revere White and his wife, Anna Lee White. Paul, a cowboy who grew up in the area, purchased the land from the parents of a childhood friend who had passed on. He began ranching it around 1913, adding onto his holding over the years and driving cattle into Denver. White passed on in 1969, but his wife and son, George, operated the ranch until 1972—the same year Jefferson Country approved its open-space program. Jeffco purchased the land in 1975 and dedicated it to Paul White's memory. The ranch buildings still stand today, and visitors can see old ranching equipment near the parking area.

A wild turkey roams across White Ranch Open Space.

A gorilla-shaped rock ponders Colorado atop a ridge in White Ranch Open Space.

The Rawhide Loop is a fitting tribute to the land, taking hikers across the old hayfields and meadows, resplendent with late-spring wildflowers, and through largely forested areas thick with ponderosa pine.

Hiking Rawhide Trail in a clockwise direction takes you down the old ranch road, now a wide singletrack dirt path that's great for hiking and biking, and into the lovely meadows. The first junction you'll encounter is Wrangler's Run, at about 1.0 mile in. You can take that to shortcut most of the hike for a 2.5-mile loop, but with little elevation change, it's lovely to continue hiking. The farther you go, the more likely you are to see the park's natural inhabitants, including mule deer, wild turkeys, and others.

At 1.7 miles the Waterhole Trail junction leads to the Sourdough Springs camping areas, with toilets and a spot to refill water. Continue north and around to begin your way back. You're rewarded with entirely different perspectives as the trail wanders through more forested land and offers views to the east of a rocky ridge before entering the central meadow near the parking lot and the old ranch equipment.

Miles and Directions

- 0.0 Start at White Ranch Park West Trailhead and head left (northwest) on the Rawhide Trail.
- 0.3 Stay on the Rawhide Trail as it passes the Belcher Hill Trail to the left.

White Ranch Open Space: Rawhide Loop

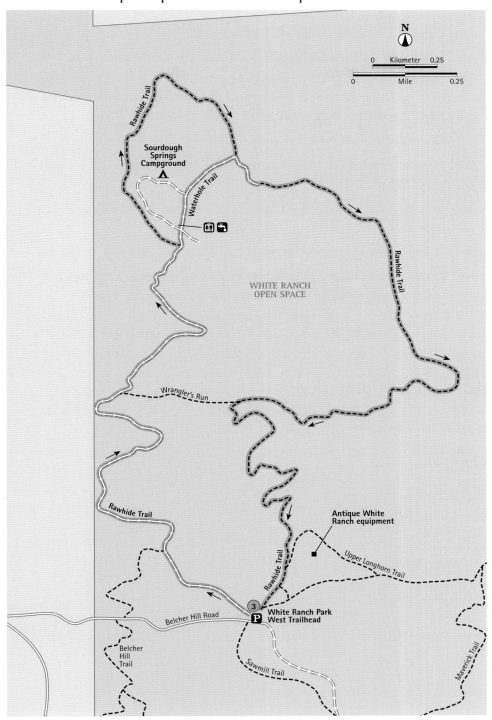

1.1 Continue northeast on the Rawhide Trail, passing the Wrangler's Run Trail junction on the right. (Bailout: Take the Wrangler's Run Trail east to shortcut across to the eastern side of the Rawhide Trail for a 2.3-mile loop.)

1.7 Go left at the Waterhole Trail junction, leaving the dirt road to continue on the Rawhide Trail, which becomes a singletrack dirt trail. (Option: Turn right on the Waterhole Trail to access toilets and water or the Sourdough Springs camping areas. Taking the Waterhole Trail across shortens the loop to 4.5 miles.)

2.4 Reach a picnic area at the northernmost and highest point of the hike.

2.5 Continue on the Rawhide Trail, bypassing the Waterhole Trail junction on the east side of the park.

3.9 Reach the low point of the hike and begin the steady, gradual climb back the trailhead.

4.1 Pass the eastern junction with Wrangler's Run; stay on the Rawhide Trail

4.9 Pass the Upper Longhorn Trail junction to return to the White Ranch Park West Trailhead. (Option: Take the Upper Longhorn Trail to visit remnants of ranch equipment.)

5.0 Arrive back at the trailhead.

Adventure Information

White Ranch. www.jeffco.us/1437/White-Ranch-Park

Outfitters

Bentgate Mountaineering. 1313 Washington Ave., Golden; (303) 271-9382; bentgate.com. Open Sun–Fri; closed Sat.

Wilderness Exchange. 2401 15th St., Ste. 100, Denver; (303) 964-0708; wildernessx.com

REI Denver Flagship. 1416 Platte St., Denver; (303) 756-3100; rei.com

Great Pre- or Post-Adventure Spots

Woody's Wood Fired Pizza. 1305 Washington Ave., Golden; (303) 277-0443; woodysgolden .com

Intact buildings at White Ranch Open Space.

Barrels & Bottles Brewery. 600 12th St., Unit 180, Golden; (720) 328-3643; barrelsbottles .com

Tributary Food Hall & Drinkery. 701 12th St., Golden; (303) 856-7225; tributarygolden.com

Hike 4 Deer Creek Canyon: Bill Couch Mountain

Starting in a grassy meadow, this hike climbs a cool, narrow canyon along Plymouth Creek, offering some shade even on hot days, making this a pleasant hike throughout the summer. From the top of Bill Couch Mountain, hikers have a lovely 360-degree view. To the east views showcase South Valley Park's flatirons and hogback, with Denver's cityscape as a northeastern backdrop. The plains stretch to the horizon to the southeast. To the west the horizon rises, pushed ever higher by tantalizing views of the Front Range Rockies.

Start: Deer Creek Canyon Trailhead

Distance: 5.6 miles out and back

Hiking time: About 3 hours

Difficulty: Easy to intermediate trail with decent elevation gain

Elevation gain: 1,390 feet

Trail surface: Dirt singletrack

Best seasons: Year-round; fantastic wildflowers in spring; decent foliage in fall

Other trail users: Equestrians, mountain bikers

Canine compatibility: Leashed dogs permitted

Land status: Jefferson County Open Space

Camping, fees, and permits: Permits required for large groups; no camping

Schedule: Open year-round, 1 hour before sunrise to 1 hour after sunset. (Park will close for muddy conditions to prevent erosion.)

Maps: USGS Indian Hills; National Geographic Trails Illustrated #100: Boulder/Golden

Nearest town: Littleton

Trail contact: Jefferson County Open Space; (303) 271-5925; jeffco.us/open-space

Finding the trailhead: From the intersection of West Ken Caryl Avenue and CO 470, turn left in 0.2 mile onto South Valley Road. Turn left in 2.1 miles to stay on South Valley Road. Turn right at the next intersection in 0.3 mile onto West Deer Creek Canyon Road. In 0.7 mile turn left onto Grizzly Drive; continue for 0.4 mile and turn right into the trailhead parking lot (13388 Grizzly Dr.). The trailhead has restrooms and water, as well as signage. GPS: N39.54308° / W105.15204°

The Hike

Another of Jefferson County's open-space gems, Deer Creek Canyon Park has more than 10 miles of trails, with multiuse trails as well as trails dedicated to hikers and equestrians, including the Meadowlark, Homesteader, and Golden Eagle Trails. Mountain bikers can test themselves on a rocky section of the Plymouth Creek Trail called "The Wall" and enjoy Red Mesa Loop, a 2.5-mile loop on the park's western side.

The land was used by the Clovis people as early as 12,000 years ago and later by members of Arapaho, Cheyenne, and Ute tribes. It was settled by the Williamsons in 1872. John Williamson, suffering from tuberculosis, was given just months to live unless he moved to a drier climate. Williamson, his wife, Annie, son, John, and Annie's niece, Esther, emigrated from Plymouth, England. They purchased the land from a squatter and began building their new homestead, Glen Plym, named for their old home. They grew hay, wheat, corn, and vegetables, irrigating with water from Plymouth Creek.

Looking east toward the top of Bill Couch Mountain.

Penstemon and scrub oak along the trail at Deer Creek Canyon.

As John had found relief from his tuberculosis in their new home, the Williamsons invited others suffering from the disease to come out. Guests who traveled from the East Coast stayed in tent houses and ate in the large dining room the family built. Folk from Denver flocked in on the weekends. Both John and his wife passed in 1911, nearly thirty years after his initial diagnosis.

Annie's niece, Esther, had married local rancher Sam Couch, and Bill Couch Mountain, which offers the best views in the area, was named for Esther's son. The park also encompasses some of the Couch homestead.

The hike on Plymouth Creek Trail begins easily enough, welcoming hikers as it travels southeast across a meadow of wild grasses and flowers speckled with yucca, prickly pear cactus, and other flora, such as scrub oak or Gambel oak, and sage. But as the trail starts climbing into Plymouth Creek's small canyon, it narrows and steepens, sometimes climbing up steps.

Thankfully, as the trail parallels the creek, taller trees, mostly pine and fir, provide shade for the most arduous part of the hike. While most are respectful, beware of mountain bikers coming down the steeper sections of the trail. Most will stay on rocks on the northwestern side of the trail during sections with stairs.

As the trail connects with the Red Mesa and Homesteader Trails, it continues to climb, albeit less steeply. Here the trail opens up to a pine-oak woodland with views to the east interspersed with grassy areas. Turn right onto the Golden Eagle Trail and lope along its south-facing side before it spirals to a small, rocky top with panoramic views. It's a great spot to stop and snack before heading back down. Look for eagles and falcons soaring by as they hunt for food.

Though close to Denver, there is a lot of wildlife in the area, including deer, mountain lions, and bears. You're not as likely to see the predators, though. It also helps to be wary of rattlesnakes sunning on the trail.

Miles and Directions

0.0   Start at Deer Creek Canyon Trailhead. Head left (south) on the Plymouth Creek Trail.

0.8   The trail crosses Plymouth Creek then travels along the trail to the left (south) of the creek.

1.0   Continue on the Plymouth Creek Trail, passing the Meadowlark Trail on the right.

1.6   At the Plymouth Creek–Plymouth Mountain Trail junction, turn right to stay on the Plymouth Creek–Homesteader Trail.

2.2   At the Plymouth Creek–Red Mesa Trail junction, continue straight.

2.4   A the Red Mesa Loop–Golden Eagle Trail junction, turn right to follow the Golden Eagle Trail.

2.8   Reach the peak of Bill Couch Mountain; head back via the same route.

5.6   Arrive back at the trailhead.

Adventure Information

White Ranch. www.jeffco.us/1437/White-Ranch-Park

Outfitters

Bentgate Mountaineering. 1313 Washington Ave., Golden; (303) 271-9382; bentgate.com. Open Sun–Fri; closed Sat.

Wilderness Exchange. 2401 15th St., Ste. 100, Denver; (303) 964-0708; wildernessx.com

REI. 5375 S Wadsworth Blvd., Lakewood; (303) 932-0600; rei.com

Deer Creek Canyon Park: Bill Couch Mountain

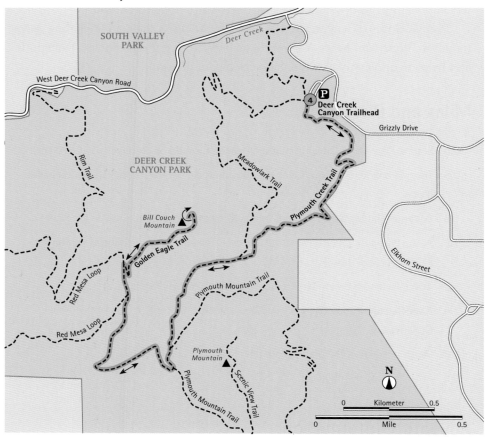

Great Pre- or Post-Adventure Spots

Green Mountain Beer Company. 2585 S Lewis Way, Lakewood; (303) 986-0201; green mountainbeercompany.com

Lariat Lodge Brewing Co. 12684 W Indore Place, Littleton; (303) 979-0797; lariatlodge brewing.com

The Flying Pig Burger Co. 5935 S Zang St., Littleton; (720) 726-4544; flyingpigburgerco .com

Hike 5 Staunton State Park: Old Mill to Mason Creek Loop

Opened in 2013, Staunton is one of Colorado's newest state parks. It has nearly 30 miles of hiking and biking trails, campsites, track-chair access, climbing, fishing, and more. This tour de Staunton takes you across grassy meadows to the park's historic cabins, the site of an abandoned lumber mill, and its highest overlooks, where trekkers get fantastic views west of nearby Lions Head and Mount Evans beyond and south to Pikes Peak, 50 or so miles away.

Start: Staunton Ranch Trailhead

Distance: 7.6-mile loop

Hiking time: About 4 hours

Difficulty: Easy to intermediate hiking with decent elevation gain on dirt trails

Elevation gain: 1,330 feet

Trail surface: Dirt road and singletrack

Best seasons: Year-round; great spring flowers, peaking in mid- to late June; lovely fall colors

Other trail users: Mountain bikers, equestrians, climbers, campers, track chairs, geocachers

Canine compatibility: Leashed dogs permitted (leash less than 6 feet long)

Land status: State park

Camping, fees, and permits: Daily park fee or annual state pass; camping permits purchasable online

Schedule: Open year-round; day-use hours 6 a.m.–10 p.m.

Maps: USGS Meridian Hill, Conifer, Pine; National Geographic Trails Illustrated #100: Boulder/Golden

Nearest town: Conifer

Trail contact: Staunton State Park; (303) 816-0912; cpw.state.co.us/placestogo/parks/Staunton/

Finding the trailhead: From the intersection of US 285 and South Elk Creek Road, go 1.5 miles to the park entrance, on the right. Pay at the visitor center, or continue to the parking lot 0.5 mile from the Elk Creek Road turnoff (12102 S Elk Creek Rd.). Visitors can also pay fees at a self-service kiosk, which accepts credit cards. GPS: N39.50052° / W105.37759°

The Hike

It took Staunton State Park a long time to sprout from a seed in the mind of Frances Hornbrook Staunton into today's vast mountain park. Staunton's parents, Drs. Rachel and Archibald Staunton, purchased an initial 160-acre plot in the area in 1918. Initially, Rachel homesteaded the land in the warmer months, providing medical care to those in the area, including Native American families, who bartered beadwork, pottery, jewelry, and rugs to pay for her services. They grew the homestead into a 1,720-acre ranch, which Frances eventually took over and managed.

Frances quietly wrote the donation of the land into her will in 1961, years after her father passed. She didn't announce the bequest until 1984. It was completed in 1986 before her death in 1989. Additional parcels were added in the late 1990s.

Oddly enough *Harvey*—the play about a 6-foot-tall imaginary rabbit friend—had a role to play in the finalization of Staunton. Mary Chase, the play's Pulitzer Prize–winning author, owned a crucial 80-acre parcel. The last parcel, which would allow access to the rest of the land without having to go through a

Blaine cabin, built in the late 1800s is among the earliest buildings still existent in Staunton State Park.

The Staunton Ranch Trail meanders through grassy, sparsely wooded areas with Staunton Rocks in the background.

subdivision, wasn't acquired until 2006. That final acquisition raised the acreage of the park to nearly 4,000 acres.

With its sweeping meadows, ponds, and forested areas butting against rocky outcrops of granitic Pikes Peak batholiths, it's no wonder the Stauntons, Chase, and others were so enamored with the area. Operating under the name Lazy V Ranch, the Staunton family also had guests and held camps on the property, hosting groups including Girl Scouts, the Lazy V Ranch for Boys, and the Mount Marion Camp for Catholic Girls.

Today a great network of well-marked and -defined trails meander through the landscape, allowing visitors to walk through aspen groves, grassy meadows speckled with wildflowers, and pines. At its northern and eastern peripheries, trails lead to towering rock formations and reveal other treasures, such as Elk Falls and endless opportunities for rock climbing. The Old Mill to Mason Creek Loop offers a chance to get the highest views as well as see the historic Staunton cabins and the remains of their lumber mill. It also offers a trio of the most impressive and expansive outlooks in the park. This hike offers a little of everything the park has to offer.

Looking west over Staunton State Park from the Pikes Peak lookout.

Heading west and north on the Staunton Ranch Trail takes you across rolling meadows shared with deer and elk. The lightly forested area is scattered with pine, fir, and aspen groves and carpeted in a rainbow of wildflowers. In late spring and summer, wild roses, gold banner, and silvery lupine are among the flowers that hedge the trail here. Yellow-flowered shrubby cinquefoil and a plethora of other wildflowers sprout among the grasses and trees.

A short hike on the trail brings you to the remnants of the shower house and cabins built on the property. These are now on the National Register of Historic Places. The loop continues and turns right at the Old Mill Road, a dirt road surrounded by thicker forests. Much of the most popular rock-climbing areas in the park, like The Pooka, are near here. This also marks the earnest climb of the trek, a mile-long climb rising 500 feet to the remains of the old lumber mill. The mill was scrapped for metal during World War II. Most of it collapsed sometime in the 1960s or 1970s, but the bunkhouse remains standing.

From here the loop makes another sharp, short ascent, gaining 100 feet of elevation in 0.2 mile. It climbs another 300 feet over the next mile, reaching a high point of 9,510 feet at the Eagle Cliffs Overlook, a great spot to rest and take in the day's adventures so far. The remainder of the loop is a relatively steady descent. Though a little lower, the next two outlooks, Pikes Peak and Catamounts, offer vistas as stunning as Eagle Cliffs.

Much of the remainder of the loop is a descent through coniferous forest. At about 5.0 miles into the hike, you begin encountering a series of low-angle switchbacks that lead to the Mason Creek Trail. This southerly trail takes you the remainder of the way back to the parking lot on the eastern side of the park.

Miles and Directions

0.0 Start at the Staunton Ranch Trailhead, on the northwestern side of the parking lot. Go left (northwest) on the Staunton Ranch Trail, walking past the Ponderosa and Spruce campsite areas.

0.8 At the Dines Meadow, Historic Cabin, and Staunton Ranch Trail, go left to visit the historic cabins.

1.3 Stay left at the trail junction to rejoin the Staunton Ranch Trail.

1.6 Cross a small bridge in a forested area.

1.7 Turn right at the junction with the Old Mill Trail and begin a gradual 2.0-mile ascent leading to the old mill ruins and the high point of the hike.

2.4 Reach the old mill site and turn right at the junction with the Mason Creek Trail.

3.4 Turn right at the Bear Paw Trail junction to gain three of the best overlooks in the park.

3.7 Reach the Eagle Cliffs Overlook, about 20-feet off the main trail, the high point of the hike.

4.4 Reach the Pikes Peak Overlook.

4.5 Reach the Catamounts Overlook.

5.0 Encounter switchbacks.

5.5 Go right (southeast) at the junction with the Mason Creek Trail and make the bulk of your descent.

7.4 Turn right (west) at the junction with the Staunton Ranch Trail to return to the trailhead.

7.6 Arrive back at the trailhead.

Staunton State Park: Old Mill to Mason Creek Loop

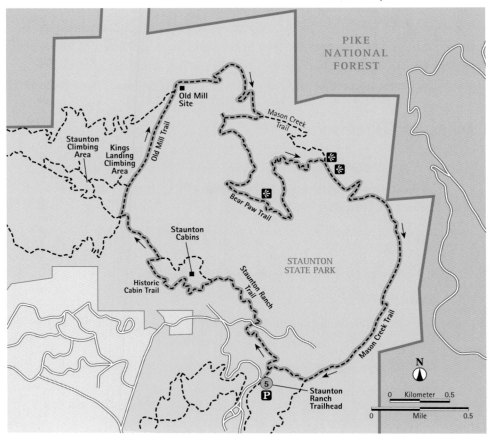

Adventure Information

Organizations

Friends of Staunton State Park (webcam). friendsofstauntonstatepark.org/webcam

Outfitters

Evergreen Mountain Sports. 10875 US 285, Ste. D101, Conifer; (303) 674-5100; evergreen mountainsports.com

Bentgate Mountaineering. 1313 Washington Ave., Golden; (303) 271-9382; bentgate.com. Open Sun–Fri; closed Sat.

Remnants of the Old Mill site at Staunton State Park. Parts of the sawmill were scrapped for metal during World War II.

REI Lakewood. 5375 S Wadsworth Blvd., Lakewood; (303) 932–0600; rei.com

Great Pre- or Post-Adventure Spots

Coney Island Boardwalk hot dog stand. 10 Old Stagecoach Rd., Bailey; (303) 838–9999; coneyislandbailey.wordpress.com

Mad Jack's Mountain Brewery. 23 Main St., Bailey; (303) 816–2337; madjacksmountain brewery.com

Green Mountain Beer Company. 2585 S Lewis Way, Lakewood; (303) 986–0201; green mountainbeercompany.com

Hike 6 Bear Peak

This bear of an ascent is one of the tougher climbs on the Front Range and a favorite of locals who want to torture their legs or train for harder adventures. Starting at an iconic I. M. Pei-designed building, the hike has a sustained incline of 2,130 feet over 1.5 miles and a total elevation gain of 2,530 feet. Adventurers who endure this StairMaster of a hike are rewarded with a lovely climb through a forested canyon and a fun rock scramble to awesome views of the entire Front Range and Rockies. On clear days you can see the Front Range's two most prominent mountains: Pikes Peak, nearly 80 miles south, and Longs Peak, about 26 miles to the northwest, as well as other fourteeners, including Mount Evans.

Start: NCAR Trailhead, National Center for Atmospheric Research

Distance: 5.5 miles out and back

Hiking time: About 4 hours

Difficulty: Difficult, featuring a tough ascent and a final scramble over rock to the top

Elevation gain: 2,530 feet

Trail surface: Dirt trail, rocky surfaces

Best seasons: Late spring through late fall

Other trail users: Hikers only (equestrians allowed on some but not all segments of this hike)

Canine compatibility: Leashed dogs permitted

Land status: City of Boulder Open Space and Mountain Parks (OSMP)

Camping, fees, and permits: No fees; off-trail permits available online

Schedule: Open year-round; NCAR Road open 6 a.m.–10 p.m.

Maps: USGS Eldorado Springs; National Geographic Trails Illustrated #100: Boulder/Golden

Nearest town: Boulder

Trail contact: OSMP, Boulder; (303) 441-3440; osmp.org

Finding the trailhead: From the intersection of CO 93 and Table Mesa Drive, head west on Table Mesa Drive for 2.5 miles to the NCAR parking lot (1850 Table Mesa Dr.). The NCAR access road opens at 6 a.m. Head southwest on NCAR Road about 200 feet from the parking lot to a large rock and signs for the trail network. Here the trail parallels the building. GPS: N39.97873° / W105.27534°

The Hike

This trek starts at the Mesa Laboratory of the National Center for Atmospheric Research (NCAR), which is housed in a unique building designed by world-renowned architect I. M. Pei. In addition to serving as a lab for NCAR scientists and researchers, the building hosts galleries and interpretive exhibitions where visitors can touch a cloud, steer a hurricane, and learn about atmospheric sciences to help people understand atmospheric science and weather—something any Colorado adventurer can stand to learn more about!

In designing the building, Pei was inspired by the cliff dwellings at Mesa Verde. To mimic the color of the reddish granite of the Flatirons, sand was sourced from a local quarry and mixed into the concrete used for the structure. It's worth a

Looking west near the top of Bear Peak, the Rockies continue to get taller.

The trail gets rockier near the top of Bear Peak.

visit. The building has a weekday cafe that closes at 1:30 p.m. and restroom facilities that visitors can use.

NCAR is a program of the National Science Foundation. It's managed and administered by the University Corporation for Atmospheric Research (UCAR), which was founded in 1960 by fourteen member universities.

The first part of this adventure is along the NCAR Trail, also called the Walter Orr Roberts Trail, named for UCAR's first president and NCAR's first director. This part of the hike, on flat trail, includes interpretive signs explaining weather and atmospheric conditions. After the interpretive signs, the trail starts a little climb over the 100-million-year-old Dakota Hogback. This feature stretches as far south as New Mexico and as far north as Wyoming.

As the trail descends from the hogback, Boulder's famous Flatirons come into view. These dramatic rock spires are part of the Fountain Formation, composed of conglomerate rock and sandstone deposited some 280 million years ago and ultimately uplifted into their current formation roughly 65 million years ago as the current Rocky Mountains grew. Softer rock and the rock around them eroded away, and today they stand like giant rocky splinters jutting into the sky, glowing in the reflected light of dawn.

Continue across the flower-speckled meadow and enter a forested area. This is your last respite before beginning the climb. After crossing Bear Canyon Creek, the climb begins.

For this adventure, stay left on the Mesa Trail at the junction with Bear Canyon Trail. Continue climbing the wide trail and head right at the junction with the Fern Canyon Trail to begin the leg-pumping ascent. The initial climb isn't too tough. But after the trail passes the Shanahan Trail to the left, the incline increases significantly, reaching up to 30 percent as the trail switchbacks up Fern Canyon on water bars and steps. Please stay on-trail here and observe signs for peregrine falcon closures to protect their nesting habitat. The toughest stretch ends as you reach the spur trail to Nebel Horn, which is worth a short side trip for a quick break and to get great views of Boulder, the Flatirons, Green Mountain, and more.

Of course there's more. From here the trail turns south, following Bear Peak's ridge. At about 2.5 miles into the climb, the forest starts thinning out, right around tree line, due to a wildfire in 2012. From here complete the 100-foot scramble across rocks to the top.

Relish the views, drink some water, and enjoy some food before returning via the same route. If you haven't had enough, you can always turn the hike into a loop and add about 2.0 miles by taking the Bear Peak West Ridge Trail from the top and connecting with the Bear Canyon Trail to return to the NCAR lot.

Miles and Directions

0.0 Start at the NCAR Trailhead and head west toward Table Mountain.

0.5 Pass a water tank to the right and continue straight at the Mesa Trail Connector junction.

Bear Peak

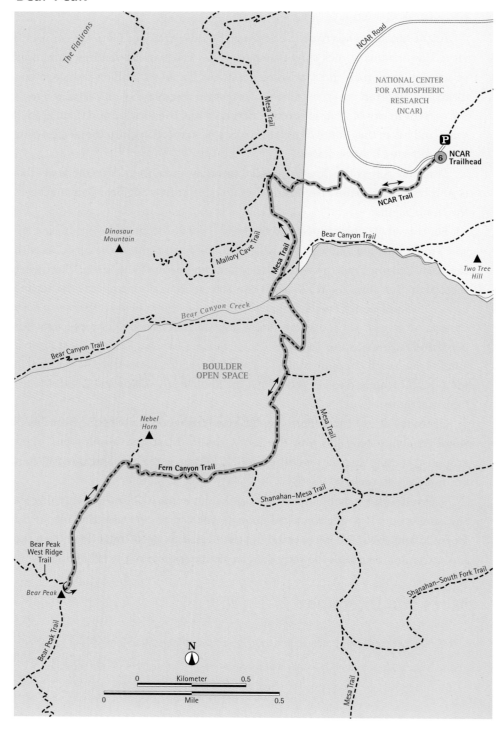

0.6 Head left (south) to stay on the Mesa Trail at the Mesa Trail Connector–Mallory Cave Trail junction.

1.0 Continue on Mesa Trail as Bear Canyon Trail joins from the left. Begin the ascent, crossing Bear Canyon Creek about 300 feet after the junction.

1.3 Turn left (south) onto the Fern Canyon Trail at the junction with the Mesa and Bear Canyon Trails.

1.4 Continue south on the Fern Canyon Trail as the Mesa Trail splits off to the right.

1.8 Continue west on the Fern Canyon Trail at its junction with the Shanahan Trail.

2.0 Begin a long series of switchbacks that last about 0.25 mile.

2.3 Pass the Nebel Horn turnoff as the trail heads southwest on Bear Peak's ridge.

2.8 Reach the top of Bear Peak at 8,458 feet. Return via the same route.

5.5 Arrive back at the NCAR Trailhead.

Adventure Information

Outfitters

Neptune Mountaineering. 633 S Broadway, Boulder; (303) 499-8866; neptunemountaineering.com

JAX Outdoor Gear. 900 South, US 287, Lafayette; (720) 266-6160; jaxgoods.com

Moosejaw. 1755 29th St., Unit 1092, Boulder; (720) 452-2432; moosejaw.com

REI Boulder. 1789 28th St., Boulder; (303) 583-9970; rei.com

Great Pre- or Post-Adventure Spots

The Post Brewing Co. 2027 13th St., Boulder; (720) 372-3341; postbrewing.com/boulder/

4 Noses Brewing Co. 8855 W 116th Circle, Broomfield; (720) 460-2797; 4nosesbrewing .com

Hike 7 Walker Ranch Loop

A prime example of a riparian habitat nestled in the foothills of Colorado, Walker Ranch is listed as a cultural site on the National Register of Historic Places and also listed on the Colorado Register of Historic Properties. This loop takes your breath away both physically, with some challenging climbs, and figuratively, with beautiful views of Indian Peaks and the Rockies and patches of wildflowers in meadows and in the shadows of Douglas fir and ponderosa pine. It's fantastic on foot, mountain bike, and horseback. However, a series of challenging steps on the eastern side of the loop means many bikers will shoulder their bikes, and it's not recommended for horses.

Start: Walker Ranch Trail access, Crescent Meadows parking lot

Distance: 7.3-mile loop

Hiking time: About 4 hours

Difficulty: Moderately difficult due to steep inclines and declines

Elevation gain: 1,560 feet

Trail surface: Dirt trails and closed, nonmotorized roads

Best seasons: Year-round

Other trail users: Cyclists, equestrians, anglers

Canine compatibility: Leashed dogs permitted

Land status: Boulder County Parks and Open Space; Eldorado Canyon State Park

Camping, fees, and permits: No fees, permits, or camping

Schedule: Open year-round, sunrise to sunset

Maps: USGS Eldorado Springs; National Geographic Trails Illustrated #100: Boulder/Golden

Nearest town: Boulder

Trail contact: Boulder County Parks and Open Space; (303) 678-6200; bouldercounty.org/open-space/parks-and-trails/walker-ranch

Special considerations: No fire of any type is allowed in the park. This includes smoking cigarettes or marijuana.

Finding the trailhead: From the intersection of CO 93 and CO 72, head west on CO 72. In 7.5 miles turn right onto Crescent Park Drive and continue for 1 mile. Turn right onto Gross Dam Road; the trailhead is 1.8 miles ahead on the right, just after passing over railroad tracks (2502–3108 Gross Dam Rd.). GPS: N39.93043° / W105.34001°

Note: There are plenty of ways to access the Walker Ranch, with three parking areas on the north side, but coming in from Crescent Meadows and Eldorado

Early spring waters flow under snow and ice on Boulder Creek.

State Canyon Park on the southwestern side, you're less likely to see as many people parked.

The Hike

With large forested areas covering much of the ranch, this hike offers some shade on hot summer days. The loop also crosses South Boulder Creek in numerous spots and parallels it in others, making for ideal spots to cool off on a hot day. In winter the hike becomes a great adventure on snowshoes and winter traction.

It's no wonder James Walker homesteaded this little paradise in 1882. But he was far from the first user of the land. Evidence shows that Native Americans used the land far earlier for hunting and fishing. Today this lush piece of land consists of 3,616 acres of open space with more than 14 miles of trails in lower montane habitat. With terrain ranging from meadows, forested slopes, and steep rocky outcrops to stream corridors, gulches, and montane shrublands, the park provides important habitat for plants and wildlife.

With many original buildings intact or restored on the Walker Homestead, it's no surprise that it's on the National Register of Historic Places as a representation of how early settlers used the land and how those uses changed to include not only homesteading and ranching but also mining and logging. The nearby railroad also impacted how the land was used.

Today the park works to preserve both legacies of the land, natural and human-created. Park resources are managed to promote wildlife habitat, and it shows in the inventory of plants and animals that live in the area, including elk, mule deer, bobcat, mountain lion, black bear, red fox, and more. Nearly a hundred bird species are found within its borders, flying through or roosting and hanging out in ponderosa pine, Douglas fir, and aspen. Boulder raspberry and mountain mahogany, as well as wide array of wildflowers, are found in the park today.

The park has felt the ravages of fires. The Eldorado Canyon Fire of 2000, for instance, changed a portion of the park's montane forests into a mix of grass- and shrub-covered areas with pockets of tree cover. You'll encounter almost all of this on the Walker Ranch Loop.

As you head northwest from the Crescent Moon area's trailhead. The trail drops into the ranch land, crossing South Boulder Creek on a bridge for the first time then paralleling it at just about 1.0 mile into the hike. Shortly thereafter, a picnic table by the Tom Davis Gulch provides a spot for a quick rest before climbing back up about 600 feet to the parking area by the Walker Ranch Homestead. As the trail heads back into lowlands, it goes through a series of switchbacks as it descends 500 feet to the next trailhead, with toilets nearby. From here the trail descends another 300 feet and crosses the South Boulder Creek again, this time on the eastern side of the park.

The next section is the hardest part of the hike, climbing up rocks and stairs for an initial 500 or so feet. At 6.0 miles the elevation gain mellows out for a bit as the trail winds around the side of a hill and then resumes climbing as it crosses over into Eldorado State Canyon Park. A little farther along, the forest opens up into grassy meadows as the trail heads east to return to the parking area.

Miles and Directions

0.0   Start at the Walker Ranch Trail access, northeast of the parking lot. Head left (north) for a clockwise loop of the park, and begin a meandering descent on a good trail.

1.0   The trail crosses a branch of the South Boulder Creek on a bridge shortly after turning sharply to the north.

1.5   The trail crosses a smaller, intermittent tributary to South Boulder Creek near a fishing access point then begins a 1.6-mile ascent.

2.5   Reach the Walker Ranch Loop trailhead (picnic and toilet facilities) as the trail turns right (easterly) and the climb eases.

3.3   Reach large switchbacks heading downhill.

4.1   The trail continues to the right (south). To the left, the Ethel Harrold Trailhead offers a picnic area and toilets about 1,000 feet from the trail.

5.0   Reach the low point of the hike at the Eldorado Canyon Trail junction; continue south a little farther before the trail turns right.

5.1   Cross South Boulder Creek on a bridge near another good fishing area; rapidly ascend on stairs and switchbacks.

5.2   The ascent becomes more gradual and, after a sharp elbow, begins heading southwest.

7.3   Arrive back at the parking area.

Walker Ranch Loop

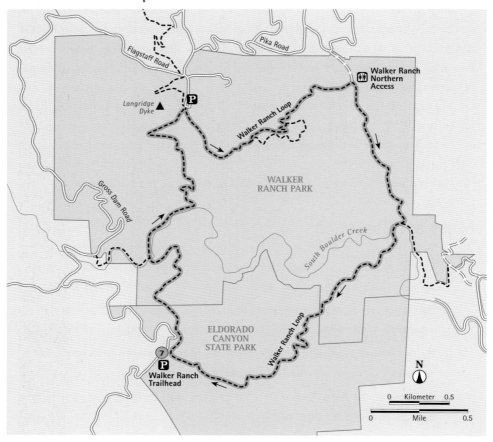

Adventure Information

Walker Ranch. bouldercounty.org/open-space/parks-and-trails/walker-ranch/

Outfitters

Neptune Mountaineering. 633 S Broadway, Boulder; (303) 499-8866; neptunemountaineering.com

JAX Outdoor Gear. 900 South, US 287, Lafayette; (720) 266 6160; jaxgoods.com

Moosejaw. 1755 29th St., Unit 1092, Boulder; (720) 452-2432; moosejaw.com

REI Boulder. 1789 28th St., Boulder; (303) 583-9970; rei.com

A fun, slushy hike through Walker Ranch on an early spring day.

Great Pre- or Post-Adventure Spots

The Post Brewing Co. 2027 13th St., Boulder; (720) 372-3341; postbrewing.com/boulder/

4 Noses Brewing Co. 8855 W 116th Circle, Broomfield; (720) 460-2797; 4nosesbrewing .com

Hike 8 Colorado Trail: Segment 2—Buffalo Creek Fire

The views of this segment of the Colorado Trail are like no other. The devastation of the 1996 Buffalo Creek Fire is abundantly apparent for almost the entirety of this segment of the trail. While grasses and shrubs are starting to grow on this once-forested part of the trail, the impacts of the fire are unavoidable here. Perhaps a benefit of the fire is that this segment now offers more spectacular views of the granitic and sandstone rocks and peaks around it.

Start: South Platte River Road Trailhead

Distance: 9.5 miles point to point

Hiking time: About 5.5 hours

Difficulty: Moderately difficult; significant elevation gain and significant exposure to sun with very little access to water

Elevation gain: 2,300 feet

Trail surface: Dirt trail, rocky surfaces

Best seasons: Late spring through late fall

Other trail users: Cyclists, equestrians

Canine compatibility: Leashed dogs permitted

Land status: Pike National Forest

Camping, fees, and permits: Use fee at Little Scraggy trailhead; no camping at South Platte River

Schedule: Open year-round, 24/7

Maps: USGS Platte Canyon, Pine; National Geographic Trails Illustrated #135: Deckers, Rampart Range

Nearest town: Buffalo Creek

Trail contact: South Platte Ranger District, Pike National Forest; (303) 275-5610; fs.usda.gov/contactus/psicc

Special considerations: There is very little water on this trail. On hot days bring more water than you're used to, just in case. Emergency water is usually available at an unmanned fire station at the northeast side. Make sure to turn the spigot off after using it. Also, many property owners in the area relish their privacy; don't park on private land, and don't trespass.

Finding the trailhead: From South Foxton Road off US 285, head east on South Foxton Road for 6.6 miles. Turn left onto West Platte River Road and continue for

You can still see damage from the Buffalo Creek Wildfire; this was once a pine-filled forest. Little Scraggy peak looms on the horizon.

5.7 miles. Turn right onto CR 97, crossing a bridge, and find a parking area on the right in 0.6 mile. There is a vault toilet here. GPS: N39.40047° / W105.16765°

The Hike

The Colorado Trail is among the highest long trails in the United States, with a higher percentage of its total mileage above 10,000 feet than any other long trail in the country. It's one of Colorado's truly remarkable adventure gems and showcases the history, geology, and heritage of the land in a way no other adventure in the state can match. It's a story of dreams realized, Coloradans' enthusiasm for the outdoors, and the power of volunteer efforts.

The nearly 500-mile-long trail travels across eight mountain ranges as it goes through six national forests and wilderness areas and traverses five major river systems, some of which help feed much of the Southwest. The trail has twenty-eight distinct segments for hikers and equestrians. It also has an 80-mile bypass near the Collegiate Peaks, which allows bikers to complete the trail without traveling across wilderness lands where they're prohibited. Across its entirety, the average elevation of the trail is 10,300 feet, with a low point of 5,500 feet at its eastern terminus at the mouth of Waterton Canyon. The trail's highest point is 13,271 feet, just below Coney Summit, closer to its southwestern terminus near Durango.

The idea for a Colorado Trail stretches back to the 1940s and the Roundup Riders and Colorado Mountain Club, but the idea was really popularized by *Colorado Magazine* publisher Merrill Hastings in 1970. However, without the passionate efforts of Gudrun "Gudy" Gaskill, first woman president of the Colorado Mountain Club and founder of the Colorado Trail Foundation (see sidebar), the trail may never have seen completion. Gaskill and hundreds of volunteers prevailed and built the trail at a cost of just $500 per mile—a fraction of the $24,000 per mile the USDA Forest Service estimated it would cost.

The whole of the Colorado Trail is impressive, gaining some 90,000 vertical feet from end to end, but if you spent all your time doing it in one year, how would you have time to explore all the rest Colorado has to offer? This segment of the Colorado Trail is among the most distinctive—a story of both tragedy and recovery. It's also fitting, as it pays homage to the Colorado Trail's most ardent advocate, starting by crossing the Gudy Gaskill Bridge over the South Platte River.

Sadly, the most outstanding features of this hike are now the scars of the Buffalo Creek Fire, sparked in 1996 by an unattended campfire near Wellington Lake. The fire raged across 12,000 acres of Pike National Forest, forever changing streambeds and drainage in the area. It's expected that it will take centuries for the forest to fully recover. Much of this segment still passes through that burn scar. However, while the trail passes through the charred remains of pine, fir, and other trunks, the ground is being rejuvenated as buckwheat, paintbrush, pasqueflower, sunflower, and other wildflowers reclaim the land.

Thanks to the fire, the geology of the area opens up to travelers in ways it hadn't for centuries. Views of Cathedral Spires and Long Scraggy Peak are now visible from much more of this trek. Those more striking features—the giant domes, rock spires, and broad flat rock—are composed of 1.1-billion-year-old Pikes Peak Granite. The metamorphic basement rock found at the trailhead is even older, and this trek takes you on that ancient story.

After crossing the Gudy Gaskill Bridge, the trail turns right and back around to pass under the bridge. It then begins the long ascent to the Top of the World

Pikes Peak to the south from the Colorado Trail. The carcasses of burnt trees wait for time to take them down.

Ridge on short sieges of switchbacks. A mile into the hike, the incline lessens and the trail enters the open burn area and passes an old quartz mine. One can only imagine now how the area would have looked when covered with pine and fir, as many of the surrounding areas are.

At about 2.3 miles the trail comes to an outcrop of pink granite. It's a good place for a rest and to take photos. After this, the trail gets back into some forest. At 4.2 miles the trail crosses an old 4x4 road; there are good places along the trail to camp if you're out for an overnight trip. A little farther, at 4.6 miles, is the high point of the trip (7,770 feet), which offers views of Chair Rocks to the west as well as other features, such as Long Scraggy Peak to the south and Raleigh Peak to the southeast. The trail now heads southeast, making a slight descent before climbing again and crossing the dirt Raleigh Peak Road, which it parallels until it gets close to the unmanned fire station. From here the trail is relatively flat to the parking area.

The trail reenters the burn area at 6.5 miles and shortly thereafter arrives at the burnt Top of the World picnic area. Continue on the trail and find the fire station on the right at 8.8 miles. The trail first parallels then crosses Deckers Road, where there's a pullout for cars. This is the end of the segment. If parking is not

GUDY GASKILL: MOTHER OF THE COLORADO TRAIL

Although the idea for the Colorado Trail stretched back to the late 1940s, without the efforts of Gudrun "Gudy" Gaskill, the Colorado Trail probably wouldn't have reached fruition. Fondly referred to as the "Mother of the Colorado Trail," she is commemorated with trails, bridges, and other features named in her honor throughout the state.

Gudy and her husband, David, joined the Colorado Mountain Club in 1952, years after the initial idea for a Rocky Mountain Trail was envisioned by the Roundup Riders and the CMC. In 1970 the organizations encouraged Bill Lucas, who headed the USDA Forest Service's efforts in the Rocky Mountains, to create such a trail with volunteer assistance. Lucas brought the idea back to Washington, DC, and invited Gaskill and Bill Ruskins to talk with the forest service. That led to passage of the Volunteers in the National Forests Act of 1972, which allowed volunteers to help improve national forestlands and bushwhacked the way for the Colorado Trail.

Although Gaskill was born in Illinois, she spent much of her childhood exploring in Colorado. Her father spent summers as a ranger in Rocky Mountain National Park. Before work he'd drop Gudy and her siblings off at a different spot in the park and pick them up after work. They spent their days hiking and playing in the vast, mountainous park. Gaskill competed as a downhill and cross-country skier. She later worked at an area lodge and climbed Longs Peak thirty-one times, according to the Colorado Women's Hall of Fame. She climbed all fifty-four of Colorado's fourteeners as well as the European Alps and other major peaks around the world. She earned an education degree at Western Colorado University and a master's degree in recreation from the University of New Mexico and raised a family of four.

Gaskill attended the first planning meeting for the Colorado Trail and never missed any of the early meetings. With all her passion and experience, it's no wonder she was soon asked to lead the task of creating the trail. Within a few years of kicking off the effort in earnest, the forest service and the Colorado Trail Foundation's predecessor signed a partnership agreement allowing the trail to be built. The route was already roughed out, and plans were in place to use primarily volunteer efforts to build trail spans to connect existing trails and forest roads.

In 1977 Gaskill became the first female president of the CMC and helped grow that organization as well as continuing to work on the Colorado Trail, soliciting donations, recruiting volunteers, and donating countless hours of her time to complete the trail, which of course included hiking on it and making sure volunteers were supported and progress was being made. Through fits and starts the trail was ultimately completed and connected in 1987. Gaskill founded the Colorado Trail Foundation in 1986 and served as its first president.

Gaskill's efforts were recognized by President Ronald Reagan's Take Pride in America Campaign and President George H. Bush's Thousand Points of Light program. The Colorado Women's Hall of Fame inducted her as a member in 2002.

Gudy Gaskill passed on in 2016, leaving a strong and lasting legacy of conservation and trail stewardship. The work she did in leading the development of the Colorado Trail through thousands of volunteers is being studied and used by other states and agencies as they build out their own trail networks and strengthen volunteer efforts.

available here, you can park at the Little Scraggy trailhead, a fee area, 1.1 mile farther on the trail. There's a vault toilet there.

Miles and Directions

0.0 Start at the South Platte River Road Trailhead and Gudy Gaskill Bridge, on the west side of the parking lot. Cross the bridge and follow the trail around and under the bridge, heading south as it follows the South Platte for a bit.

0.2 Almost immediately after the trail turns right, encounter switchbacks as the trail climbs west, steeply at first then more gradually.

1.0 Enter the burn area and, shortly after, pass an abandoned quartz mine, on the left (south) side of the trail.

2.3 The trail passes around an outcrop of pink granite and reenters some forest area.

4.2 The trail comes close to an old 4x4 road near good areas for camping.

4.6 Reach the high point of the hike and follow the trail as it elbows sharply south.

Colorado Trail: Segment 2—Buffalo Creek Fire

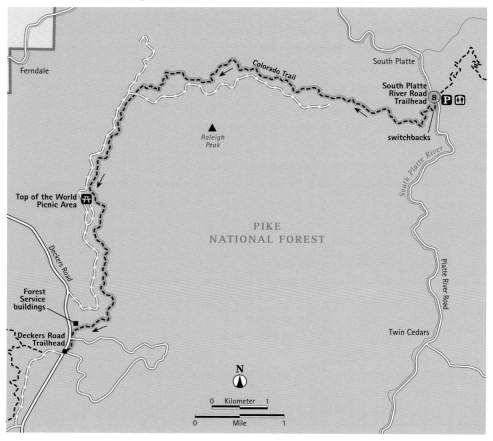

5.4 The trail crosses the closed Raleigh Peak Road. From here the hike is relatively flat.

6.5 Reenter the burn area.

6.9 Reach the Top of the World picnic area.

8.8 Cross FR 538; shortly after, reach an unmanned fire station to the right of the trail, which has emergency water on its northeast side.

9.1 The trail bears left as it parallels Deckers Road (Jefferson CR 126).

9.5 The segment ends at a small parking pullout across the road. Alternatively, the Colorado Trail continues another 1.1 miles to the Little Scraggy Trailhead, a USDA Forest Service campground with a toilet and fee parking.

Adventure Information

Colorado Trail #1776—Segment 2. fs.usda.gov/recarea/psicc/recreation/hiking/recarea/?recid=82634&actid=51

Organizations

The Colorado Trail Foundation. coloradotrail.org

Outfitters

Evergreen Mountain Sports. 10875 US 285, Ste. D101, Conifer; (303) 674-5100; evergreen mountainsports.com

Bentgate Mountaineering. 1313 Washington Ave., Golden; (303) 271-9382; bentgate.com. Open Sun–Fri; closed Sat.

REI Lakewood. 5375 S Wadsworth Blvd., Lakewood; (303) 932-0600; rei.com

Great Pre- or Post-Adventure Spots

Coney Island Boardwalk hot dog stand. 10 Old Stagecoach Rd., Bailey; (303) 838-9999; coneyislandbailey.wordpress.com

Mad Jack's Mountain Brewery. 23 Main St., Bailey; (303) 816-2337; madjacksmountain brewery.com

Green Mountain Beer Company. 2585 S Lewis Way, Lakewood; (303) 986-0201; green mountainbeercompany.com

Hike 9 Florissant Fossil Beds National Monument

The majority of the more than 40,000 fossilized specimens collected at this national monument and sent to museums around the world aren't dinosaurs or mammoths. Walking the monument's family-friendly trails will take visitors past much larger fossils—the remains of petrified redwood trees, the largest of which is 14 feet across. The monument has 15 miles of hiking trails as well as a visitor center where people can learn more about the monument's fascinating history.

Start: Florissant Fossil Beds National Monument Visitor Center

Distance: 5.8-mile loop

Hiking time: About 3 hours

Difficulty: Easy hiking on gently rising and falling terrain

Elevation gain: Minimal

Trail surface: Dirt and sand trails

Best seasons: Year-round

Other trail users: Hikers only

Canine compatibility: Service animals only

Land status: National Park Service

Camping, fees, and permits: Weekly passes sold onsite

Schedule: Visitor center open 9 a.m.–4:30 p.m. Park closes 4:30 p.m. in winter and 5 p.m. in summer; closed Thanksgiving, Christmas, and New Year's Day.

Maps: USGS Lake George; National Geographic Trails Illustrated #137: Pikes Peak, Cañon City

Nearest town: Woodland Park

Trail contact: National Park Service; (719) 748-3253; nps.gov/flfo/index.htm

Finding the trailhead: From the intersection of CO 67 and US 24 in Woodland Park, head west on US 24 for 8.3 miles. Turn right onto CR 42 and continue for 5.8 miles. Turn right onto CR 1 and then left in 0.9 mile at the sign for Florissant Fossil Beds National Monument. Continue 0.2 mile to the parking lot (15807 Teller CR 1). GPS: N38.91367° / W105.28586°

The Hike

Knowing that you're walking through history every time you go out for a hike is a wonderful feeling—the trees, rocks, streams, and rivers all have a story to tell. But there are few places where time has kept a historic record like Florissant Fossil Beds National Monument—one you're actually walking over with every step.

That's the legacy of the monument, thanks to Lake Florissant and the now-extinct Thirtynine Mile volcanic area nearby. The area experienced significant volcanic activity in the late Eocene era, about 34 million years ago. The numerous eruptions provided a toxic environment for all life in the area, causing mass die-offs.

Plants, animals, and insects poisoned by the volcanic environment died and fell into the lake, where microalgae known as diatoms were digesting silica from the ash, blooming in the lake, and then dying. All of this together resulted in micro-thin layers of ash-clay deposits called couplets blanketing the dead biota. Each subsequent layer compacted those below it, preserving the biota in "paper shales," which produced the fossils still being discovered here today, some of

A 34 million-year-old fossilized redwood stump at Florissant National Monument.

The Charlotte Hill Homestead at
Florissant National Monument.

which are hidden perhaps just inches, feet, and yards beneath the monument's
trails today.

There's more to the story of course; the petrified redwoods in the park were
also created in this period. It's estimated that they could have towered about 200
feet above the forest floor back then, but they too were undone by the volcanic
activity, their roots suffocated by silica-rich mudflows that hardened them and
made them ready for mineralization. Some of those trees are estimated to have
lived up to 700 years. These ancestral redwoods aren't the same as the redwoods
growing in California today, but tell of the environs of that long-distant period.
The remains show that it was much warmer and humid in the area back then, like
a giant jungle of trees crowding out the sun.

You can take all this in on a hike of the land, saving the best for last. Head
west on the Hornbek Wildlife Loop, with forest to your left and meadows to
the right. You can continue to the right and take the Hornbek Loop around or
continue straight, taking the Boulder Creek Trail into the forest for a slightly
longer trek. On this loop the trail crosses Boulder Creek at 1.3 miles and begins

to loop around, reentering meadows filled with wildflowers and then paralleling the creek for a little more than a mile.

The Boulder Creek Trail rejoins the Hornbek Loop at 2.2 miles, providing an option to return to the visitor center or continue on to a much more modern part of the monument's history, the Hornbek Homestead.

This easy trail continues to follow the creek for a little longer then arcs more northward and takes a right at 3.1 miles. From here you have a good view of the Hornbek Homestead, which was established by the twice-widowed Adeline Hornbek in 1878. It was reportedly the first two-story house in the valley. Here she raised four children and eventually married a third man, Frederick Sticksel, when she 66. She passed on in 1905 at the age of 71. The home is now listed on the National Register of Historic Places. It was purchased in 1973, four years after President Richard Nixon declared the fossil beds a national monument at the urging of local citizens and scientists who wanted to preserve the land for its significance.

After visiting the homestead the trail continues on, crossing CR 1 twice and looping back around. Just shy of the parking lot, turn right onto the easy Petrified Forest loop trail and see some of the world's largest petrified tree remains, including the "Big Stump," 14 feet across. The loop ends at the visitor center and right by the parking lot.

Miles and Directions

0.0   Start at the visitor center and head west on the Boulder Creek Trail.

0.4   Continue on the Boulder Creek Trail, passing the Hornbek Wildlife Loop trail junction.

0.6   Continue on the Boulder Creek Trail as it passes the Sawmill Loop junction.

1.3   Stay on the Boulder Creek Trail as It crosses Boulder Creek. (Option: Add 0.1 mile to the trek by taking the Boulder Creek Loop Trail here.)

2.2   Continue hiking straight (northeast) on the Hornbek Wildlife Loop.

3.1   Cross a creek as the trail reaches its northeasternmost point.

3.3   Pass the Hornbek Homestead buildings.

3.4   Cross CR 1.

4.5   Cross Grape Creek on a small bridge.

Florissant Fossil Beds National Monument

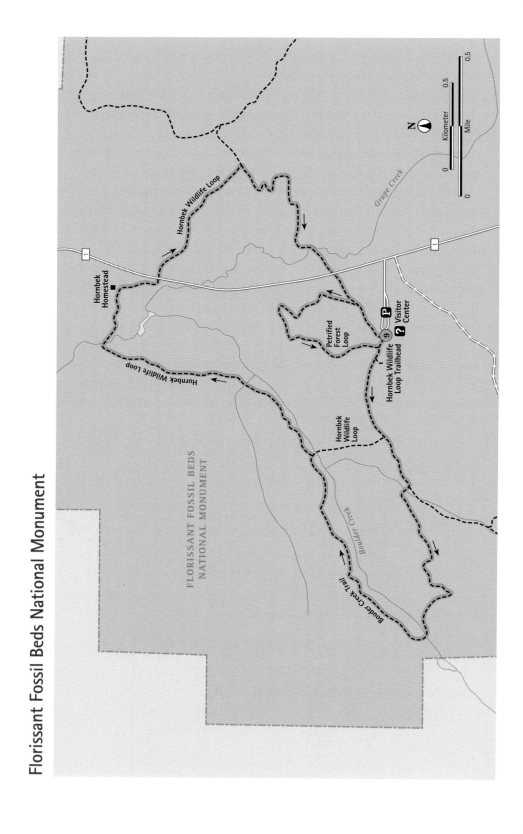

4.8 Turn right onto the Petrified Forest Loop.

5.8 Arrive back at the visitor center.

Adventure Information

Florissant Fossil Beds National Monument. nps.gov/flfo/planyourvisit/index.htm

"The Story of Adeline Hornbek." nps.gov/flfo/learn/historyculture/adeline-hornbek.htm

Organizations

The Friends of the Florissant Fossil Beds. fossilbeds.org/about/

Outfitters

Mountain Chalet. 15 N Nevada Ave., Colorado Springs; (719) 633-0732; mtnchalet.com

Wilderness Exchange. 2401 15th St., Ste. 100, Denver; (303) 964-0708; wildernessx.com

REI Greenwood Village. 9000 E Peakview Ave., Greenwood Village; (303) 221-7758; rei.com

REI Colorado Springs. 1376 E Woodmen Rd., Colorado Springs; (719) 260-1455; rei.com

Great Pre- or Post-Adventure Spots

Iron Tree Table & Taps. 37 Costello Ave., Florissant; (719) 748-0124; iron-tree-table-and
-taps.business.site

Manitou Brewing Co. 725 Manitou Ave., Manitou Springs; (719) 282-7709; manitoubrew
ing.com

Penny Arcade. 900 Manitou Ave., Manitou Springs; (719) 685-9815; facebook.com/
manitouspringspennyarcade

Hike 10 Harrison Plane Crash Site via the Ice Cave Cliffs Trail

This moderately difficult trail offers a fair amount of solitude compared with many on the Front Range. It also offers plenty of tree coverage as it leapfrogs from creek to creek and climbs into forest openings showcasing Pikes Peak Granite domes and spires before reaching a somber, hidden artifact—the remnants of a World War II fighter plane.

> **Start:** Palmer Lake Reservoir trailhead
>
> **Distance:** 10.8 miles out and back
>
> **Hiking time:** About 5.75 hours
>
> **Difficulty:** Intermediate to difficult due to some trail finding and steeper trail sections
>
> **Elevation gain:** About 2,060 feet
>
> **Trail surface:** Dirt
>
> **Best seasons:** Year-round
>
> **Other trail users:** None
>
> **Canine compatibility:** No dogs permitted
>
> **Land status:** Palmer Lake and Pike National Forest
>
> **Camping, fees, and permits:** No fees at Palmer Lake Reservoir trailhead
>
> **Schedule:** Open year-round
>
> **Maps:** USGS Palmer Lake; National Geographic Trails Illustrated #135: Deckers, Rampart Range
>
> **Nearest town:** Palmer Lake
>
> **Trail contact:** Palmer Lake; (719) 481-2953; townofpalmerlake.com. Pike National Forest, Pikes Peak Ranger District, 601 South Weber, Colorado Springs 80903; (719) 636-1602; fs.usda.gov/detail/psicc/about-forest/districts/?cid=fsm9_032731.
>
> **Finding the trailhead:** From I-25 exit 163, take CR 404 west toward Palmer Lake for 2.5 miles. Turn left onto Spruce Mountain Road; in 0.1 mile continue left on CO 105. Continue for 0.3 mile and turn right onto Glenway Street. In 0.2 mile turn left onto High Street. In 0.1 mile turn left onto South Valley Road and then make an immediate right onto Old Carriage Road. Follow this to a small parking lot (365 Glenside Rd.). There is a trail kiosk on the western side of the lot. GPS: N39.11881° / W104.92135°

The Hike

This beautiful hike stays largely under forest canopy, making it a great hike on a summer day; swaths of aspen, streamside willows, cottonwoods, Rocky Mountain scrub oak, and Gambel oak make for a fantastically colorful fall hike too. With the thick forest canopy, old man's beard lichen on pines, and rich, vibrant underbrush in sections, parts of this trail wouldn't seem out of place in the Northeast. However, from its start it's undeniably a Rocky Mountain hike.

Starting at the Rampart Range Fault in Palmer Lake and following the path of North Monument Creek, the trail heads west on Balance Rock Road as it passes between Chautauqua Mountain to the south and Sundance Mountain to the north. Just after passing Lower Palmer Lake Reservoir on the trail, the western face of Sundance Mountain is flanked by Ice Cave Creek, a gorgeous cut in the mountain, full of large boulders.

In about 50 feet you reach the trailhead for the Ice Cave Creek–Winding Stairs Trail. Bear right onto the trail, initially climbing a series of sharp switchbacks before paralleling the babbling creek. In this stretch there are some great opportunities to view the expanse of the eastern planes, mounds, and mesas beyond Palmer Lake. Some of this mile-long climb is on narrow, difficult singletrack trail,

Touching wild grasses along the Sidney Harrison Trail.

The Sidney Harrison plane crash site. Harrison was transporting a Cessna O-1 Bird Dog in 1952 and got lost in a snowstorm.

but the trail is easy to follow and there are plenty of holds to grab onto. As the trail climbs out of the Ice Cave Creek ravine, it crosses the creek then reaches a junction with the Swank Trail and heads right, gradually climbing through the forest. In spring and summer, white and pink geranium, wood lily, pinedrops, and columbine are found here. Shortly thereafter cross Levi Creek, a small seasonal stream, and begin paralleling it on the trail.

Pass the junction with the Ice Cave Cliffs Trail and begin an easy mile-long descent through a ponderosa forest. The trail continues north until it intersects the Sidney Harrison Connector Trail at Cook Creek in a flat spot. Turn left onto the connecter and work your way through willows and brush. The trail is easy to see, but the area is overgrown and the trail can be marshy here as it follows the creek for a bit. The trail leaves this creek bed at 4.0 miles, cuts through a small meadow lined with aspen, and then begins the toughest climb of the day on a steep ridge, gaining about 400 feet in 0.5 mile on a good trail.

After the climb, reach the Sidney Harrison Trail junction. Take stock of the area—the connector trail is easy to miss on the way back—and head left on the good, relatively level trail. The forest is thinner here, and there are some fantastic views of Pikes Peak Granite spires across a drainage. Follow the trail as it makes a J-arc to the day's goal.

At the end of the arc, you'll find the most unique feature of this out-and-back adventure: the wreckage of Capt. Sidney Harrison's Cessna O-1 Bird Dog, a World War II–era plane, which crashed during a snowstorm in 1952. Harrison, a veteran of both World War II and the Korean War, had fought in both France and Germany. He was transporting the plane from Wichita to Buckley Air Force Base in Aurora, just outside Denver, when it went down. The wreckage is a somber but beautiful memorial to the war hero. The wreckage is amazingly intact considering it has been there for more than sixty years. Unfortunately, people have vandalized it over the years, shooting at it or leaving their names on the fuselage. Don't be one of them.

The trek back is easier but has some tough re-ascends. However, coming back into the Ice Cave Creek ravine reveals some of the best views of the day.

Looking east from the Winding Stairs Trail to mesas.

Harrison Plane Crash Site via the Ice Cave Cliffs Trail

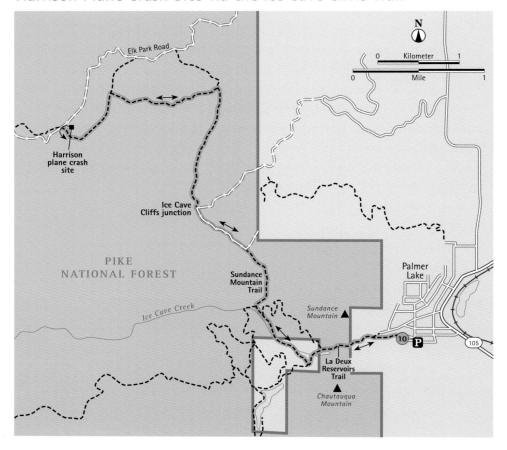

Miles and Directions

0.0   Start at the Palmer Lake Reservoir Trailhead and head west on the La Deux Reservoirs Trail.

0.2   The trail joins Balanced Rock Road, which is closed to motorized traffic.

0.6   The trail passes the eastern side of Lower Palmer Reservoir.

0.8   Beyond the western side of the reservoir, turn right at the Winding Stairs–Ice Cave Creek Trailhead and start an ascent on a series of short switchbacks.

1.3   The trail crosses Ice Cave Creek.

1.5   Stay left at the junction with Swank and Sundance Valley Trails.

1.6 At the next trail junction, stay right to remain on the Swank Trail and resume the ascent. The trail ascends 400 feet over the next mile.

2.1 Stay left at the junction with the Sundance Mountain Trail.

2.7 At the junction with the Ice Cave Cliffs Trail, continue straight as the trail gently descends.

3.8 Turn left at the Sidney Harrison Connector Trail junction and cross Crook Creek in a marshy area.

4.1 The trail begins its most difficult ascent, rising 500 feet over 0.6 mile.

4.7 At the Sidney Harrison Crash Site Trail junction, turn left. (Take stock of the trail junction. There is no marker, and it's easy to miss on the way back.)

5.4 After an easy final ascent through aspen and coniferous forest, reach the Harrison Plane Crash Site. Return via the same route.

10.8 Arrive back at the trailhead.

Adventure Information

Outfitters

Mountain Chalet. 15 N Nevada Ave., Colorado Springs; (719) 633-0732; mtnchalet.com

Wilderness Exchange. 2401 15th St., Ste. 100, Denver; (303) 964-0708; wildernessx.com

REI Greenwood Village. 9000 E Peakview Ave., Greenwood Village; (303) 221-7758; rei.com

REI Colorado Springs. 1376 E Woodmen Rd., Colorado Springs; (719) 260-1455; rei.com

Great Pre- or Post-Adventure Spots

Rock House Ice Cream & More. 24 Hwy. 105, Palmer Lake; (719) 488-6917; rockhouseicecream.com

Burly Brewing Co. 680 Atchison Way, Ste. 800, Castle Rock; (720) 486-0541; burlybrewing.com

Pikes Peak Brewing Co. 1756 Lake Woodmoor Dr., Monument; (719) 208-4098; pikespeakbrewing.com

Hike 11 Devil's Head Fire Lookout

This family-friendly hike is a chance to channel your inner Jack Kerouac to be a temporary Dharma Bum. A short hike with moderate elevation gain leads to the last working fire lookout on Colorado's Front Range. The tower has an awe-inspiring 360-degree panorama. Built in 1951, the Devil's Head Fire Lookout is on the National Register of Historic Places. Primarily used by hikers, there are numerous rock climbing routes in the area as well. It's a heavily used area, so please practice Leave No Trace principles and don't litter.

Start: Devil's Head Lookout Trailhead #611, Pike and San Isabel National Forests

Distance: 2.7 miles out and back

Hiking time: About 2 hours

Difficulty: Easy to moderate hiking on wide trails, with steep ascents on steps and the final stairs to the fire tower

Elevation gain: About 870 feet

Trail surface: Dirt and stairs

Best seasons: Apr or May–Dec 1; access road closed in winter

Other trail users: Rock climbers

Canine compatibility: Leashed dogs permitted

Land status: Pike and San Isabel National Forests

Maps: USGS Devil's Head; National Geographic Trails Illustrated #135: Deckers, Rampart Range

Nearest town: Sedalia

Trail contact: Pike National Forest, Pikes Peak Ranger District; (719) 553-1404; fs .usda.gov/recarea/psicc/recreation/hiking/recarea/?recid=12927&tactid=50

Finding the trailhead: In Sedalia, head south on CO 67 at the intersection with US 85. In 9.9 miles turn left (south) onto Rampart Range Road and continue 9.2 miles to the trailhead. Rampart Range Road is closed annually by December 1; the USDA Forest Service tries to reopen it by April 1. GPS: N39.26935° / W105.10500°

The Hike

At 9,748 feet above sea level, the Devil's Head Fire Lookout sits atop the highest point in the Rampart Range. With few peaks nearby, the lookout tower offers awesome, unparalleled views in every direction—Pikes Peak is easily seen 33

Devils Head Fire Tower lookout from afar.

miles to the south, Grays Peak is 45 miles to the northwest, and Longs Peak is visible 75 miles to the north. On a clear day you can see 100 miles in every direction from the tower! While oft-snowcapped peaks grace the western backdrop, its foreground is covered with countless forested peaks, cut through with bands of reddish-pink Pikes Peak Granite, standing like waves frozen in time. Closer peaks and blocks of rock show the dramatic domes and spires formed by the ancient granite.

The current fire tower is actually the third at Devil's Head. The first was built in 1912, just seven years after the USDA Forest Service was created and six after creation of Pike National Forest. Then it was little more than a table bolted to the rock with a firefinder on it. Fire spotters used a log shelter near the firefinder as protection in storms and called fires in to authorities. That structure was replaced with a 10 x 10-foot glass-enclosed observatory that housed the firefinder and a telephone. A set of wood stairs and a railing to the lookout were built in 1921. Fire spotters spent six months a year in the tiny enclosure, seeking to protect the forests from fires for thirty-two years.

The current structure was built in 1951 by Fort Carson Company A, 973rd Engineer Construction Battalion. They dismantled the old fire tower and hauled several tons of brick, steel, lumber, water, and cement over the 2.5-mile trail with

Looking west to the snowcapped tops of the Rockies from the lookout tower.

a small forest service tractor and mules. In 1991 the structure was listed on the National Register of Historic Places. It still serves as an active fire lookout and may be open to the public when staffed. When not staffed, visitors can usually climb the 143 steps to the observation deck, but the windows will be shuttered.

Usually staffed from late May to early September, the tower was largely staffed by one man, Billy Ellis. He and his wife, Margaret, lived at the cabin at the meadowy base of the fire tower every summer from 1984 until he retired in June 2019 at the age of 87.

The small meadow below the massive granite block of Devil's Head is a fantastic place for a respite after the 1.3-mile hike to the top. With a picnic area and interpretive signage, visitors can learn more about the history of the forest and fire spotters before making the final climb or returning to the trailhead.

From the parking lot, the wide dirt trail is easy to find. You're quickly engulfed in a dense fir and pine forest. There are great views all along the trail, but some of the best are found when the trail takes elbow-sharp turns and as it passes giant boulders of granite.

On the way down, consider taking the Zinn Overlook Trail, about 0.2 mile from the top. This little 0.3-mile trail has some rock-climbing routes and a great overview of the rolling foothills to the south.

Devil's Head Fire Lookout

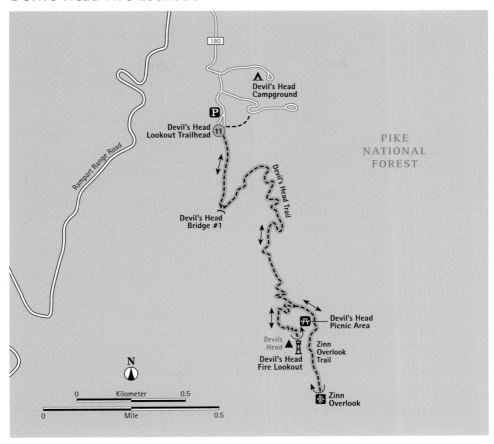

On this heavily trafficked trail, it's important to practice Leave No Trace principles. This is a good opportunity to teach little ones by having them collect some "trail treasures," like dropped water bottles or bits of plastic wrappers.

Miles and Directions

0.0 Start at the Devil's Head Lookout Trailhead (#611) and follow the easy, well-marked trail.

0.2 Cross a bridge then encounter large boulders left of the trail.

0.9 Encounter more large boulders on the right side of the trail.

1.0 The trail begins some easy switchbacks below the final ascent.

1.1 Pass the Zinn Overlook Trail and continue to the Devil's Head Fire Lookout (Option: Take the overlook trail for a lovely little side trip that adds 0.6 mile to the hike.)

1.2 Reach the ranger's cabin below the Devil's Head Fire Lookout, where there is a picnic area and interpretive signs about the history of the fire tower.

1.3 If the tower is open, climb the 143 stairs to the lookout. Return via the same route.

2.7 Arrive back at the trailhead.

Adventure Information

Outfitters

Mountain Chalet. 15 N Nevada Ave., Colorado Springs; (719) 633-0732; mtnchalet.com

Wilderness Exchange. 2401 15th St., Ste. 100, Denver; (303) 964-0708; wildernessx.com

REI Greenwood Village. 9000 E Peakview Ave., Greenwood Village; (303) 221-7758; rei.com

Great Pre- or Post-Adventure Spots

Sedalia Bakery. 4110 Rio Grande Ave., Sedalia; (303) 815-3656; facebook.com/sedaliabakery

Burly Brewing Co. 680 Atchison Way, Ste. 800, Castle Rock; (720) 486-0541; burlybrewing .com

Rockyard Brewing Company. 880 Castleton Rd., Castle Rock; (303) 814-9273; rockyard.com

Hike 12 Mts. Bierstadt and Evans via the Sawtooth

Evans is the closest fourteener to Denver, and people can drive to its peak. Bierstadt is likely the most hiked fourteener because of its easy access and its proximity to Denver. So why put this hike in an adventure guide? The Sawtooth! This burly, rocky route is a challenging, fun Class 3 scramble connecting two of Colorado's most famous fourteeners. The rocky Sawtooth offers some limited exposure then empties out into an amazing alpine meadow with alpine wildflowers. The return route brings you into a gorgeous gully teeming with wildlife, flowers, and waterfalls in wet years.

Start: West slope from Guanella Pass Trailhead

Distance: 10.1-mile loop

Trailhead elevation: 11,210 feet

Hiking time: About 9 hours

Difficulty: Very difficult, requiring Class 1 to Class 3 climbing and scrambling

Elevation gain: More than 3,700 feet

Trail surface: Dirt, scree, rock

Best seasons: Mid-May–Oct

Other trail users: Mountaineers, snowshoers, skiers

Canine compatibility: Leashed dogs permitted

Land status: Arapaho National Forest, Mount Evans Wilderness

Camping, fees, and permits: No fees; camping spots along Guanella Pass

Schedule: Open year-round

Maps: USGS Mount Evans; National Geographic Trails Illustrated #104: Idaho
   Springs, Georgetown, Loveland Pass

Nearest town: Georgetown, Idaho Springs

Trail contact: Arapaho National Forest; (970) 295-6600. USDA Forest Service,
   Clear Creek Ranger Station; (303) 567-3000.

Special considerations: Start this hike early! It's a long 10.1 miles with a lot of
   elevation gain and both technical hiking and scrambling. You'll want to be off the
   peaks before any nasty weather comes in. It's a good idea to be off Evans no later
   than 1 p.m., even better to be off its peak by 11 a.m. And never, never be afraid
   to turn around earlier than you had planned should the need arise. The mountains
   will still be there for another attempt.

Finding the trailhead: From I-70 take exit 228 to Georgetown and the junction of
   US 6 and Argentine Street. Head south on Argentine for 0.6 mile. Turn left onto

6th Street then right in 2 blocks onto Rose Street. Head south on Rose Street for 4 blocks and turn right onto 2nd Street. At 1 mile the road becomes Guanella Pass Road; follow this for 10 miles to reach the pass at 11 miles. The trailhead is on the left in a paved parking lot. There's an overfill parking lot on the right. GPS: N39.59650° / W105.71033°

The Hike

You see it from Guanella Pass, the rugged gray granite of the Sawtooth as the ridgeline drops south and east from the top of Mount Bierstadt—like someone chipped away a nice, smooth traverse over to the other side, leaving jagged teeth. You see it and think: *Yeah! I got this!* And weather permitting, you do.

The whole of the Sawtooth is doable. There are some scary moments if you're going solo or haven't tried something like this before, but if you take your time and route-find, you'll find the path described here. This trek is worth the time and effort because the Sawtooth connects the Chicago Peaks, as they're known. On their own, they're both easy hikes, but this combination adds a little more

The fierce gendarme guarding the rest of The Sawtooth. Climb up and to the right of the tower on trail fragments.

to the journey. Though they're called the Chicago Peaks, neither has much of a connection to the windy city—except, perhaps, on bad-weather days.

Albert Bierstadt, a landscape painter who likely made one of the first ascents of his namesake mountain in the 1860s with William Byers, actually named Mount Evans "Mount Rosa." He was honoring both Monte Rosa in Switzerland and Rosalie Ludlow, his future wife. Bierstadt was remembered for paintings like 12 × 7-foot *Storm in the Mountains*, based on his sketches of the area. The moniker Mount Rosa was short-lived however. In 1895 Colorado legislators voted to rename the peak Mount Evans to honor John Evans, Colorado's second territorial governor. Evans was honored for helping establish Colorado as a state and as a railroad entrepreneur whose work helped the state flourish in its early years. In an interesting twist, the other peak was named for Bierstadt thanks to Denver high school botany teacher Ellsworth Bethel, who first suggested the name.

The first feature you come across on this adventure is The Willows—a maze of short willows that cover a marshy area. Thankfully, boardwalks make it easier to traverse this area while also reducing human impact. Deer and elk are known to inhabit this area but normally don't have much interaction with humans. From here it's easy to see the trail as it winds its way up the western face of Bierstadt. Follow the trail to the top, and when everyone else turns around, keep going. The Sawtooth begins on the eastern side of Bierstadt, with a snowfield that persists through most of the year.

Now look for a trail that works its way close to the ridgeline below a tall gendarme (rock tower). As you get closer to the gendarme, climb over the rocks below its right side and look for trail fragments to help guide you through. This is the toughest part of the day. After that, the trail works its way up, to the left, and finally curves back around to the right on a decent ledge. Staying close to the rock wall here will make it seem a little less scary.

After the trail curves back around to the right (east), it enters alpine tundra, an area filled with low-growing flowers like the alpine forget-me-not, moss campion, alpine pussytoes, and more—flowers you won't notice unless you're looking down. At these higher elevations you might hear picas and marmots, but mountain goats and bighorn sheep are also known to inhabit the area. Continue heading east and Mount Evans finally comes into view. Following cairns, continue east until you reach the Mount Evans Summit Trail and take that to the top. When someone asks if you drove to the top, smile.

Sunset calling, looking west hiking on the boardwalk to Guanella Pass Trailhead.

Cross back over the same meadow, but instead of heading back toward the Sawtooth, head a little farther north and then east to follow trails into Scott Gomer Gully, which crosses back and forth over Scott Gomer Creek. It's a steep, somewhat difficult descent on a lot of scree but rewarding as it opens up into a beautiful, verdant cirque below the Sawtooth before the trail works its way back toward The Willows. Tighten you shoes or boots before you enter this area—the muck will actually suck the footwear off your feet if you don't. Find the board-walk on the left side of The Willows and hike on out.

Miles and Directions

0.0   Start at the Guanella Pass Trailhead and head east on a great trail.

0.2   The trail becomes a series of boardwalks as it goes through The Willows.

0.3   Cross the last of the boardwalks and continue hiking on the excellent dirt path as it comes close to and passes Deadman Lake on the left (north).

0.8   After passing over Scott Gomer Creek, follow the trail as it bears southeast.

1.1   The trail begins a gradual incline and begins a series of switchbacks.

Mts. Bierstadt and Evans via the Sawtooth

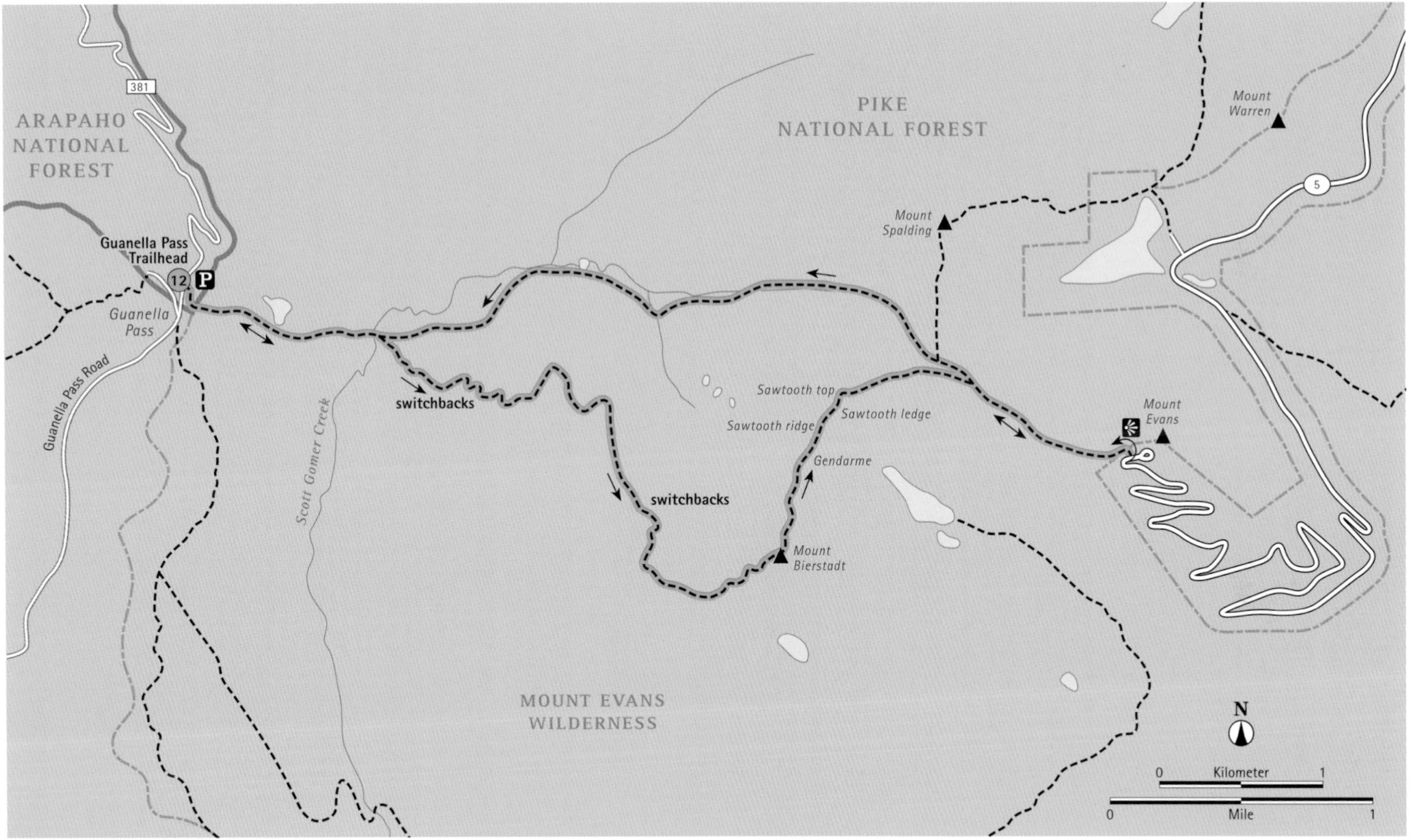

ARAPAHO NATIONAL FOREST

381

PIKE NATIONAL FOREST

Mount Warren

5

Mount Evans

Mount Spalding

Sawtooth top

Sawtooth ridge

Sawtooth ledge

Gendarme

Mount Bierstadt

switchbacks

switchbacks

Scott Gomer Creek

MOUNT EVANS WILDERNESS

Guanella Pass Trailhead

P

12

Guanella Pass

Guanella Pass Road

N

Kilometer

Mile

0   1

2.2 Exit tree line and begin hiking southeast.

2.9 The trail turns left, heading east up and up to Bierstadt's peak.

3.6 Reach Bierstadt's peak. Continue over to its northern side and descend over a gnarly snowfield (MICROspikes and a mountaineering ax are needed).

3.8 Climb up to a gendarme and stay to its right (east) side for fun Class 3 scrambling.

4.0 Begin climbing along the Class 3 Sawtooth ridge after the gendarme by ascending a gully to a notch on the ridge; pass through the notch and turn right.

4.1 Begin working your way around a narrow ledge, which becomes easier and wider as you continue (staying to the right keeps you on more-solid rock).

4.2 Follow the ridge and take a sharp right turn to reach the top of the ledge, heading east toward Mount Evans. Look back; breathe. From here the trail turns east and returns to Class 2, easier trekking over alpine meadows.

4.6 Start following the cairns that lead toward Mount Evans. (Option: By heading northeast across the path to Scott Gomer Gully, you can bail out without continuing to Mount Evans.)

5.5 Continue following cairns and an increasingly more defined trail to the peak of Mount Evans to the east. Just below the summit of Mount Evans, cross the road and follow the good trail to the peak. Begin returning down the same route.

6.4 Look for trail fragments on the right leading north and west across the meadow into Scott Gomer Gully.

6.8 Continue into the gully and head west, following braided, scree-covered trails and trail fragments that lead into the valley.

7.0 The trail gets much steeper as it descends back toward Guanella Pass.

7.2 The descent mellows as the trail starts entering willow marshes.

7.9 Reach the willow marshes and a small pond. Look for drier areas to trek through. It's very hard to stay on-trail, but staying left (south) of the creek offers the best chance of finding a trail that leads back to main trail through the willows.

8.8 Near a crossing of Scott Gomer Creek, look for an opportunity to return to the boardwalk across the willow maze.

10.1 Arrive back at the trailhead.

Looking west across the Sawtooth route to Bierstadt, Abyss Lake is in the basin below.

Adventure Information

Outfitters

FERAL. 1630 Miner St., Idaho Springs; (303) 829-5681; feralmountainco.com

Bentgate Mountaineering. 1313 Washington Ave., Golden; (303) 271-9382; bentgate.com. Open Sun–Fri; closed Sat.

Great Pre- or Post-Adventure Spots

Westbound & Down Brewing Company. 1617 Miner St., Idaho Springs; (720) 502-3121; westboundanddown.com

Tommyknocker Brewery & Pub. 1401 Miner St., Idaho Springs; (303) 567-4419; tommy knocker.com

Dillon Dam Brewery. 100 Little Dam St., Dillon; (970) 262-7777; dambrewery.com

The Alpine Restaurant and Bar. 1106 Rose St., Georgetown; (303) 569-0200; alpinerestau rantgeorgetown.com

Hike 13 Horsetooth Mountain and Falls Loop

This giant molar of a rock sits above Horsetooth Reservoir, the highest point around Fort Collins and a popular destination for everything from paddleboarding and road biking to rock climbing and scuba diving. This moderately difficult adventure takes you to hidden waterfalls and the top of it all for the best views in the region.

Start: Horsetooth Rock Trailhead

Distance: 7.4-mile loop

Hiking time: About 4 hours

Difficulty: Intermediate hike with decent elevation gains and losses

Elevation gain: 1,700 feet

Trail surface: Mainly dirt trails

Best seasons: Year-round

Other trail users: None

Canine compatibility: Leashed dogs permitted

Land status: Managed by Larimer County

Camping, fees, and permits: Daily use and camping fees

Schedule: Open year-round

Maps: USGS Horsetooth Reservoir

Nearest town: Fort Collins

Trail contact: Larimer County; (970) 498-7000; larimer.org

Finding the trailhead: From the intersection of Harmony Road and College Avenue, head west for 2.3 miles on Harmony. Continue for 6.5 miles as Harmony Road becomes W CR 38E. Turn right into the parking lot (6550 W CR 38E), pay the fee, and park. The trailhead is on the north side of the lot. GPS: N40.52409° / W105.18106°

The Hike

Known today as Horsetooth Rock, this cracked monolith has a rich history connected with humans. Native American lore says this rock is the cleaved heart of a giant that kept anyone from hunting the bison, antelope, and deer in the Valley of Contentment (now Horsetooth Reservoir) below it.

Whether the giant was maleficent to everyone or beneficent to the animals in the valley (stories differ), Chief Maunamoku and his tribe needed food as a drought had wiped out their food supplies. Knowing there were animals in the

Looking west toward Horsetooth from across the reservoir.

valley but perhaps scared of the giant's wrath, Maunamoku and his tribe concocted a plan. They tricked the giant's protector, a nighthawk, into leaving the giant while it slept. Maunamoku then used a tomahawk from the heavens to cleave the giant's heart in middle, then on the right and left, creating the distinctive spires of the rock. The next morning, when the tribe awoke, the heart had turned to stone. It's a far more romantic interpretation of how the formation got its current name, which isn't attributed to anyone in particular. It likely came from traders and settlers who agreed that it looked like a horse's tooth.

The geologic history of Horsetooth goes much further back. The metamorphic and igneous rock that makes up the feature is nearly 2 billion years old.

Even though the end goal was the same—ensuring people had access to sustainable food sources—the Valley of Contentment was drastically changed in 1949 when the Horsetooth Reservoir dams were completed, forming the now 6.5-mile-long reservoir that supplies Fort Collins, Greeley, and other, smaller towns in the region as well as farmers and ranchers in the Poudre River basin.

The reservoir is part of the larger Colorado–Big Thompson Project. In the 1930s, as the Dust Bowl struck the eastern plains, farmers and legislators asked the federal government to intervene. The Big Thompson project and Horsetooth Reservoir are part of that effort. The idea was to move water from the western side of Colorado, where it was plenty, to the eastern side of the state, where more stable water supplies were needed for ranching and farming, as well as the growing population base. The solution was to divert western-slope waters to reservoirs on the east side of the Rockies via a 13.2-mile tunnel. President Franklin Roosevelt authorized the project in 1937, which took twenty years to complete. Horsetooth was completed in 1949 and delivered its first water to users in 1951.

In creating the reservoir, the remnants of an entire town were flooded. That town, Stout, sat on the southern side of Horsetooth. While much of the town was relocated, some of the original buildings, like the schoolhouse, are now underwater.

This adventure takes you to Horsetooth Falls, a natural waterfall in the park, to the top of this overlook and the highest point in the region. From the top of Horsetooth Rock, you can imagine the buildings and the history of the old, drowned town to the south; beyond that you can see the top of Longs Peak, the northernmost fourteener. Longs, about 30 miles away, is on the southeastern side of Rocky Mountain National Park.

Beyond the earthen dams on the east side of the reservoir, you can see the sprawling metropolis and farms and ranches the reservoir feeds.

Miles and Directions

0.0 Start at the Horsetooth Rock Trailhead and head right (east) on the Horsetooth Falls Trail.

1.0 Come to short spur for Horsetooth Falls; turn left.

1.1 Arrive at Horsetooth Falls. Return to main trail network and turn left (north).

1.2 Turn left onto the Spring Creek Trail.

1.6 At the junction of the Horsetooth Falls, Soderberg, and Spring Creek Trails, continue on the Spring Creek Trail.

2.0 Continue on the Spring Creek Trail at its junction with the Wathan Trail. (Option: You can bail out from the longer hike by taking the Wathan Trail.)

3.2 Turn left onto Tower Road at its junction with the Spring Creek and Mill Creek Trails.

3.3 At the Towers Road–West Ridge Trail junction, turn left onto the West Ridge Trail.

4.0 At the junction of the West Ridge and Pirate Trails, continue left (south).

4.7 At the junction with West Ridge and Wathan Trails, continue straight.

Horsetooth Mountain and Falls Loop

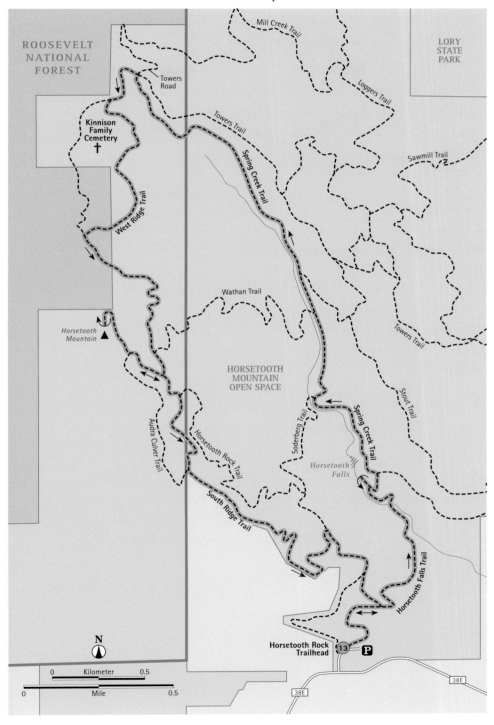

ROOSEVELT
NATIONAL
FOREST

LORY
STATE
PARK

Mill Creek Trail

Towers
Road

Loggers Trail

Towers Trail

Kinnison
Family
Cemetery

Sawmill Trail

West Ridge Trail

Spring Creek Trail

Wathan Trail

Horsetooth
Mountain

Towers Trail

HORSETOOTH
MOUNTAIN
OPEN SPACE

Stout Trail

Soderberg Trail

Spring Creek Trail

Audra Culver Trail

Horsetooth Rock Trail

Horsetooth
Falls

South Ridge Trail

Horsetooth Falls Trail

N

Horsetooth Rock
Trailhead

13

P

0   Kilometer   0.5

0   Mile   0.5

38E

38E

4.8   Turn right onto the Horsetooth Rock Trail.

4.9   Pass the Audra Culver Trail junction.

5.2   Reach the top of Horsetooth Mountain; return to the Horsetooth Rock Trail.

5.4   Pass the Audra Culver Trail junction again; continue straight on the Horsetooth Rock Trail.

5.5   Come to the junction with the South Ridge Trail; continue on the South Ridge Trail.

5.9   Pass the Audra Culver Trail and stay on the South Ridge Trail.

6.7   At the South Ridge–Horsetooth Rock Trail junction, turn right to return to the trailhead.

7.4   Arrive back at the trailhead.

Adventure Information

City of Fort Collins NOCO Trail Report. gisweb.fcgov.com/Html5Viewer/Index .html?viewer=trail%20status

Horsetooth Reservoir. larimer.org/naturalresources/parks/horsetooth-reservoir

Outfitters

JAX Outdoor Gear. 1200 N College Ave., Fort Collins; (970) 221-0544; jaxgoods.com

REI Fort Collins. 4025 S College Ave., Fort Collins; (970) 223-0123, rei.com

Great Pre- or Post-Adventure Spots

CooperSmith's Pub & Brewing. #5 Old Town Square, Fort Collins; (970) 498-0483; cooper smithspub.com

McClellan's Brewing Co. 1035 S Taft Hill Rd., Fort Collins; (970) 568-8473; mcclellans brewingcompany.com

Odell Brewing. 800 E Lincoln Ave., Fort Collins; (970) 498-9070; odellbrewing.com

Hike 14 DeCaLiBron Loop

One of the best adventures to make you feel like a badass, the DeCaLiBron Loop climbs four of Colorado's fifty-eight peaks over 14,000 feet high. You'll pass over 14,148-foot Mount Democrat; hop over 14,238-foot Mount Cameron, a subpeak of 14,286-foot Mount Lincoln; and finally summit 14,172-foot Mount Bross—all in one day. Collectively these peaks are known as the Democrat Group, and this loop is the easiest way to summit multiple fourteeners in one day in the state!

Start: Kite Lake Trailhead

Distance: 6.8-mile loop

Trailhead elevation: 12,000 feet

Hiking time: About 5 hours

Difficulty: Moderately difficult (up to Class 2) hiking; some route finding required

Elevation gain: 2,980 feet

Trail surface: Mostly talus

Best seasons: Summer and fall (snowshoeing and skiing in winter)

Other trail users: None

Canine compatibility: Leashed dogs permitted

Land status: Pike National Forest

Camping, fees, and permits: Parking and campsite fees; campsites available on a first-come, first-served basis

Schedule: Open year-round (road access limited by snow in winter)

Maps: USGS Alma, Climax; National Geographic Trails Illustrated #109: Breckenridge, Tennessee Pass

Nearest town: Alma, Fairplay

Trail contact: Pike National Forest; (719) 553-1400. USDA Forest Service South Park Ranger District; (719) 836-2031; fs.usda.gov/recarea/psicc/recreation/camping-cabins/recarea/?recid=12844&tactid=29. Park County Sheriff's Office; (719) 836-2494.

Finding the trailhead: From CO 9 in Alma, go west on Kite Lake Road (CR 8), a poorly marked dirt road in the middle of Alma. It's by the Alma Fire House and Mining Museum, housed in an old log cabin. Follow the road for 6 miles along Buckskin Gulch to reach Kite Lake. The last mile is rougher, but most two-wheel-drive vehicles should be able to navigate the road in summer. The road closes at Paris Mill in winter, which is 3 miles from Kite Lake. There are two parking areas. The upper area has some campsites and requires users to pay a fee; the lower area doesn't. The well-marked trailhead is near restrooms on the south side of Kite Lake. GPS: N39.32789° / W106.12939°

The Hike

Trail tips: Start this trek early. Aim to have all four peaks done by noon at the latest to avoid lightning storms. It's best to hike this popular trail early in the day and during the week, when there's less traffic. Keep in mind that you don't have to make the full loop. If someone in your party is unable to complete the loop, the group can easily hike down the trail and back to the trailhead.

There is no cluster of fourteeners in Colorado as close to one another as this cluster of mountains in the Mosquito Range. Although known as the Democrat Group, these peaks could just as easily be called the political group. Wilbur Stone, a drafter of the Colorado Constitution, gave Mount Lincoln, the tallest and northwesternmost mountain in this cluster, its name in 1861. Miners from the south who lived and worked in the area were upset that it was named for the first Republican president and began calling Buckskin Peak, the southernmost

The terrain changes significantly from Democrat to Cameron.

mountain in the group, "Mount Democrat." By 1883 that name was showing up on official maps from the Land Office Survey.

Mount Bross was named for Illinois Lieutenant Governor William Bross, who served from 1865 to 1869. Bross owned mining property near Alma and spent time out there. On a climb of Mount Lincoln in 1868, he allegedly enjoyed the trip so much that he sang a doxology on the summit. Local miners started calling the northeasternmost peak in the cluster "Mount Bross," which it remains today.

Mount Cameron, which isn't technically a fourteener (it's just about 50 feet short of being considered an independent peak by local standards and traditions), has a connection to politics as well. Some say it was named for Union general Robert Alexander Cameron, who served during the Civil War. Cameron also helped establish Colorado Agricultural Colonies in Fort Collins and Greeley during the 1870s. Another possibility is that it was named for Simon Cameron, a Republican senator from Pennsylvania, who had served as President Lincoln's first secretary of war.

All these mountains were heavily mined, and you can see tailings piles and remnants of mining equipment around the mountains. On the initial ascent, the trail passes the Kentucky Belle Mine, a gold and silver mine started in 1900, at 12,400 feet. The actual summit of Mount Bross is technically not open to hikers because the Colorado Fourteeners Initiative hasn't been able get in touch with all the entities and people that have claims on that peak's summit.

The trail that connects these mountains is easy to follow and well cairned. It also largely echoes the shape of Kite Lake, looking a lot like an old-fashioned diamond-shaped kite.

The trek begins by heading up to the ridge that connects Lincoln and Cameron to Democrat. The trail then heads left (west) to climb the dark granite of Mount Democrat. The trail returns to the ridge and continues heading northwest toward Cameron and Lincoln on an easy, wide saddle. As the trail starts climbing a ridge to Cameron and Lincoln, the rock changes dramatically, lightening in color to a nearly white granite mixed with clay-colored shale. It looks like you're walking on Mars.

After climbing over Mount Cameron and gaining Lincoln 0.5 mile farther, retrace the route, but just before re-ascending Cameron, take a trail that heads south, dropping into the saddle between Bross and Lincoln. Then begin the ascent to the day's last fourteener, Bross. Officially, Bross's summit is on property containing mining claims; hikers aren't supposed to climb the 20 or so feet to the true summit from the trail. The Colorado Fourteeners Initiative recommends skirting the summit. Return down a ridge on the mountain's west face before entering a gully and arriving back at the trailhead.

Miles and Directions

0.0 Start at the Kite Lake Trailhead. Bear left and follow the well-established but blocked dirt road past the lake in an easterly direction to the ruins of the Kentucky Belle Mine.

0.5 The trail takes a sharp right turn for a short dogleg then turns left and resumes its trajectory up the mountain.

0.8 The trail goes left toward Mount Democrat and begins a relatively gentle ascent with switchbacks.

1.3 Gain the saddle between Mount Lincoln and Mount Cameron. Take the trail to the left, following the sign to Mount Democrat, and begin hiking across some small switchbacks to Mount Democrat's false summit.

1.7 The path curls around the false summit, revealing Mount Democrat's true summit.

1.9 Achieve Mount Democrat's summit at 14,148 feet. Head back down the same trail.

2.4 At the junction with the trail back to Kite Lake, turn left, heading northeast on a well-worn talus trail.

3.3 Ascend Mount Cameron's peak and continue on the trail.

3.7 Reach the peak of Mount Lincoln. Return down the same path.

4.1 Take the trail to the left, heading toward Mount Bross.

5.3 Reach the path below the summit of Mount Bross (about 20 feet below the true summit).

5.7 Turn left, descending southwest on the ridgeline toward the trailhead.

6.3 Turn right, crossing back over the streambed, and enter the gully heading south.

6.4 Turn left and continue heading down the gully.

6.6 Cross a small streambed, heading northwest, and exit the gully between Bross and South Bross.

6.8 Arrive back at the trailhead.

DeCaLiBron Loop

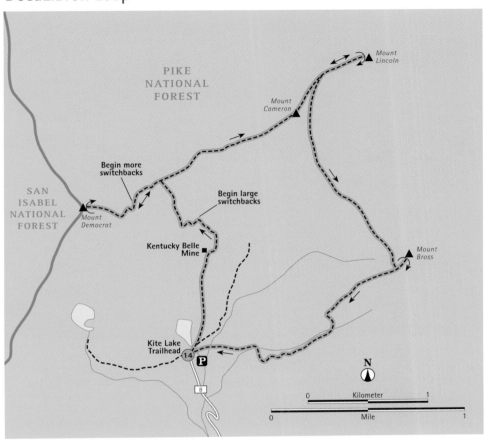

Adventure Information

Outfitters

High Alpine Sports. 525 Main St., Fairplay; (719) 836-0201; highalpinesports.com

Mountain Outfitters. 112 S Ridge St., Breckenridge; (970) 453-2201; mtnoutfitters.com

Great Pre- or Post-Adventure Spots

South Park Brewing. 297½ US 285, Fairplay; (719) 836-1932; southparkbrewingco.com

Mount Democrat overlooking Kite Lake.

Broken Compass Brewing. 68 Continental Ct., B12, Breckenridge; (970) 368-2772; broken compassbrewing.com

Breckenridge Brewery & Pub. 600 S Main St., Breckenridge; (970) 453-1550; breckbrew .com

Breckenridge Distillery. 1925 Airport Rd., Breckenridge; (970) 547-9759; breckenridgedis tillery.com

Downstairs at Eric's. 111 S Main St., Breckenridge; (970) 453-1401; downstairsaterics.com/ new

Hike 15 Castlewood Canyon: Rimrock to Creek Bottom Loop

When people think of adventure in Colorado, their head snaps to the mountains. It's true, there are countless adventures there, but the Colorado Plateau also has its own treasures. Castlewood Canyon is one of the more remarkable ones. The small canyon is home to four distinct ecosystems, including Black Forest, which is unique to the area. It's also home to unusual geology and once was the source of a flood that caused significant destruction in Denver.

Start: The Homestead Trailhead

Distance: 4.4-mile loop

Hiking time: About 2 hours

Difficulty: Easy hiking on dirt trails

Elevation gain: About 600 feet

Trail surface: Dirt

Best seasons: Spring through fall

Other trail users: Hikers only

Camping, fees, and permits: Daily fee

Schedule: Open sunrise to sunset

Canine compatibility: Leashed dogs permitted (leashes 6 feet or less)

Land status: State Park

Maps: USGS Castle Rock South, Russellville Gulch

Nearest town: Franktown

Trail contact: Castlewood Canyon State Park, 2989 S Hwy. 83, Franktown 80116; (303) 688-5242; cpw.state.co.us/placestogo/parks/CastlewoodCanyon/Pages/default.aspx

Finding the trailhead: From I-25 exit 184 (CO 86), head east on CO 86 as it becomes Founders Parkway. In 4.2 miles turn left onto CO 86 E and continue for 10 miles. In 4.6 miles turn right on North Castlewood Canyon Road. Continue on the road for 2.2 miles. Stop at the kiosk to pay the entry fee, then continue on the road for 0.1 mile to park in the lot on the left (858 S Castlewood Canyon Rd.). There are vault toilets at the trailhead. GPS: N39.35979° / W104.76822°

The Hike

Originally called Wildcat Canyon by the miners and loggers who were the first white settlers in the area in the 1860s, it later became known as Castlewood Canyon. By the 1880s families, farmers, and ranchers were homesteading in the area, drawn by the promise of readily accessible irrigation water. In 1889, in a bid to further improve the ability to provide water for farmers and other users, a 600-foot-long, 92-foot-high dam was planned; it was built in 1890. The dam always had some seepage, showing structural problems early on. On August 2, 1933, a squall raised the water level from 6 feet below its spillway crest to overflowing it by 1 foot in about 1 hour. About an hour later the dam was breached, discharging water down Cherry Creek at a rate of 126,000 cubic feet per second, explains Lee Mauney in a case study of Castlewood Canyon Dam for the Association of State Dam Safety Officials.

"The flood wave first passed through rural farmland and washed out county bridges. It reached the outskirts of Denver between 5 and 6 a.m. There were two flood waves reported, an initial wave probably caused by water spilling from and overtopping the dam, and then a larger, more destructive wave approaching 15 feet high. By 7 a.m., six hours after the breach, the flood wave made it to downtown Denver, flooding businesses and homes with an estimated discharge of 15,000 cfs."

Thankfully the flood caused by the dam breach killed only two people in Denver, but it caused over $1 million in damages at the dawn of the Great Depression. The remains of the ill-fated dam are still in place in Castlewood Canyon, near the northern terminus of this hike. Below the dam you can see the impact of the flood on Cherry Creek.

For example, a 55-million-year-old rock layer was made visible by the violent power washing delivered by the flood. That layer of Dawson Arkose contains plant and animal fossils showing that the region was once a tropical rain forest. It's a softer rock layer than what's above it. Volcanic eruptions in the Thirtynine Mile volcanic area, about 90 miles away near Salida, reached the area minutes after the explosion 36.7 million years ago. Melted rock and superheated ash fell on the land, instantly burying the layer underneath. This deposit is known as Wall Mountain Tuff (rhyolite). This normally shiny rock is found across the park as pieces with sharp angles and tiny holes; the color varies from pink to purple, gray, or brown. That layer is covered with 34-million-year-old Castle Rock

Looking over Castlewood Canyon by Rimrock Loop.

Conglomerate, probably the most identifiable rock in the park. This conglomerate rock was created when sediment mixed with much, much older rocks and boulders and glued into place, like an ancient super concrete. It's easy to see these contrasting rock layers when hiking through the canyon, and they make for interesting climbing over continually variable surfaces.

Equally as interesting about Castlewood are the four distinct ecosystems in the park. Within 2,636 acres, there are grasslands, montane forests, Fontaine scrublands, and riparian habitats. These welcome a diverse mix of flora and fauna. Nearly 200 bird species have been identified in the park, and this is a place that cottontail rabbit, coyote, ground squirrel, mule deer, porcupine, and red fox call home.

With lots of scrub oak and aspen in the area, it's also a great place to go leaf-peeping in fall, particularly with Pikes Peak to the south and Devil's Head to the west.

Miles and Directions

0.0   Start at The Homestead Trailhead and head south.

Castlewood Canyon: Rimrock to Creek Bottom Loop

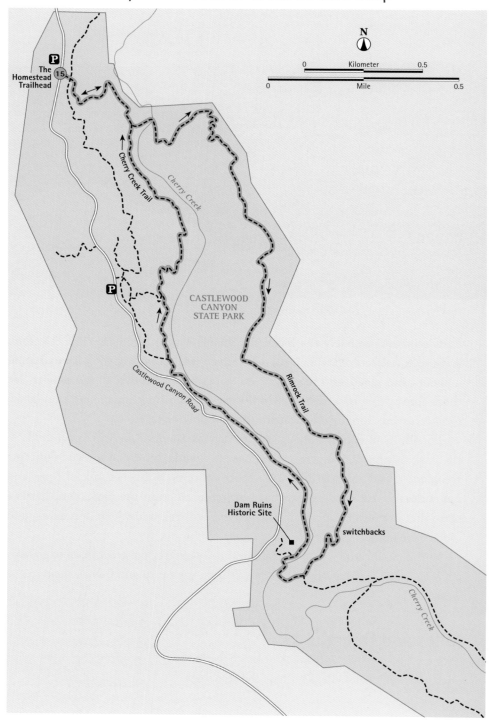

0.4 Turn left onto the Rimrock Trail.

0.7 Begin an ascent up short switchbacks for the next 0.1 mile, heading south.

2.2 Begin hiking some switchbacks down into the canyon.

2.4 At the Rimrock Canyon–Dam Trail junction, turn right, then cross Cherry Creek.

2.6 Pass the Castlewood Canyon Dam; continue heading north.

3.3 Continue straight on the Cherry Creek Trail as a spur heads left to a parking area.

3.5 Continue straight on the Rimrock Trail at another spur to parking areas.

4.1 Return to top of the Rimrock loop; keep straight to return to trailhead.

4.4 Arrive back at the trailhead.

Adventure Information

Outfitters

Mountain Chalet. 15 N Nevada Ave., Colorado Springs; (719) 633-0732; mtnchalet.com

Wilderness Exchange. 2401 15th Street, Ste. 100, Denver; (303) 964-0708; wildernessx.com

REI Greenwood Village. 9000 E Peakview Ave., Greenwood Village; (303) 221-7758; rei.com

Great Pre- or Post-Adventure Spots

Sedalia Bakery. 4110 Rio Grande Ave., Sedalia; (303) 815-3656; facebook.com/sedaliabakery

Burly Brewing Co. 680 Atchison Way, Ste. 800, Castle Rock; (720) 486-0541; burlybrewing.com

Rockyard Brewing Company. 880 Castleton Rd., Castle Rock; (303) 814-9273; rockyard.com

Hike 16 Paint Mines Interpretive Park Loop

The eastern grasslands hide this awesome, unique feature from passersby's eyes, but those in the know—from Native Americans 10,000 years ago to locals today—know that this geologically stunning park's colorful hoodoos and spires make it one the most unique areas in Colorado. Surrounded by prairie, the area teems with jack-rabbits, mule deer, pronghorn, and more while hawks and falcons soar overhead, searching for prey like Preble's meadow jumping mouse. At just about 750 acres, Paint Mines Interpretive Park is a family-friendly adventure with interpretive signage to explain the area's geology, ecology, and human history and prehistory.

Start: Paint Mines Road Trailhead

Distance: 3.9-mile loop

Hiking time: About 1.75 hours

Difficulty: Easy, with wide trails and little elevation change

Elevation change: Minimal

Trail surface: Pea gravel and dirt

Best seasons: Year-round

Other trail users: None

Canine compatibility: No dogs permitted

Land status: El Paso County Parks

Camping, fees, and permits: None

Schedule: Open dawn to dark

Maps: USGS Calhan

Nearest town: Calhan

Trail contact: El Paso County Parks Headquarters, 2002 Creek Crossing, Colorado Springs 80906; (719) 520-6375; elpasoco.com/parks

Special considerations: The hoodoos are extremely fragile. No climbing or other activities are permitted on the formations, which are particularly colorful after a rainfall.

Finding the trailhead: From the intersection of US 24 and Yoder Street on the east side of Calhan, head south on Yoder Street for 0.7 mile. Turn left onto Paint Mine Road; continue 1.4 miles and turn into the parking lot at Paint Mines Interpretive Park (29582–29752 Paint Mine Rd.). There is a vault toilet there. GPS: N39.02045° / W104.27408°

The Hike

Rain and wind have etched a story at Paint Mines Interpretive Park for tens of thousands of years, carving a canyon in miniature in badlands soils. This has revealed an even more fascinating story of the historical ecology and geology of Colorado and the formation of the Rockies as far back as 70 million years. That was when the current Rocky Mountains started rising from the inland Cretaceous Seaway during the Laramide orogeny. The orogeny began uplifting a batholith formed more than a billion years ago, creating mountains like nearby Pikes Peak. Formations like Garden of the Gods, the Dakota Hogback, and the Flatirons near Boulder appeared as softer sedimentary rock eroded into sand. The Denver Basin formed on the eastern plains of Colorado and was filled with sediment from those erosive forces.

The area became a rain forest about 64 million years ago—the remains of trees are still found petrified in the area and throughout Colorado, as at Florissant Fossil Beds, creating a soil layer up to 20 feet deep known as paleosol. This was then covered with silt that eroded from Pikes Peak and the Rockies and hardened into a white sandstone over time, creating the badlands soil comprising the park. Iron oxides in the sandstone tinted it. Erosion and gullying over

Detail of the colors of hoodoos at Paint Mines Interpretive Park.

more recent times have exposed these colorful layers of selenite clay and jasper, with wind and water eroding them into the delicate hoodoos and spires we see today. Depending on the concentrations of iron oxides, the clays turned different colors, from browns, purples, reds, and maroons to yellow or gray.

The Paint Mines were discovered by the Clovis people, ancestors to Native Americans, at least 10,000 years ago when they were hunting mammoth and giant bison on the plains; some evidence shows that they even chased bison over cliffs. They used the colorful clays in their earthenware and ceremonial paints. Archaeologists have discovered artifacts from Cody complex peoples (6,000–8,000 BC). They also found artifacts from the more recent Apishapa culture (AD 1,000–1,400).

American homesteaders came much, much later, in the 1880s, as the railroad expanded west. Dad McRae was likely the first to scout and buy the land in 1887. A year later, in 1888, "Two-fisted" Michael Calahan built a water tower and loading platform for the railroad and named the town Calahan. Somehow, by the time the trail depot was built in 1906, the town had become known as Calhan. By the 1890s, settlers were already quarrying the clays at the Paint Mines and hauling them to Denver and Pueblo, where they were used for fire brick, pottery, and tile. As time wore on into the 1900s, people stopped using the colorful clays and mining the land for it. Calhan's residents used the area for picnics and Easter sunrise services. Others partied in the gullies among the hoodoos.

In 1997 El Paso County began buying the land to preserve it, closed the area, and conducted archaeological and geologic surveys to learn about its history. The county enlisted volunteers to clean up the area and build trails. Funding for the project was secured through Great Outdoors Colorado (COCO) and The Conservation Fund. Less than ten years later, in June 2005, Paint Mines Interpretive Park opened to the public. Today, in addition to being a park, Paint Mines is a living geological and archaeological laboratory that's still in the process of eroding. It's also recognized as the Calhan Paint Mines Archaeological District by the National Park Service, listed on the National Register of Historic Places.

You can take this all in on an easy, well-marked trail. To save the best, most dramatic sites for last, start by heading northeast, traveling through grasslands populated by native short- and mid-grasses like blue grama and buffalo grass. You'll also notice mountain mahogany, chokecherry, wild rose, and low sagebrush in areas where streambeds hold more water. These areas host bunnies and jackrabbits, jumping mice, frogs, short-horned lizard, and more.

Three hoodoos come together to form an arch.

Also present are Swainson's hawks, owls, ducks, mourning doves, and western meadowlarks.

To the east, blades of wind turbines sweep in their graceful arcs, providing clean energy and a backdrop over the plains' rolling hills. The path never comes close enough to the base of their towers, but it does head south, closer to them, before working its way back into the valley close to the hoodoos. As the trail loops around and intersects itself, you can choose to complete the figure-eight loop by heading east and around, gaining some glimpses of the hoodoos to the west from above, as recommended here, or continue straight ahead to the hoodoos themselves.

When you reach the hoodoos—those colorful towering structures that look like they're straight out of a Wile E. Coyote cartoon—look down at their base and at the trail. This is where water is still carving the gullies deeper. Without the roots of grasses and other flora to fix the soft clays in place, the formations are still eroding. The trail underfoot is actually an ephemeral stream that flows after rains, carrying sediment out. It's important to stay on the marked trails here and not climb or play on the hoodoos, no matter how fun it looks. They're extremely delicate; hopefully, with care, they will remain for years to come.

Paint Mines Interpretive Park Loop

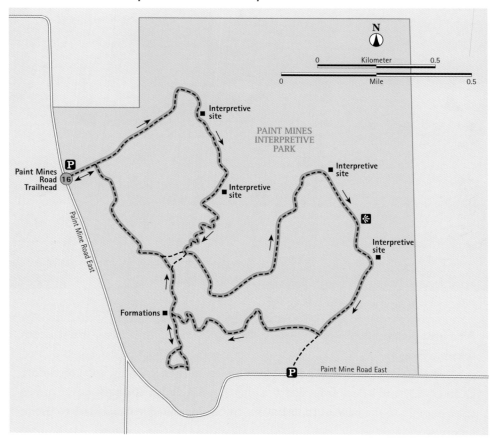

Miles and Directions

0.0 Start at the Paint Mines Road Trailhead (west trailhead) and head east.

0.1 Just before 0.1 mile, reach the junction where the loop completes. Continue straight, heading northeast on the trail.

0.4 Reach the northeasternmost part of the trail; continue as the trail turns to the southeast and descends further, reaching a low elevation point for the trail. The trail begins to climb again as it starts heading more southerly.

1.1 After winding through a lovely meadow, turn left to continue south on the trail; follow it as it starts to head in a more southeasterly direction.

1.3 The trail continues to climb before an easy descent.

1.7 The trail reaches another low point before climbing toward the Paint Mines.

2.9 Reach the Paint Mines and enjoy the awesome sights.

3.1 Begin a gradual ascent out of the Paint Mines.

3.4 Reach a point where loops connect on the trail; head left (north) on the Paint Mines Trail to return to trailhead.

3.8 Return to the initial trail junction and turn left (west), back toward the trailhead and parking area.

3.9 Arrive back at the trailhead.

Adventure Information

Organizations

El Paso County Parks Friends Group. communityservices.elpasoco.com/community-outreach-division/friends-groups/

Outfitters

Mountain Chalet. 15 N Nevada Ave., Colorado Springs; (719) 633-0732; mtnchalet.com

REI Greenwood Village. 9000 E Peakview Ave., Greenwood Village; (303) 221-7758; rei.com

REI Colorado Springs. 1376 E Woodmen Rd., Colorado Springs; (719) 260-1455; rei.com

Great Pre- or Post-Adventure Spots

Go kart racing at SBR Motorsports Park. 21430 Spencer Rd., Calhan; (719) 492-2635; sbrmotorsportspark.com

Rooster's Grille & Pizzaria. 1000 5th St., Calhan; (719) 347-3280; roostersgrille.com

Burly Brewing Co. 680 Atchison Way, Ste. 800, Castle Rock; (720) 486-0541; burlybrewing.com

Rockyard Brewing Company. 880 Castleton Rd., Castle Rock; (303) 814-9273; rockyard.com

Manitou Brewing Co. 725 Manitou Ave., Manitou Springs; (719) 282-7709; manitoubrewing.com

Penny Arcade. 900 Manitou Ave., Manitou Springs; (719) 685-9815; facebook.com/manitouspringspennyarcade

Hike 17 Monarch Lake to Lone Eagle Peak

Named for Charles "Lone Eagle" Lindbergh and rising nearly 2,000 feet above Mirror Lake, 11,946-foot Lone Eagle Peak is one of the most dramatic and iconic peaks in Colorado. The majestic, monolithic mountain of gray granite is found at the end of a beautiful alpine hike following two streams. The area abounds with wildflowers, waterfalls, and wildlife, among them moose, elk, and black bear. It's a great day hike or camping trip, and the fall colors are fantastic.

Start: Monarch Lake Trailhead, Arapaho National Forest

Distance: 14.3 miles out and back

Hiking time: About 7.5 hours

Difficulty: Intermediate trekking on good, well-marked trails

Elevation gain: About 2,000 feet

Trail surface: Dirt, rock

Best seasons: Late spring through fall; access road closed Nov 15–June 15

Other trail users: Backpackers, rock climbers, hunters, anglers, equestrians (only to Cascade Falls)

Canine compatibility: Leashed dogs permitted

Land status: Arapaho National Forest

Camping, fees, and permits: Recreation pass or daily fee required; camping permits required June 1–Sept 15

Schedule: Open 24/7

Maps: USGS Monarch Lake; National Geographic Trails Illustrated #102: Indian Peaks, Gold Hills

Nearest town: Granby

Trail contact: Arapaho National Forest, Sulphur Ranger District, 9 Ten Mile Dr., Granby 80446; (970) 887-4100; fs.usda.gov/recarea/arp/recarea/?recid=28658

Special considerations: In summer and into the fall, this is a popular area. Although camping permits are issued, the camping is backcountry. This is wilderness and there are black bears in the area. Plan accordingly if camping.

Finding the trailhead: From the intersection of US 40 and US 34 in Granby, take US 34, heading northeast for 5.4 miles toward Grand Lake. Turn right onto CR 6 and continue for 9.5 miles to the parking area. The trailhead is southeast of the lot, by Monarch Lake. There is a vault toilet and picnic area by the trailhead. GPS: N40.11091° / W105.74600°

Waterfalls along the trail to Lone Eagle Peak.

The Hike

The story behind Lone Eagle Peak's name—even though it would deserve the name on its own merits—involves a glacier owned by Boulder, a city engineer turned promoter, and a young daredevil pilot named Charles Lindbergh. Before Lindbergh became a household name for making the first solo transatlantic flight in 1927—coincidentally, the same year Boulder became the only city in the United States to own a glacier—he was a penniless pilot, traveling from town to town, giving people rides for $5 a flight.

Boulder City Engineer Fred Fair was hired in 1904 to engineer water systems tapping high-mountain streams and glaciers to supply Boulder with water, which to this day sources some water from the Arapaho Glacier. He realized that glaciers near Boulder could be tourist attractions as well and was promoting them as such in magazines across the country. As the idea gained traction, the Denver & Interurban Railroad hopped on the advertising train, renaming itself the Glacier Route. To further promote glacial tourism in the region, in 1923 they cooked up the idea of offering a $1,000 prize to anyone who would land a plane on St. Vrain Glacier, which had a more gradual slope than the larger Arapaho Glacier.

Lindbergh happened to be in Boulder that summer offering rides. Hearing that Lindbergh was up for the challenge, Fair met Lindbergh in a field at the edge of Hayden Lake. Fair said Lindbergh was a "hungry-looking youngster with a bashful grin." According to Fair, Lindbergh looked him straight in the eye and said: "Sure, I'll land on the glacier. I know I can do it, and I certainly could use that $1,000. I don't care if I never get her off there. You can see for yourself that it wouldn't be much loss."

Lindbergh's plane at the time was a tattered Curtiss "Jenny." Fair said that though its canvas cover fluttered in the breeze, "the engine purred smoothly and circled gracefully in flight." Still, Fair worried that the "suicide-crate" of a plane might not make the landing, which would draw the wrong type of publicity. So the proposed Lindbergh flight never happened.

After Lindbergh made his historic flight in May 1927, Fair named the previously unnamed peak near St. Vrain Glacier "Lindbergh Peak." However, the US Board on Geographic Names doesn't allow a peak to be named for a living individual. Instead it became Lone Eagle Peak, for one of Lindbergh's nicknames. One can imagine that when Lindbergh flew over the Rockies in the *Spirit of St. Louis* in August 1927, he tipped his wings to the mountain.

Charlie Mertens takes in the majestic Lone Eagle Peak. ERIN NUTINI, COURTESY OF NUTINI PHOTOGRAPHY

The peak is located in the Indian Peaks Wilderness, just a few miles south of Rocky Mountain National Park's southwestern edge. Its northern face is the most photographed and is photographed most from Mirror Lake. The hike to it is a fairy tale, following alpine lakes and two mountain creeks with some crossings as it passes through pine forests interspersed with aspen stands and meadows, ever climbing toward its objective. The trail passes numerous waterfalls, perhaps the biggest of which is Cascade Falls at 4.4 miles. Hikers are rewarded with stunning views of Lone Eagle Peak only when they make it to Mirror Lake. Before that, the inclines and forests hide the mountain.

While this adventure only covers the hike to Lone Eagle Peak, there are numerous ways to summit it. It can be hiked as a Class 4 scramble with a fair amount of exposure on its northeast side. It can also be climbed as a multi-pitch 5.7 trad route on its north face; other 5.10+ routes are available on its north and east faces.

Miles and Directions

0.0   Start at the Monarch Lake Trailhead, on the northwest side of Monarch Lake, and head southwest on the Cascade Creek Trail.

0.8   Reach the northeastern side of Monarch Lake and continue on the Cascade Creek Trail as you head into the Indian Peaks Wilderness.

1.5   Go left at the junction where Cascade Creek joins the Buchanan Creek Trail; begin ascending as the trail stays close to Buchanan Creek.

1.9   Encounter an initial series of switchbacks.

2.5   Pass Shelter Rock (no camping in the area, as it's within 100 feet of the trail).

3.1   At the Cascade Creek–Buchanan Pass Trail junction, continue straight (west) as the Buchanan Pass Trail heads left. The trail continues its gradual climb.

3.3   The trail crosses Buchanan Creek and, shortly after, starts following Cascade Creek.

4.4   Reach Cascade Falls.

6.0   Turn right at the junction with Pawnee Pass Trail (USFS #907) and take the Cascade Creek Trail to Crater Lake. The trail levels out for a bit before a final climb to Crater Lake.

6.7   As the trail nears Mirror Lake, it resumes climbing. Skirt the northwest side of Mirror Lake and climb the final 50 or so feet to Crater Lake.

Monarch Lake to Lone Eagle Peak

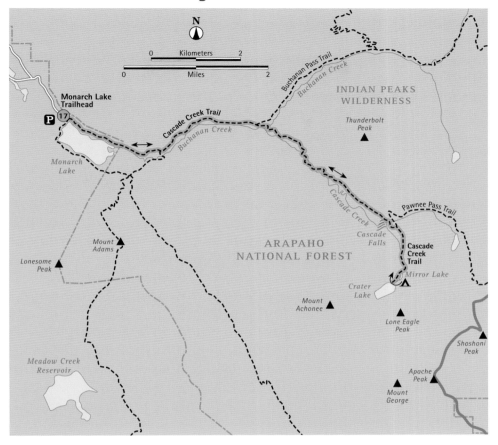

7.1 Reach Crater Lake and look for places to take pictures of iconic Lone Eagle Peak across the southwestern side of the lake (there are campsites near its northeastern side). Return the way you came

14.3 Arrive back at the trailhead.

Adventure Information

Monarch Lake. fs.usda.gov/recarea/arp/recreation/hiking/recarea/?recid=28566&actid=51

Cascade Trail #1: fs.usda.gov/recarea/arp/recreation/hiking/recarea/?recid=28658&actid=50

Outfitters

Two Pines Supply. 150 E Agate Ave., Granby; (970) 363-4054; twopinessupply.com

Great Pre- or Post-Adventure Spots

Never Summer Brewing Co. 62 E Agate Ave., Granby; (970) 887-0333; neversummerbrewing co.com

Fraser River Beer Company. 218 Eisenhower Dr., Fraser; (720) 352-1874; fraserriverbeerco .com

Maverick's Grille. 15 E Agate Ave., Granby; (970) 887-9000; mavericksgrille.com

Hike 18 American Lakes Trail to Snow Lake

This picturesque hike to alpine lakes just north of the Never Summer Wilderness and Rocky Mountain National Park offers stunning views of the Rockies and Nokhu Crags in an alpine cirque. With more than 600 moose in the park, it's also prime moose-viewing country. This out-and-back adventure is suitable for most and makes for a good, albeit tough, day. It also makes an excellent camping trip.

Start: American Lakes Trailhead, State Forest State Park

Distance: 6.9 miles out and back

Hiking time: About 4 hours

Difficulty: Moderately difficult hiking due to elevation gain

Elevation gain: Nearly 1,700 feet

Trail surface: Dirt road and dirt trail

Best seasons: Year-round

Other trail users: Campers, mountain bikers, equestrians, anglers; hunting and snow sports in season

Canine compatibility: Leashed dogs permitted (leash 6 feet long or less)

Land status: State Forest State Park

Camping, fees, and permits: Day pass fees (pay at kiosks when office is closed); additional fees for camping

Schedule: Open 24/7

Maps: USGS Mount Richthofen; National Geographic Trails Illustrated #114: Walden, Gould

Nearest town: Walden

Trail contact: State Forest State Park, 56750 Hwy. 14, Walden 80480; (970) 723-8366; cpw.state.co.us/placestogo/parks/StateForest

Special considerations: Most negative encounters with moose are caused by dogs. Please keep them leashed and quiet. If you see moose too close for comfort, move behind trees.

Finding the trailhead: From the intersection of US 287 and CO 14 (Powder Canyon Road), head west on CO 14 for 61 miles. Turn left on CR 62 and follow it for 0.6 mile; continue straight on CR 62A until it ends in a dirt lot in 0.9 mile. The trailhead is on the east side of the lot. GPS: N40.50493° / W105.88408°

The Hike

The hike to Snow Lake in State Forest State Park is the northernmost adventure in this book. On the northwest side of Rocky Mountain National Park, the 71,000-acre state park has over 90 miles of hiking trails and 130 miles of trails open to mountain biking. Visitors to the park can cross over into national forest and Rocky Mountain National Park in the backcountry, and this trail enters Medicine Bow–Routt National Forest at Snow Lake. State Forest Sate Park's ecosystems include mountain meadows; riparian zones; wetlands; cold climate sand dunes; and lodgepole pine, subalpine, and aspen forests; and it is the only state park with an alpine tundra habitat.

Considered the moose-viewing capital of Colorado, the area is now home to more than 600 moose. The state transplanted twenty-four moose to the area in 1978 and 1979, and they have thrived among the lodgepole pine forests near riparian zones, like those near the Michigan River and along this adventure. Other large ungulate mammals are highly visible in the park as well as moose. It's estimated that there are 5,000 to 6,000 elk and 5,000 to 6,000 mule deer in the area, as well as 1,100 to 1,200 pronghorn and two herds of bighorn sheep. Pronghorn are found in lower altitude sagebrush areas; elk find year-round food and

A moose calf milking its mother.

Beautiful fall foliage near Michigan Lakes with Static Peak and Snow Lake above, Nokhu Crags on the right.

habitat in the area, in summer eating grasses and forbs in mountain meadows and riparian areas. In winter they find forage in shrublands and aspen stands and rest and find thermal cover in closed-canopy forests.

This hike travels through subalpine forest, characterized by Engelmann spruce and subalpine fir with some lodgepole pine, and alpine tundra, which has low-lying grasses, sedges, rushes, and forbs as well as lichen-painted rock. It also has many flowers, including marsh marigold and alpine forget-me-not. The alpine tundra feeds bighorn sheep and birds like the white-tailed ptarmigan and American pipit. Other biomes in the park include wetlands, home to river otters and beavers, as well as the only cold climate sand dunes in the state. Mule deer winter near the park's East and North Sand Dunes and use meadows, riparian areas, and forests the rest of the year.

The hike takes you through prime moose-viewing country on easy trails with moderate inclines. It then opens into a rolling alpine tundra meadow, takes trekkers to the Michigan Lakes, and ends at Snow Lake at 11,525 feet. In summer, alpine wildflowers and grasses populate this alpine tundra, giving off a lovely aroma. In the fall, low-growing willows and other alpine growth create a rusty mosaic of colors as their leaves change.

Snow Lake offers stunning close-up views of the Nokhu Crags in a gorgeous cirque. The crags, composed of shale metamorphosed into hornfels, were called *Neaha-no-xhu* ("eagles nest") in the Arapaho language. True to their name, golden and bald eagles have been spotted near the crags. Looking back to the northeast from Snow Lake, Thunder Mountain and Lulu Mountain are nearby; a little farther off is 12,265-foot Iron Mountain.

Miles and Directions

0.0 Start at the American Lakes Trailhead, heading southeast, and follow it up an easy fire road.

0.5 Cross a small bridge.

1.1 The trail crosses the Michigan Ditch Trail; continue straight.

1.8 At the junction with the Thunder Pass Mountain Trail, stay right on the American Lakes Trail.

1.9 Cross the Michigan River on another bridge; begin climbing up a series of easy switchbacks, which last for about 0.8 mile.

3.1 Continue straight at the junction with the Thunder Pass Mountain Trail (on the left). The trail continues west, following the northeastern side of both Michigan Lakes.

3.4 The trail leaves the northwestern side of the second Michigan Lake as it makes a final, 250-foot ascent to Snow Lake. Return via the same route.

6.9 Arrive back at the trailhead.

Adventure Information

Outfitters

JAX Outdoor Gear. 1200 N College Ave., Fort Collins; (970) 221-0544; jaxgoods.com

REI Fort Collins. 4025 S College Ave., Fort Collins; (970) 223-0123; rei.com

Great Pre- or Post-Adventure Spots

CooperSmith's Pub & Brewing. #5 Old Town Square, Fort Collins; (970) 498-0483; coopersmithspub.com

American Lakes Trail to Snow Lake

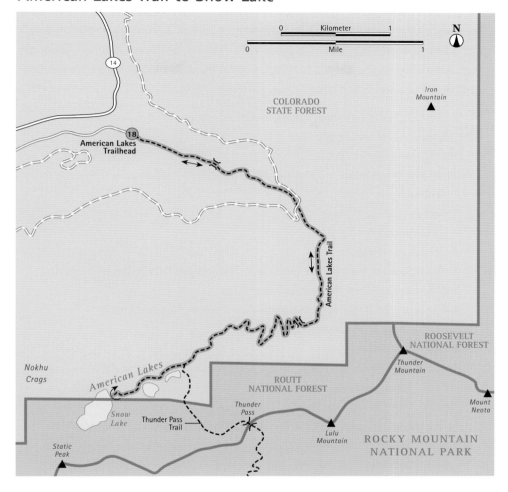

McClellan's Brewing Co. 1035 S Taft Hill Rd., Fort Collins; (970) 568-8473; mcclellans brewingcompany.com

Odell Brewing. 800 E Lincoln Ave., Fort Collins; (970) 498-9070; odellbrewing.com

All Smoked Up BBQ. 476 Main St., Walden; (970) 218-4626; facebook.com/All-Smoked-Up -BBQ-1571218409590552/

Mountain Tap Brewery. 910 Yampa St., Steamboat Springs; (970) 879-6646; mountaintap brewery.com

Hike 19 Shadow Mountain Fire Lookout

A beautiful year-round hike on a heavily forested trail with moderate elevation gain, this hike takes you to the last of four fire lookout towers in Rocky Mountain National Park. Although the fire lookout is closed, there are still fantastic views from the top of Kawuneeche and Grand Lake Valleys as well as the surrounding lakes to the west.

Start: East Shore Trailhead, Shadow Mountain National Recreation Area

Distance: 8.8 miles out and back

Hiking time: About 5 hours

Difficulty: Intermediately difficult hike on good, well-marked trails with decent elevation gain

Elevation gain: 1,900 feet

Trail surface: Dirt

Best seasons: Year-round

Other trail users: Equestrians; cross-country skiers and snowshoers in winter

Canine compatibility: Leashed dogs permitted

Land status: Rocky Mountain National Park, Arapaho National Forest

Camping, fees, and permits: Daily use fee

Schedule: Open 24/7

Maps: USGS Shadow Mountain, Grand Lake; National Geographic Trails Illustrated #200: Rocky Mountain National Park

Nearest town: Grand Lake

Trail contact: Arapaho National Forest, Sulphur Ranger District, 9 Ten Mile Dr., Granby 80446; (970) 887-4100; fs.usda.gov/recarea/arp/recarea/?recid=28592. Rocky Mountain National Park, 1000 US 36, Estes Park 80517; (970) 586-1206; nps.gov/romo/index.htm.

Finding the trailhead: From the intersection of US 40 and US 34 in Granby, take US 34 northeast toward Grand Lake for 14 miles. Turn right onto West Portal Road and continue for 0.3 mile. Turn right onto Center Drive and continue 0.2 mile. Turn left onto Marina Drive then take the first right (Shadow Mountain Drive) in 450 feet. Stay on Shadow Mountain Drive for 0.2 mile and turn right onto Jericho Road. Continue for 0.5 mile then turn right into the parking area. There are vault toilets at the parking area. The trailhead is on the east side of the lot. GPS: N40.24028° / W105.82589°

The Hike

The three-story Shadow Mountain Fire Lookout, also known as the Shadow Mountain Patrol Cabin, is the last of four fire tower lookouts in Rocky Mountain National Park. The tower was built by the Civilian Conservation Corps in 1933. A couple usually occupied the lookout tower in fire season, sharing lookout duties to watch for fires in the forested lands. However, like almost all fire towers in Colorado, it was shuttered as other means of detecting fires were adopted. Its last active fire season was 1968. The lookout tower was added to the National Register of Historic Places in 1978 and was restored in the mid-1990s. However, as of early 2019, the catwalk on the lookout's third story remained closed.

Though the lookout is closed, the hike to the top of Shadow Mountain is still worth the effort. It offers a peek into Rocky Mountain National Park and fantastic views of the Continental Divide, the usually snowcapped peaks of the Never Summer Wilderness, Grand County, and the valley of Fraser River. It also offers

The southwest view from the top of Shadow Mountain.

Shadow Mountain Fire Tower.

an awesome view of Shadow Mountain Lake, Grand Lake, and Lake Granby. These lakes are vital water sources for Colorado's eastern slopes and plains.

Grand Lake is north of the fire tower. At 1.5 miles long, 1 mile across, and up to 389 feet deep, it is the largest and deepest natural lake in Colorado. A glacial lake, it was first formed between 30,000 and 10,000 years ago during the Pinedale glaciation. The lake is naturally damned by a glacial terminal moraine. The Utes called it Spirit Lake, believing that departed souls dwelled in its cold waters.

Both Shadow Mountain Lake, west of the fire tower, and Lake Granby, south of the tower, are larger, man-made lakes. All three are part of the Colorado–Big Thompson (C-BT) project to divert water from Colorado's western slopes to its eastern slopes. Lake Granby is the second-largest reservoir in Colorado's Rockies and the third largest in the state. Water from Lake Granby is pumped up to Shadow Mountain Lake and flows by gravity to Grand Lake. From Grand Lake, water flows into the 13.1-mile-long Alva B. Adams Tunnel, dropping almost 0.5 mile as it flows through five hydroelectric plants, traveling under the Continental Divide to the Front Range. The power generated drives pumps on Colorado's western slope, which push those waters to Lake Granby. Excess power produced by the generators is sold to Colorado's electric grid. The water emerges on the

Front Range in numerous reservoirs, including Horsetooth Reservoir above Fort Collins.

The Continental Divide isn't far. In fact, the hike to Shadow Mountain starts on the Continental Divide Trail and follows it along the eastern shore of Shadow Mountain Lake until 1.5 miles, when the Shadow Mountain Trail heads left and up through a pine forest. Though the pines are thick and provide great shadows, they're riddled with dead trees, many of which are likely beetle-killed.

The trail continues to gain altitude as it climbs through the forest, mostly on large zigzags across the western slopes of Shadow Mountain. The final approach to the peak, as the trail turns to the north, is the steepest section, but it's short.

Miles and Directions

0.0 Start at the East Shore Trailhead and head right (south) on the East Shore (N103) and Continental Divide Trails, following the shore of Shadow Mountain Lake.

0.7 The trail crosses from the Arapaho National Recreation Area into Rocky Mountain National Park.

1.5 At the junction with the Shadow Mountain Trail, turn left and begin the ascent.

1.7 The trail elbows back and heads north up a forested ridgeline.

2.4 The trail comes to another elbow and heads south for a short bit.

2.7 At yet another elbow, the trail resumes its northerly direction.

3.1 The trail turns right, heading southeast.

3.9 The trail comes to another elbow and heads north.

4.0 On the final push to the top, the trail turns right again.

4.1 As the climb eases near the top, the trail turns to the left.

4.2 The trail makes a final left turn.

4.4 Reach the Shadow Mountain Fire Lookout. Return via the same route.

8.8 Arrive back at the trailhead.

Adventure Information

Shadow Mountain Reservoir. fs.usda.gov/Internet/FSE_DOCUMENTS/fseprd516852.pdf

Shadow Mountain Fire Lookout

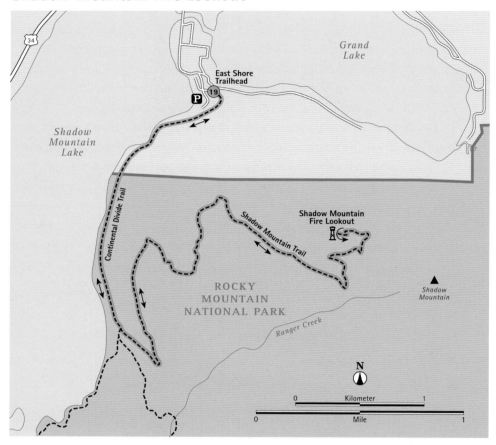

Outfitters

Two Pines Supply. 150 E Agate Ave., Granby; (970) 363-4054; twopinessupply.com

Great Pre- or Post-Adventure Spots

The World's End Brewpub. 813 Grand Ave., Grand Lake; (970) 509-9970; worldsendbrew pub.com

Sagebrush BBQ & Grill. 1101 Grand Ave., Grand Lake; (970) 627-1404; sagebrushbbq.com

Fraser River Beer Company. 218 Eisenhower Dr., Fraser; (720) 352-1874; fraserriverbeerco .com

CLIMBING ADVENTURES

Colorado is a land of rock. All across the state, cliffs and canyons, geological uprisings and erosion have created incredible opportunities for climbing that draw people from around the world. This book covers some of the state's most amazing areas, from Eldorado Canyon and Shelf Road to other areas as well-loved but not necessarily as well-known. From single-pitch sport climbs to epic trad multi-pitch adventures, there's something for every climber in here. A few uber-popular areas didn't make the cut, like Red Rocks Canyon, Rocky Mountain National Park, and Eleven Mile Canyon. Here you'll find places offering hundreds of routes and epic days. People spend lifetimes exploring the rock face, finding the perfect place for the next cam as the ground melts away below.

A climbing access sign in Staunton State Park.

Climb 20 Clear Creek Canyon: Creekside

One of the closest, quickest getaways from Denver, where people can lose themselves in a cornucopia of adventures, is Clear Creek Canyon, just west of Golden. With hiking, mountain biking, whitewater rafting, climbing, and more, the canyon offers an abundance of outdoor activities—but let's hone in on climbing.

The canyon has everything from multi-pitch and trad routes to fantastic sport routes and bouldering over frothy Clear Creek. It has something to offer everyone, from the casual climber to extreme athletes looking to challenge themselves. But with nearly 1,000 listed routes at ninety crags listed on Mountain Project, it's hard to know which spots to take on for the first time and what times of day and year are the best to explore a crag. While the easiest, quickest crag to access is Canal Zone—just 0.25 mile into Clear Creek Canyon, it's also the busiest. Waiting to get a chance to climb one of the crag's twenty routes can be like sitting in traffic on I-70 on a Sunday. *Note:* Some of the crags in Clear Creek Canyon, particularly the lower part of the canyon, are closed February 1 to July 31, for raptor and eagle nesting.

There are perhaps two "walls with it all" in Clear Creek Canyon: Wall of the '90s and Creekside. Between the two crags, there are sixteen classic routes and more than sixty known routes. The crags offer overhang, crack, granite, slab climbing, and more. However, the one real wall with it all in this canyon is Creekside. It has at least thirty-six climbing routes, ranging from 5.6 to 5.12d or 5.13+, meaning it has a little something for everyone.

Climbing type: Trad, sport, multi-pitch
Difficulty: 5.6–5.13+
Rock type: Varies; granitic, metamorphic slab
Best seasons: Year-round. The western side gets less sun, so it's good for summer climbing. The eastern side gets more direct sunlight and is good for morning climbs in summer and cold days in winter.
Land status: Jefferson County Open Space
Maps: USGS Squaw Pass; National Geographic Trails Illustrated #100: Boulder, Golden
Nearest town: Golden
Camping, fees, and permits: No fees or camping; no parking after dark
Contact: Jefferson County Open Space; (303) 271-5925; www.jeffco.us/1196/Clear-Creek-Canyon-Park

Creekside on Clear Creek Canyon from the Other Safari wall.

Getting there: From the intersection of US 6 and CO 93, head west on US 6. Drive 12 miles into the canyon. Turn left at the light and continue through Tunnel 5; there is a small parking lot on the left with a few spaces. Park here or alongside the northern side of the road, on the creek side. GPS: N39.74292° / W105.40629°

Finding the crag: This massive rock actually has four different access points and two different places to park, about 0.25 mile from each other on US 6 West. Access the eastern side, which has classic four-star-rated climbs like Playin' Hooky (5.8, 4 pitches) and Solid Gold (5.12a, 5 pitches), from across the Catslab lot on the northwestern side of US 6. If parked in the lot, carefully cross over US 6 (cars speed through this area very quickly) and head east toward Tunnel 5. Step over the cement barricade—as of 2020 there's a deep notch in it—and look for the trail that heads to the left, following the north side of the creek. Follow the creek west for 0.2 mile, passing the climbing crags The Doghouse, Other Critters, and The Safari on your right side. Those crags are about 350 feet up the canyon side. The Solid Gold area is the first crag you'll reach. GPS: N39.74184° W105.40993°

The Climb

"Clear Creek Canyon is my home, and I feel fortunate to call it my local crag," says Kevin Capps, who founded Denver Mountain Guiding in 2010 and wrote *Rock Climbing Clear Creek Canyon*. "I have only been climbing here since 2009, but I feel like I have been a part of the final frontier of the canyon's development, racking up nearly one hundred first ascents. The right side of Creekside is the perfect section of wall for a moderate climber that is looking to push their boundaries by testing out some of the classic multi-pitch climbs like Playin' Hooky, Black Gold, or even Creek Dance. Playin' Hooky is by far the most popular multi-pitch sport climb on the Front Range, so if you're going on a weekend, be prepared for a party.

"Creekside has an impressive all-star lineup with the classic Playin' Hooky 5.8, which gives you a taste of some of the best metamorphic slab climbing Colorado has to offer! For even more of a challenge, test your abilities on Solid Gold, a steep and exposed headwall that goes at 5.12a," Capps says.

Best Routes

Playin' Hooky (5.8, sport), 4 pitches, 10 draws: This epic climb shares its first two pitches with Solid Gold and can be climbed with a 70-meter rope as one pitch. It starts to the right of the dihedral and roof and climbs left to an overhanging belay. Belay your partner here or stretch the rope to the second belay station, on a good ledge with multiple anchors. **Pitch 1:** 10 bolts. **Pitch 2:** 8 bolts. Both are 2-bolt anchors. **Pitch 3 (5.6):** 6 bolts, 2-bolt anchor. After climbing to the left of the seas, look up to the right to climb slab. The anchors are about midway up this pitch. **Pitch 4 (5.8):** 10 bolts, 2-bolt anchor. Continue up the slab, going straight toward a small, vertical finish. **Descent:** Rappel the route, stopping at each anchor with a 60-meter rope. With a 70-meter rope, the last two anchors can be combined.

A look at prominent features on Creekside. A route setter (in blue) is setting a new sport route on the right.

Solid Gold (5.12a), 5 pitches, 12 draws: Aptly named. This route shares the first two pitches with Playin' Hooky (above). **Pitch 3 (5.7):** 7 bolts, 2-bolt anchor. Climb left over fourth-class terrain and continue to a belay spot. **Pitch 4 (5.12a):** 10 bolts, 2-bolt anchor. This pitch starts with a crumbly face ascent—watch out for loosening any rocks! After an initially sketchy band of rock, the pitch reaches a solid vertical rock face that climbs over some small roofs. There's a small ledge by the anchors to belay from. **Pitch 5 (5.11d):** 12 bolts, 2-bolt anchor. This final pitch starts out with its hardest moves, climbing up and to the left before resuming a vertical face climb to finish on easier slab. **Descent:** Rappel the route, stopping at every belay station.

Big Bro's Watchin' (5.11, trad/sport mix), 6 pitches, full rack to 4-inch cam, 5 draws: This spicy route requires a rack up to a #4 cam, at least 9 draws, and an anchor. It starts with a Class 5 climb just left of the lower dihedral to anchor in on a 1-bolt anchor backed up with a cam. The first two pitches are rated 5.9. The first pitch ends parallel to the top of the dihedral. The next pitch climbs over a flake to easier terrain. **Pitch 3 (5.11a):** This ledgy face reaches a thin crack and continues climbing to reach a hanging anchor. **Pitch 4 (5.11b):** From the hanging anchor you can place a #4 cam horizontally in a crack. Climb left over a bulge to a hand-size crack to a crux move. **Pitch 5 (5.10d):** Climb an overhanging stemming corner jam over the roof to next, exposed belay station. **Pitch 6:** Either rappel from this belay station or scramble to the final anchors and move over the anchors on Solid Gold to rappel to the bottom.

Adventure Information

Outfitters

Bentgate Mountaineering. 1313 Washington Ave., Golden; (303) 271-9382; bentgate.com. Open Sun–Fri; closed Sat.

Wilderness Exchange. 2401 15th St., Ste. 100, Denver; (303) 964-0708; wildernessx.com

Vital Outdoors. 1224 Washington Ave., Golden; (303) 215-1644; vitaloutdoors.com

REI Denver Flagship. 1416 Platte St., Denver; (303) 756-3100; rei.com

Clear Creek Canyon Park: Creekside

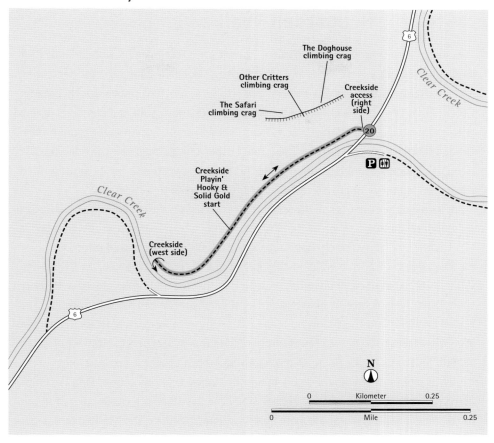

Great Pre- or Post-Adventure Spots

Woody's Wood Fired Pizza. 1305 Washington Ave., Golden; (303) 277-0443; woodysgolden.com

Barrels & Bottles Brewery. 600 12th St., Unit 180, Golden; (720) 328-3643; barrelsbottles.com

Mountain Toad Brewing. 900 Washington Ave., Golden; (720) 638-3244; mountaintoadbrewing.com

Tributary Food Hall & Drinkery. 701 12th St., Golden; (303) 856-7225; tributarygolden.com

Climb 21 Eldorado Canyon State Park: Redgarden Wall

The steep, daunting walls of Eldorado Canyon are a technicolor wonderland; rock tripe—fluorescent yellow, sage, and other crustose lichens—paints the red sandstone and quartzite as the canyon towers more than 1,000 feet above South Boulder Creek. At its base is 1.6-billion-year-old granite. In short, Eldo is a climber's dream with more than 1,000 mainly trad routes tucked away in less than 0.5 square mile. Graded harder than most areas (a 5.9 most other places might be considered a 5.7 here), it's quickly overwhelming. People get Eldo'd—awestruck—by its stoutly rated routes on chimneys, sharp arêtes, broad roofs, and generally sheer walls.

It's no wonder the Utes sheltered in the canyon walls during winter. Similarly, it's no wonder Eldorado Canyon State Park was founded by passionate climbing legends like Layton Kor, Gerry Roach, Bob Culp, Lynn Hill, Beth Bennett, and others.

The largest of all the walls in the park, and the "wall with it all," is Redgarden Wall. It's a 700-foot-tall behemoth of jutting sandstone and broken teeth with more than 1,000 feet of face. It boasts some of the canyon's most famous lines like The Naked Edge, T2, and The Yellow Spur and easier ones like Rewritten. In all, Redgarden Wall has at least 300 named routes, from relatively easy learners like the 5.4, 4-pitch Pseudo Sidetrack to the 5.13c, 2-pitch Centaur—both of which are trad lines.

With plenty of shade and walls facing in almost every direction, Eldo is climbable year-round. Spring and fall are generally the best times to climb most of it, but north-facing walls generally remain cool in summer, while walls like Redgarden get a lot of southern and western exposure, making them better to climb on cooler days or on mornings of hot days.

Climbing type: Primarily trad multi-pitch climbing, with some sport routes and anchors

Difficulty: 5.4–5.13c

Rock type: Chiefly Fountain Formation sandstone and quartzite

Best seasons: Spring through fall

Land status: Colorado State Park

Maps: USGS Eldorado Springs; National Geographic Trails Illustrated #100: Boulder, Golden

Nearest town: Boulder

Camping, fees, and permits: Vehicle and pedestrian fees, payable at entrance station during office hours or at kiosk when office is closed; no camping

Redgarden Wall, Tower Two to the right, Tower One left of that, the Middle Buttress, and Hot Spur.

Contact: Eldorado Canyon Park, 9 Kneale Rd., Eldorado Springs 80025; (303) 494-3943; cpw.state.co.us/placestogo/parks/EldoradoCanyon

Special considerations: Certain areas on Redgarden Wall are closed for raptor roosting and nesting. These closures are generally Feb 1–July 31. The top pitches of Naked Edge are closed; also closed is the stretch of upper rock between the Naked Edge and The Sidetrack.

Getting there: From the parking area at the intersection of CO 93 and CO 170, head west and south on CO 170 for 3.5 miles, arriving at the parking area. There are toilets at the entrance and at Supremacy Rock. Bring WAG bags if needed. *Note:* Eldo has limited parking and is extremely popular—particularly on the weekends. If your group has multiple vehicles park as many as possible at the parking lot on CO 93 and take as few vehicles into the canyon as possible. GPS: N39.93127° W105.28163°

Finding the crag: Cross the South Boulder Creek Bridge and then turn left (west), following the creek on its northern side. In 0.1 mile access to climbing at Redgarden Wall starts on the right. The trail climbs north up the wall for about 0.5 mile. There are more than 300 routes on this section of wall. GPS: N39.93156° / W105.28187°

The Climb

The Redgarden Wall is the biggest, tallest wall in Eldo. Some climbs have as many as eight pitches, making for epic days on the wall as it climbs 700 feet from its base. The wall dominates the north side of the canyon and includes four distinct summits (from the creek to the west): Tower Two, Tower One, Lumpe Tower, and Middle Buttress. Features include vertical faces, big ramps, roofs, and sharp arêtes.

Redgarden's variety and length have attracted some of the best climbers from around the world. "Tommy Caldwell and his climbing partner were doing laps up the Naked Edge and all kinds of other really hard climbs," says Rebecca Slyder, a former park ranger in the area. "We'd come in at 6 a.m. and they would already be up on midway, on their fourth and fifth laps of the day."

Slyder says she's hoping to climb Naked Edge, a 5.11b trad climb, one day. "It's really beautiful and really amazing that climbers have climbed that route," she says. "There are a lot of wonderful stories behind it. Sure, it's a really hard grade, and it would be amazing if I ever got the opportunity to climb that." Of routes Slyder's done, she says, "Rewritten was probably my favorite climb over there. It's not terribly hard but it is an Eldo grade. It is a really fun multi-pitch route. It's a truly awesome feeling to top out on that route, because basically you're right on top of a canyon on the north side."

Best Routes

Touch and Go (5.9, trad), full rack, lots of nuts, cams to 3-inch, 1 pitch: This popular line on Tower Two is a great start to the Naked Edge. The route begins as the trail heads away from the creek and starts climbing up the hill after exiting a patch of shrubby trees. It's below a thin, slanted roof. Climb under the roof and head up to the left on flakes into a short corner. Climb a sloping ramp then traverse left to a right-facing corner. Layback and stem up to a ledge with two bolts. **Descent:** Rappel 125 feet with two ropes to the ground from here, or continue up to Anthill Direct or the Naked Edge.

The Naked Edge (5.11b, trad), full rack, lots of nuts and stoppers, cams to 3-inch, 6 pitches: One of the most famous climbs in Eldo as well as Colorado. It features hard climbing with lots of exposure, great positioning, and a direct line. It starts at the anchors of Touch and Go. Climb Touch and Go's belay ledge and

Redgarden Wall, Towers One and Two.

work left on a ramp to a bolted belay ledge below Naked Edge. **Pitch 1 (5.11a):** Climb a thin finger crack right of edge, stemming for 75 feet to reach a 2-bolt anchor. **Pitch 2 (5.9+):** A face climb left of a slab above the belay leads to a leaning roof. Traverse left around the arête then jam a thin crack to an exposed belay. **Pitch 3 (5.6):** An easier climb to an awkward mantle. Work right to a sloping ledge under an overhanging chimney. **Pitch 4 (5.11a):** This pitch climbs difficult cracks and corners to the top of a chimney slot. Climb over the roof capping the slot to reach a small ledge. **Pitch 5 (5.11a):** Climb the shallow corner (5.11a) to the right of a hanging prow. There's a layback to an overhanging crack for major hand jams. Look for a small stance on the right to make the next anchor. **Pitch 6:** Climb left around the arête then climb up easy slabs to the summit. **Descent:** East Slabs or Rappel Descent (see below).

Tower Two (5.11a, trad), full rack, up to 8 pitches: This classic Eldo climb on Tower Two is just uphill of Touch and Go. It starts below a long roof. There's a drilled piton above it. **Pitch 1 (5.11):** Starting on burly flakes, climb over the roof, the crux move, to clip into the fixed piton—consider a stick clip if not too confident. From there climb rightward on steep but moderate rock on a left-angling ramp to a bolted belay. **Pitch 2 (5.8):** Continuing up the ramp to the west, follow the shallow chimney to a stance in a slot cave. **Pitch 3:** With a long rope this can

THE HISTORY OF CLIMBING AT ELDORADO CANYON

Best known to climbers as Eldo, Eldorado Canyon has been an adventurist's mecca since the early 1900s, when it was known as "The Coney Island of the West." Then the canyon housed high-end hotels, swimming pools, ballrooms, roller- and ice-skating rinks, and other attractions, including its world-famous hot springs. People came to use the cabins and stables and to bask in the steep canyon walls, drawing up to 40,000 visitors a day—first by rail and then by car.

Given the sheer height of the canyon's walls, it's no wonder that people have always sought new challenges on them. One of the earliest aerialists to grace the canyon was Ivy Baldwin, a former international high-wire acrobat. In 1907 he began doing a high-wire act 400 feet above the canyon floor, walking across a 7/8-inch-thick steel cable that spanned 672 feet between The Bastille and the Wind Tower. The traverse took a little over 12 minutes, and his feat continued to delight canyon visitors over the weekends for decades. He made his last crossing in 1948 on his 82nd birthday. The walk was re-created by then 24-year-old slackliner Taylor VanAllen in October 2016. VanAllen made the crossing in tribute to Baldwin and to raise funds for trail building and anchors in the park.

Although Baldwin and VanAllen soared between the park's mammoth rocks, visitors accessed the tops of the canyon via the "Crazy Stairs" built in 1908. The rickety flights of wooden stairs zigzagged nearly 600 feet up the canyon walls.

The more modern climbing history of Eldo beings in the 1950s with legendary climbers and mountaineers like Layton Kor, Gerry Roach, Bob Culp, and Royal Robbins. Kor was known for putting up first ascents in Yosemite, Longs Peak, Utah, and elsewhere in the United States. He established Tower Two in 1959 and the Yellow Spur in 1960. Both Redgarden Wall routes remain classics today.

Although climbing was a male-dominated sport in its early days, Eldorado Canyon had notable, strong women climbers in its early days too. By the early 1970s climbers like Molly Higgins, Diana Hunter, Sue Giller, and Connie Hilliard were known for climbing and leading tough routes.

Early climbers in the canyon were sometimes called marmots. Dirtbags from the start, they sometimes hid in trunks or under seats of vehicles to avoid paying the landowner, Bill Fowler, 25 cents to access the cliffs for climbing. Fowler had wanted to sell the land to the state for years. Around 1975 it became known that the Conda Mine Co. was interested in purchasing the canyon to turn it into a gravel pit. That turned the ragtag group of climbers and others who loved hiking and recreating in the canyon into activists. They ultimately prevailed upon the state, which bought the land in 1978 and turned it into the park it is today.

The canyon still draws internationally renowned climbers like Lynn Hill, Tommy Caldwell, and Sasha DiGiulian to its walls to pay homage to climbing's legacy, to train, and to challenge themselves for the next big adventure.

be combined with Pitch 2. Climb up and left to the beginning of the next ramp west. Move the belay to the other side of the ramp. **Pitch 4 (5.9):** Climb 60 feet in a shallow black gully to a narrow shelf. Traverse left to a finger crack that climbs to the left. Anchor at a small stance in the crack to belay. **Pitch 5 (5.7):** Continue climbing the widening crack to reach a large, right-facing dihedral; climb the slab ramp on the slab face. Belay below the large roof. **Pitch 6 (5.9):** Though rated a 5.9, as you climb left from the overhanging side of the dihedral, the red band of rock is rotten and slip potential is significant. **Pitches 7 and 8:** Continue up the ramp to a large tree in the saddle that's west of Tower Two. **Descent:** East Slabs or Rappel Descent (see below).

The Yellow Spur (5.10a, trad), full rack and nuts, cams to 3-inch, 7 pitches: This is another of Colorado's most famous routes. On Tower One (just west of Tower Two, about 500 feet up the hill), climb a ledge at the base of the wall and start the route by some trees below roofs. **Pitch 1 (5.10a):** Below the largest roof, climb to the left edge of the roof and angle up right on easier rock to a belay by a tree. **Pitch 2 (5.8):** Climb left to a right-facing dihedral, then climb up to a belay by a tree on a horizontal band of rock. **Pitch 3 (5.8):** Climb a corner to a ledge for an easy pull over a small roof, then stem up a dihedral to the next ledge for a belay. **Pitch 4 (5.4):** Traverse to the right on the ledge to a large dihedral, reaching a belay below a big roof. **Pitch 5 (5.8):** Find the traverse under the roof and climb around an arête and into the next corner; climb out to a belay stance on the rock ridge. **Pitch 6 (5.10a):** Climb on a thin crack to a step on a vertical

Looking up from the bottom of Rewritten.

face. Climb past pitons to reach a stance on a flake. Continue climbing to a small corner to reach a belay stance on the arête. **Alt. Pitch 6 (5.7):** Take the Robbins Traverse to the left from the flake stance. Climb the headwall on the left to reach the belay stance on the ridge. **Pitch 7 (5.6):** Climb the exposed arête to the summit. **Descent:** East Slabs or Rappel Descent (see below).

Rewritten (5.7, trad), full rack up to 3-inch, extra slings for tie-offs, nuts and a 48-inch runner for horns, up to 6 pitches: This easier classic on the Middle Buttress is farther west up the wall. **Pitch 1 (5.6):** Climb a ramp to the left to reach steep rock, passing the bulge on an arête. Traverse right and climb the crack to a belay behind a secure flake. **Pitch 2 (5.4):** Climb up the broken chimney to Red Ledge, then climb left to the eyebolt anchor. **Pitch 3 (5.5):** Head directly up from the belay, passing some blocks, and finish the pitch on top of a chimney for a belay stance. **Pitch 4 (5.7):** Make an exposed but good traverse to the left across the face, and climb the thin crack to the somewhat exposed belay. **Pitch 5 (5.5):** On Rubuffat's Arête, start on the right side then work up to the arête's left side. This pitch ends on an airy belay stance atop the arête (slings will tie off the horns). **Pitch 6 (5.5):** An easy crack climb of the face to the summit. These final pitches can be combined. **Descent:** This is farther up the wall than the other climbs listed here and has a different descending route. Scramble to

Eldorado Canyon State Park: Redgarden Wall

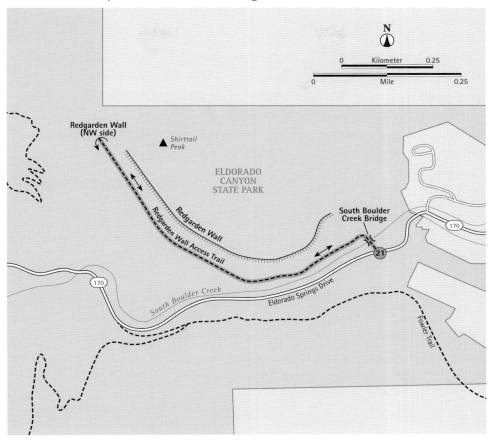

the north 500 feet to a cairn on the next summit to find a path that leads west to the base of the wall.

Descents

East Slabs

Although all descents are difficult here, the East Slabs descent is the easiest for Tower Two. That said, it becomes more hazardous when wet or dark. Consider roping up for some parts. Scramble east and southeast into steep gullies between the summits to east-sloping slabs into a narrow wooded gully. There is some downclimbing here, more so if you lose the easiest route. Find a wide bouldery gully leading southeast between Hawk-Eagle Ridge and Redgarden's East Slabs. From here, trek the rocky trail past Wind Tower to the creek and bridge.

Rappel Descent

Make four single-rope rappels on the rappel line above Ruper on Lumpe Tower. Downclimb to reach it, optionally rap from a tree. Rappel 1: Find an anchor at the notch, then rappel 85 feet to reach a ledge with a tree. Rappel 2: Rappel from the tree to reach a large section of Red Ledge. Find the next rappel station to the north on a ledge under Swanson Arête's base. There is a 2-bolt anchor at the top of West Chimney. Rappels 3 and 4: Find two short bolted rappel routes to reach the ground.

Adventure Information

Outfitters

Neptune Mountaineering. 633 S Broadway, Boulder; (303) 499-8866; neptunemountaineering.com

JAX Outdoor Gear. 900 South, US 287, Lafayette; (720) 266-6160; jaxgoods.com

REI Boulder. 1789 28th St., Boulder; (303) 583-9970; rei.com

Moosejaw. 1755 29th St., Unit 1092, Boulder; (720) 452-2432; moosejaw.com

Vital Outdoors. 1224 Washington Ave., Golden; (303) 215-1644; vitaloutdoors.com

Great Pre- or Post-Adventure Spots

The Post Brewing Co. 2027 13th St., Boulder; (720) 372-3341; postbrewing.com/boulder/

4 Noses Brewing Co. 8855 W 116th Circle, Broomfield; (720) 460-2797; 4nosesbrewing .com

Woody's Wood Fired Pizza. 1305 Washington Ave., Golden; (303) 277-0443; woodysgolden .com

Barrels & Bottles Brewery. 600 12th St., Unit 180, Golden; (720) 328-3643; barrelsbottles .com

Climb 22 Staunton State Park: The Pooka

One of Colorado's newest state parks also has some of its newest climbing areas. Some of the areas might have been climbed previously, but they had been off-limits since 1986. In summer 2012, a year before the park opened, there were almost no climbing routes in the park. A group of local climbers were invited to the park to establish routes, and when it opened in 2013 about sixty routes had been developed. Almost all the routes were developed at Staunton Rocks; other areas, like Elk Creek Spires and Lion's Head, were left untouched at the time. Now there are nearly 200 established routes in the park.

Staunton offers a good mix of trad and sport climbing with some top-rope access. While most of the nearly 4,000-acre park is forested, it also contains Pikes Peak batholiths with large domes, spires, and slabs of Pikes Peak Granite. The most impressive wall is Lion's Head, rising some 600 feet from the ground and is likely ripe for some FAs (first ascents).

The heart of climbing here is at Staunton Rocks. The area has over one hundred routes at more than ten climbing areas. The stoutest climbs are found in The Dungeon, which has numerous routes in the 5.13 range. But the "wall with it all" has to be The Pooka, which has more than twenty-six routes—a mix of multi-pitch, trad, and sport. Climbers delight in a mix of jugs, chicken heads, flakes, cracks, and of course the schmeary slab that's typical of Pikes Peak Granite, a reddish granite with a coarse-grained but often not too sharp surface. As they climb out of the trees, mostly pines near the climbing area, they get awesome views of the Rockies and, to the south, stately Pikes Peak.

As some routes in the park are long, it's recommended that climbers use a 70-meter rope. If climbing trad routes, a full rack up to a 3-inch cam and nuts is recommend. Tricams can also be helpful.

Climbing type: Mostly sport with trad and some top rope and boulders
Difficulty: 5.4–5.13d
Rock type: Pikes Peak Granite
Best seasons: Year–round
Other trail users: Mountain bikers, equestrians, campers, track chairs, geocachers
Canine compatibility: Leashed dogs permitted (leash less than 6 feet long)
Land status: Staunton State Park
Maps: USGS Meridian Hill, Conifer, Pine; National Geographic Trails Illustrated
  #100: Boulder, Golden

Nearest town: Conifer

Camping, fees, and permits: Daily park fee or annual state pass; camping permits purchasable online

Schedule: Open year-round; day-use hours 6 a.m.–10 p.m.

Contact: Staunton State Park, Pine; (303) 816-0912; cpw.state.co.us/placestogo/parks/Staunton/Pages/RockClimbing.aspx

Getting there: From the intersection of US 285 and South Elk Creek Road, go 1.5 miles to the park entrance, on the right. Pay at the visitor center or continue to the parking lot, 0.5 mile from the Elk Creek road turnoff. Visitors can also pay at a self-service kiosk, which accepts credit cards. GPS: N39.50051° / W105.37808°

Finding the crag: From the Ranch Hand trailhead on the northwestern side of the parking lot, go left (northwest) on Staunton Ranch Trail, walking past the Ponderosa and Spruce campsite areas. At 1.6 miles cross a small bridge in a forested area. At 1.7 miles turn right at the junction with the Old Mill Trail. At 1.9 miles from the trailhead, turn left at the trail sign for climbing access. In 350

The base of The Pooka, Big Squirrels Don't Cry on the left, Ricochet Rabbit on the right.

feet turn right to reach The Pooka, which is to the right in about 250 feet. GPS: N39.51599° / W105.39287°

The Climb

The Pooka is the first climbing spot off the Old Mill Trail. The massive buttress is about 500 feet long and is divided into three climbing areas. Kings Landing is on the left (southwest side); the largest area is Canyon Amphitheater, in the middle; and right of the buttress on its northwest shoulder is Astronomy Wall. The easiest climbs in the area are at Kings Landing, which is a good place to practice lead climbs on short, fun routes, like Night King or Winter Is Coming. The toughest climb is Planck Time in Canyon Amphitheater. Canyon Amphitheater is the biggest section of wall and will probably see more development.

Helmets are especially recommended in the area, even for belayers, as it's a newer climbing area, and smaller rocks have fallen off during climbs. Also, a 70-meter rope is recommended for the Canyon Amphitheater and Astronomy Wall—some of these climbs are longer, and a 60-meter rope, especially one that may have been shortened, might not be long enough.

Though most of the belay spots in the area are thinly forested, the rock face sees sun throughout the day but gets some shade in the late afternoon. Belays to second pitches also see sun.

Routes are listed from left to right.

Best Routes

Winter Is Coming (5.6, sport): 1 pitch, 7 draws. On Kings Landing, this fun short climb is ideal for a first lead or a warm-up for bigger climbs. In the center of the main wall here, find the middle of three bolted routes. It has a black water streak. This well-bolted route starts climbing left over a slab then progresses relatively straight. Staying in the black streak itself offers the most interesting climbing.

Follow That Thief (5.9+, sport): 2 pitches, 13 draws. In the Canyon Amphitheater, this route combines the 5.6 Cookie Thief with Follow That Thief for a total of 160 feet of climbing; it can feasibly be done in pitch, but it's not recommended. **Pitch 1 (5.6), 13 bolts:** Start Cookie Thief on the left side of the small canyon and climb the well-bolted, well-featured Cookie Thief to a 2-bolt anchor. Continue to

A wide view of the Canyon Amphitheater at the Pooka. Plenty of routes to be discovered!

the upper part of the amphitheater wall to a wide shelf with stunning views for a belay. **Pitch 2 (5.9+), 11 bolts:** Pull a small roof on gray, blackish rock to the left of the giant red roof. Work to the dihedral and stem to the anchor at the top of the rock. **Descent:** Rappel or lower off the anchors.

Ricochet Rabbit (5.10d, sport): 1 pitch, 15 draws. At Canyon Amphitheater on the right side of the canyon wall, find this challenging 5.10d route. Start on the black rock just right of a dirty flake. The well-featured route climbs up to the left on grayer rock before crossing a reddish band. It then reaches a small, exposed face with some good positioning requiring powerful moves to reach an anchor on the headwall. **Descent:** Rappel or lower off the anchors.

Restaurant at the End of the Universe (5.10, sport): 1 pitch, 12 bolts. On Astronomy Wall, find this fun 5.10 route just left of Dark Matter (5.9), which climbs the dark water streak in a dihedral, and about 5 feet right of a dirty crack. The route starts on a larger blocky-surfaced bulge that leads to smaller blocks. The bulge is the crux. **Descent:** Rappel or lower off the anchors

Staunton State Park: The Pooka

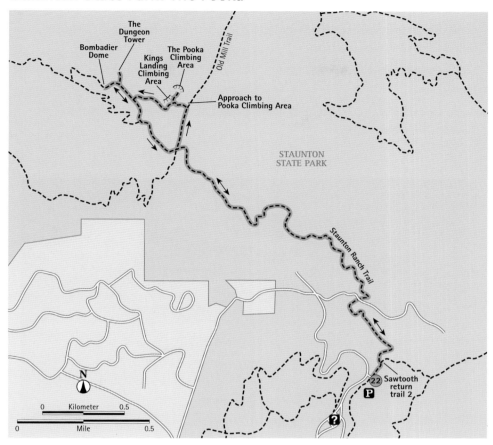

Adventure Information

Staunton State Park (webcam). friendsofstauntonstatepark.org/webcam

Outfitters

Evergreen Mountain Sports. 10875 US 285, Ste. D101, Conifer; (303) 674-5100; evergreen mountainsports.com

Bentgate Mountaineering. 1313 Washington Ave., Golden; (303) 271-9382; bentgate.com. Open Sun–Fri; closed Sat.

REI Lakewood. 5375 S Wadsworth Blvd., Lakewood; (303) 932-0600; rei.com

Great Pre- or Post-Adventure Spots

Coney Island Boardwalk hot dog stand. 10 Old Stagecoach Rd., Bailey; (303) 838-9999; coneyislandbailey.wordpress.com

Mad Jack's Mountain Brewery. 23 Main St., Bailey; (303) 816-2337; madjacksmountain brewery.com

Green Mountain Beer Company. 2585 S Lewis Way, Lakewood; (303) 986-0201; green mountainbeercompany.com

Mule deer talking at Staunton State Park.

Climb 23 Boulder Canyon: Castle Rock

This gorgeous, 17-mile canyon is composed of Precambrian granitic rock, carved and sculpted by Boulder Creek for millennia. Walls of gray and tan cliffs soar hundreds of feet up from the creek bed, while nearby pine-forested peaks top out almost 1,000 feet above. The area is loved by outdoor enthusiasts of every ilk, from climber to hikers and anglers. Its prized, sheer granitic canyon walls have drawn climbers for well over half a century. There are over one hundred climbing areas and nearly 1,700 named routes in the canyon.

Just 10 minutes outside of Boulder and easily accessible from CO 119—almost all are within a 20-minute hike from the road—many of these climbing areas are popular post-work and weekend spots. Crags like Happy Hour, Blob Rock, and The Dome get constant attention, and, as the name Happy Hour implies, sometimes you're waiting in line to climb, just as you would at a bar after a long day's work—but the lines at the crags are way, way better. Castle Rock is a popular, storied spot as well, with first ascents made by "hardman" climbers as early as the 1950s and other routes made famous by legends like Royal Robbins. But it's farther up the canyon and not as congested as some other crags on weekdays and some weekends.

Routes in the canyon are a mix of single and multi-pitch sport and trad routes, and some areas, like Happy Hour, also offer good opportunities for top-rope setups. Many crags are roadside, but some are across the creek and accessed via Tyrolean traverse. Beware of heavy runoff in spring and early summer when attempting to cross the creek.

Climbing type: Trad, sport, multi-pitch

Difficulty: 5.6–5.14

Rock type: Granite

Best seasons: Year-round

Land status: Roosevelt National Forest, Boulder, Boulder County, private

Maps: USGS Boulder, Gold Hill, Tungsten; National Geographic Trails Illustrated #100: Boulder, Golden

Nearest town: Boulder, Nederland

Camping, fees, and permits: No fees; no camping in the canyon

Contact: USDA Forest Service, Boulder Ranger District, 2140 Yarmouth Ave., Boulder 80301; (303) 541-2500; fs.usda.gov/activity/arp/recreation/climbing

Special considerations: Ownership of the canyon is complicated, as parts of it fall under city, county, private, and USDA Forest Service lands. Hence some areas are primarily bolted, while others, like Castle Rock, are primarily trad. Please be respectful of "No trespassing" signs and stay on-trail and at the crag. As with many climbing areas in Colorado, crags are excellent nesting areas for falcons and other raptors, and some areas are closed Feb 1–July 31 for their protection. Please respect those closures as well.

Getting there: From the intersection of Broadway (CO 93) and Boulder Canyon Drive (CO 119), head west on CO 119 for 12.5 miles. Castle Rock is on the left side of the road in a large, dirt pullout that surrounds the impressive rock. If meeting up with others, consider parking one or more vehicles in Boulder. Lots off Boulder Canyon Drive before 6th are popular places to consolidate vehicles. GPS: N39.97920° / W105.45504°

Finding the crag: The crag is at the pullout. If you don't see it, you're at the wrong spot!

The Climb

There are at least eighty routes on this royal, 350-foot-tall rock at the top of Boulder Canyon. Almost all routes on the massive rock are crack-based, multi-pitch trad lines, and at least one famous line on the rock has five pitches. The easiest routes on the rock, including Jackson's Wall (5.6) and Cussin' Crack (5.7), are on the west side of the road near the pullout. There are some tough boulder problems on the rock as well, like the V13 Free Range. The hardest route is Deadline, a test piece rated 5.13+–5.14-.

When climbing routes in the area, bring a full rack with cams up to 4 inches. Also required are minicams like TCUs, a full set of nuts, and plenty of slings and alpine draws. Off-width climbs can require bigger cams.

The only side of Castle Rock that doesn't have routes is the north side, which faces the road. The crag gets plenty of sun throughout the day, and climbers can move to stay in the shade or sun as needed.

One of the most famous routes at Castle Rock is Athlete's Feat, a 5.11a first free climbed by Royal Robbins and belayed by Pat Ament in 1964. The 5-pitch climb was at that time the most sustained free climb in the United States. Robbins did the climb in Swiss Tretorn tennis shoes.

To descend, most climbs have rappel anchors, but climbers can also down-climb the north side of the summit to a pine tree with a rappel chain. The rock can be slick after a rain or winter snow. From there scramble down Class 3 and 4 ramps and ledges.

Best Routes

Routes are listed left to right.

By Gully (5.9+, off-width trad), cams up to 7 inches, 2 pitches: A body-size off-width FA'd by Royal Robbins and Pat Ament in 1964. The right of two big off-width cracks on the west face of the rock; the left is Coffin Crack (5.10b). **Pitch 1 (5.9):** Start with boulder moves to reach an insecure crack; thrutch through the crack to two slots, and climb out of the crack to belay atop Coffin Crack or rappel from anchors to the right. **Pitch 2 (5.9–5.10):** Climb over a roof and climb up the gully to rappel or lower.

Cussin' Crack (5.7 or 5.8, trad), 3 pitches: Just left of the giant overhanging roof on the rock's southwest side, start climbing a big cleft. **Pitch 1 (5.5 or 5.8):** For the 5.5 variation climb the chimney up the cleft (5.5) or climb the 5.8 slab on the right to a trough. Exit left after 65 feet on a ramp, climb a bit and find a belay

The southwest side of Castle Rock. Upper part of By Gully shown.

stance below a corner. **Pitch 2 (5.7):** Climb Cussin' Crack, the V-slot. Find a ledge atop the crack to belay. **Pitch 3:** Scramble to the top on easy rock.

Athlete's Feat (5.11a, trad), 5 pitches: Once the toughest free climb in the United States! On the southeast side of Castle Rock, find a pointed boulder next to the road. **Pitch 1 (5.11a):** The crux is a mantle move above the boulder onto the sloping slab. Belay at the 2-bolt anchor above the slab. **Pitch 2 (5.10d):** Layback on the bulging corner above the anchor. Then jam on an easier crack to the next belay. **Pitch 3 (5.10b):** On this next corner crack, layback or jam about 45 feet to a belay; be aware of some loose flakes in the wide crack up top. **Pitch 4 (5.10b):** Climb a slabby corner to a 2-bolt anchor on the left. You can make two 100-foot rappels to the ground here or continue on. **Pitch 5 (5.8 or 5.9):** For the 5.9, climb to the top via a crack above the last belay. For the 5.8, move to the left to summit a corner climb.

Country Club Crack (5.11c, trad/sport), 2 pitches: This two-pitch toughie is another Boulder Canyon classic, FA'd in 1956 by Ted Rouillard and Cleve McCarty. There are fixed pins on this route, but it can be climbed with a standard rack. **Pitch 1 (5.11c):** Starting with the crux, begin by manteling on polished holds to pass two bolts to gain an awkward hand crack. Jam up to The Bar, the airy belay ledge at 65 feet. **Pitch 2 (5.11a):** Jam the long hand crack to pull over a small roof and move left to jam an insecure finger crack. Or find easier rock to the right to reach a 2-bolt anchor. Rappel with double ropes, or rappel to the pitch on anchors.

Adventure Information

Outfitters

Bentgate Mountaineering. 1313 Washington Ave., Golden; (303) 271-9382; bentgate.com. Open Sun–Fri; closed Sat.

Wilderness Exchange. 2401 15th St., Ste. 100, Denver; (303) 964-0708; wildernessx.com

Vital Outdoors. 1224 Washington Ave., Golden; (303) 215-1644; vitaloutdoors.com

REI Denver Flagship. 1416 Platte St., Denver; (303) 756-3100; rei.com

Boulder Canyon: Castle Rock

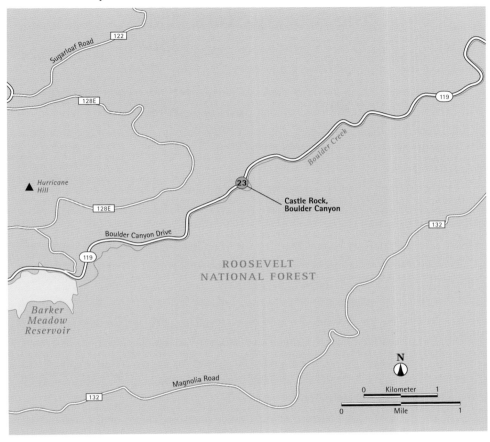

Great Pre- or Post-Adventure Spots

Woody's Wood Fired Pizza. 1305 Washington Ave., Golden; (303) 277-0443; woodysgolden .com

Barrels & Bottles Brewery. 600 12th St., Unit 180, Golden; (720) 328-3643; barrelsbottles .com

Tributary Food Hall & Drinkery. 701 12th St., Golden; (303) 856-7225; tributarygolden.com

Climb 24 Castlewood Canyon: The Grocery Store Walls

Castlewood Canyon is a surprise. East of Castle Rock, it's an interesting geological formation carved into the high plains, showcasing the tumultuous history of geology in Colorado. Etched into the land by Cherry Creek, the canyon tells a story of volcanoes, ancient oceans, tropical rain forests, and the erosion of the Rocky Mountains, current and ancestral. As a climber, it's fascinating to find all these rock types sandwiched together in just 40- to 60-foot-tall rock walls in various shelves as the canyon deepens.

There are more than 600 explored climbing routes and boulders in the canyon. Notable walls include Realm of the Venusian Love Goddess, Wendell Spire, the Grocery Store Walls, and nearby Neanderthal Wall. The short walls contain a mix of trad, sport, and top-rope areas, and there's a lot of bouldering in the park as well. With forty-four routes, the Grocery Store Walls is the "wall with it all" in the park. It has everything from 5.4 trad routes to 5.12 routes.

The canyon is capped with a 34-million-year-old layer of Castle Rock Conglomerate, formed by the erosion of the Rockies. Brought by water and cemented into place, the top of Castlewood Canyon's walls are relatively flat and easy to access, making it a great area for top roping and educating people about outdoor rock climbing, such as how to set up anchors using either chains and rings provided or building your own anchor system.

At the base of Castlewood Canyon's walls is a softer layer of Dawson Arkose deposited some 55 million years ago as the soils, flora, and fauna of an ancient tropical forest were compacted and turned into stone. That layer was then covered with volcanic rhyolite from eruptions in the Thirtynine Mile volcanic area, about 90 miles away. This Wall Mountain Tuff buried the Dawson Arkose with hard rock that formed quickly, producing rock with sharp angles and tiny holes. All that is now covered with the conglomerate rock made of smaller pieces of harder rock cemented into place by silicates over 34 million years ago.

Thanks to diverse ecosystems, there's a lot of wildlife in the park. Most of it is fox and deer, as well as raptors. There are also rattlesnakes in the area, so be sure to pay attention on the crags and in sunny rocky areas. As with many climbing areas in Colorado, there are seasonal closures for raptor breeding in Castlewood Canyon. Please respect the closures. However, the specific areas described in this book are not subject to closure.

Looking down climbing routes at the Grocery Store Walls in Castlewood Canyon

Climbing type: Trad, sport, top rope, bouldering

Difficulty: 5.4–5.12

Rock type: Varies; conglomerate, rhyolite, sandstone

Best seasons: Spring through fall

Other trail users: Hikers only

Canine compatibility: Leashed dogs permitted (leashes no longer than 6 feet)

Maps: USGS Castle Rock South, Russellville Gulch

Nearest town: Franktown

Camping, fees, and permits: Daily fee

Schedule: Open sunrise to sunset

Contact: Castlewood Canyon State Park, 2989 S CO 83, Franktown 80116; (303) 688-5242; cpw.state.co.us/placestogo/parks/CastlewoodCanyon/Pages/default .aspx

Getting there: From 1-25 exit 184 (CO 86), head east on CO 86 as it becomes Founders Parkway. In 4.2 miles turn left onto CO 86 E and stay on it for 10 miles. In 4.6 miles turn right onto North Castlewood Canyon Road. Continue on the road for 2.2 miles. Stop at the kiosk to pay the entry fee. Continue on the road for 0.7 mile to park in the lot on your left. There are vault toilets at the trailhead. GPS: N39.35289° / W104.76605°

Finding the Crag: After parking in the large lot, cross the street to find a signed climber's trail. Follow it for about 400 feet to reach the base of the cliffs.

The Climb

There are lots of good areas to climb in Castlewood Canyon, but the roughly 300 feet of the Grocery Store Walls has some of the widest variety of climbing in the canyon. On its north side there's easy access to the top roping area for the whole wall. It's also a bouldering area with a good cave and problems ranging from V1 to V7. To its south, as the wall breaks into more jagged spires, it's called Neanderthal Wall. One of the best areas of the wall has some of the most fun routes; Donut Hole and Hot Fudge are among them.

Best Routes

Donut Hole (5.11a, top rope): Easily visible from the approach is the Donut Hole, a human-size hole in the rock and the dominant feature of this 5.11a climb. The route begins directly below it and climbs straight to a roof. From undercling-ing the roof, gain crimpy handholds on the front, work over the lip, and climb

Rebeccca Slyder topping out on the Grocery Store Walls at Castlewood Canyon.

Castlewood Canyon: The Grocery Store Walls

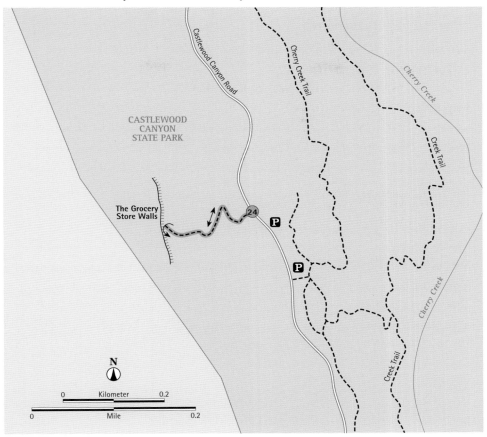

the face into the hole. From there, work to the right in a corner and finish the last part of Hot Fudge.

Hot Fudge (5.8+, trad, top rope): A fun, short roof and crack climb just right of Donut Hole. Instead of climbing over the roof, climb to the undercling and work right. Follow the crack as it heads up, and climb behind the flake behind Donut Hole. Continue to the top. Shares the same bolts with Donut Hole.

Peaches and Scream (5.6 trad, top rope): A great, short pitch for learning leaders. This line starts about 10 feet north of Hot Fudge. Gain a solid ledge to climb a crack on a solid flake. There are generous holes for footholds on the lower portion of this route. Good handholds throughout.

Caramel Corner (5.5 trad, top rope): A kid-friendly climb. Toward the northern side of Grocery Store Walls, find a large corner system with large steps and a ramp on ledgy rock with good footholds throughout. This is an easy, fun climb with a lot of surface variety; climbers can play with many cracks, pockets, and other features to gain the top.

Adventure Information

Outfitters

Mountain Chalet. 15 N Nevada Ave., Colorado Springs; (719) 633-0732; mtnchalet.com

Wilderness Exchange. 2401 15th St., Ste. 100, Denver; (303) 964-0708; wildernessx.com

REI Greenwood Village. 9000 E Peakview Ave., Greenwood Village; (303) 221-7758; rei.com

Great Pre- or Post-Adventure Spots

Sedalia Bakery. 4110 Rio Grande Ave., Sedalia; (303) 815-3656; facebook.com/sedaliabakery

Burly Brewing Co. 680 Atchison Way, Ste. 800, Castle Rock; (720) 486-0541; burlybrewing .com

Rockyard Brewing Company. 880 Castleton Rd, Castle Rock; (303) 814-9273; rockyard.com

Climb 25 Horsetooth Reservoir: Duncan's Ridge

The nearly 2-billion-year-old molar of Horsetooth Rock looms over the west side of Horsetooth Reservoir, looking east across the placid lake waters to much, much younger rock ridges and boulders composed of 100-million-year-old Dakota Sandstone. Climbers have flocked to Horsetooth Reservoir almost since it was fully dammed and filled. The damming of the reservoir was completed in 1949; it filled for the first time in 1951. By the 1960s John Gill, the father of modern bouldering, was putting up routes in the area while a professor at Colorado State University in Fort Collins. It's no wonder. The giant boulders and short ridges are ideal for complex problems and short climbs, making it one of the best places to boulder in Colorado.

Though its reddish ridge walls don't have the tall grandeur of Colorado's canyons and granite peaks, Horsetooth does offer some shorter roped climbs. One of the best areas in the reservoir for both is Duncan's Ridge. While climbers are focused on the best crag, the giant reservoir is home to tons of outdoor activities and is a popular place for locals to recreate. On almost any day you can find people in boats or paddleboarding on the water or hiking, road biking, and mountain biking. Heck, people even scuba dive there, viewing the drowned remnants of a town called Stout on its southern side.

Climbing type: Trad, top rope, bouldering

Difficulty: 5.6–5.11, V3–V9

Rock type: Dakota Sandstone

Best seasons: Year-round

Other trail users: None

Canine compatibility: Leashed dogs permitted

Land status: Managed by Larimer County

Maps: USGS Horsetooth Reservoir

Nearest town: Fort Collins

Camping, fees, and permits: Daily fees and camping fees required

Schedule: Open year-round

Contact: Larimer County; (970) 498-7000; larimer.org

Getting there: From the intersection of Harmony Road and College Avenue, head west for 2.3 miles on West Harmony Road. Continue on the same road for 1.9 miles as it becomes West CR 38E. Turn right onto South Centennial Drive. In 0.4 mile find parking in a dirt roadside lot. GPS: N40.53655° / W105.14391°

Under the roof of Roof Route.

Finding the crag: On the west side of the road, find a sign for Duncan's Ridge and hike the short trail west to the ridge, less than 5 minutes. There are options to set up a rope here for top roping climbs or to rappel in. Otherwise, you can easily hike the path down to the climbing and bouldering areas.

The Climb

There's a short, stubby ridge on the east side of the road here. That's Piano Ridge, a popular spot for bouldering, but it's too short for much else. On the western side of the road, it's relatively flat. But hiking west on a good trail leads to the top of Duncan's Ridge, the closest roped climbing to Fort Collins. From here you can choose to get to the bottom of Duncan's Ridge a couple of different ways. You can set up a top rope and rappel in or follow the trail to a short Class 3/Class 4 scramble to the bottom of the ridge.

Although Gill may have popularized bouldering here, the ridge is named for Duncan Ferguson, who was known for spending countless hours here training. He and other climbers rope soloed and used trad gear on the rocks, working on their head game for longer highball boulder projects. More recently, some have established bolted anchors at the top of the ridge, but others, perhaps hailing the early legacy of rock climbing, have chopped those bolts off. A trad rack with nuts and cams, as well as some slings to hang horns and/or create anchors, will provide pro here.

The Northern Colorado Climbers Coalition, which advocates for climbing in the region, worked with Larimer Country to develop fixed anchors at the top of Duncan's Ridge in an effort to keep the area open to climbers and increase the sustainability of climbing in the area.

The routes on Duncan's Ridge offer a wide variety of climbing difficulty, ranging from 5.4 to 5.12. In addition, classic boulder problems in the area, like The Chronic, are rated at a stout V11. The rock has big, bulging features, overhanging roofs, and cracks, making it ideal for climbing. The ridge faces primarily west but curves a little to the south as it comes closer to the reservoir's waters. As such, it gets lots of sunlight throughout the day, but especially later in the day. Climbing

A look at the Duncan's Ridge climbing area.

in summer can get hot, and in winter the afternoon sun radiating off the rocks helps warm them up.

Best Routes

Roof Route (5.10, trad): Just right of the approach trail and gully, the Roof Route's most prominent feature is, well, the roof, which is close to the top of the climb. From the bottom right of the roof, climb a crack in the dihedral and transition to the middle under a small roof. Then climb up under the big roof and find good holds as you transition to the face and larger jugs above.

Liberty's Last Stand (5.8, trad): This route is south, right of the prominent roof feature of the Roof Route and just right of a small gully to the ridge. The route has a small roof feature about 15 feet up that leads to a decently featured face climb.

Boulder, Mother's Finest (V9): One of the tougher problems in the area. Look for a cube-shaped rock visible from the ridge. The Mother Boulder is behind this. The route starts from sitting, a left-hand pinch, and a right-hand crimp. Find an undercling with your right hand and continue on underclings.

Adventure Information

Organizations

Northern Colorado Climbers Coalition. nococlimbing.org

Outfitters

JAX Outdoor Gear. 1200 N College Ave., Fort Collins; (970) 221-0544; jaxgoods.com

REI Fort Collins. 4025 S College Ave., Fort Collins; (970) 223-0123; rei.com

Great Pre- or Post-Adventure Spots

CooperSmith's Pub & Brewing. #5 Old Town Square, Fort Collins; (970) 498-0483; coopersmithspub.com

Horsetooth Reservoir: Duncan's Ridge

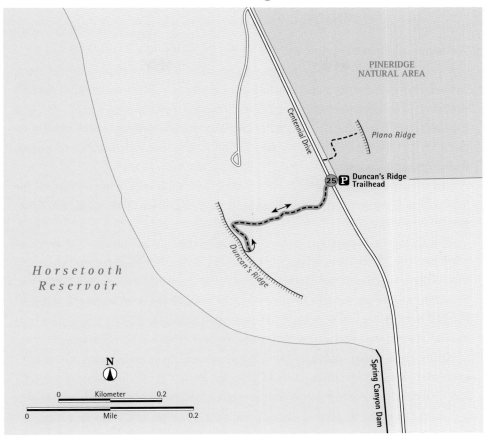

McClellan's Brewing Co. 1035 S Taft Hill Rd., Fort Collins; (970) 568-8473; mcclellans brewingcompany.com

Odell Brewing. 800 E Lincoln Ave., Fort Collins; (970) 498-9070; odellbrewing.com

Climb 26 Poudre Canyon: The Narrows— Twilight Area

The names of Poudre Canyon and the Cache La Poudre River come from a multi-day's winter storm in the early 1800s. Around 1825, some say 1836, a winter storm snowed in a group of French-Canadian trappers with William Ashley's fur trading company. After the storm, to lighten their load and cross the river, they hid extra supplies, largely gunpowder, in a pit. "Cache la poudre" translates to "the hiding place of the powder." Presumably they found it, but that detail is lost to history while the name endures.

It's no surprise they wanted to lighten their load. Who knew what lay around the next corner of the deep, mysterious canyon—its walls quickly rising more than 1,000 feet in some places?

The Cache La Poudre has been cutting into the 1.5-billion-year-old Precambrian bedrock for millions of years, carving the deep, V-shaped trench separating the northern reaches of the Mummy Range to its south and the Laramie Mountains to its north. The river runs for roughly 40 miles through much of Roosevelt National Forest's northern reaches, exposing Precambrian granites, schists, and gneisses. It has left scarred, raw rock faces, buttresses, and spires all along the canyon.

Other Front Range canyons, like Clear Creek and Boulder Canyons, are shorter and wider. The Poudre's narrowness and length, as well as lack of valuable minerals and distance from more metropolitan areas and major transportation corridors in the state, have helped keep it wilder than most of Colorado's other river systems, and made it Colorado's only nationally designated Wild and Scenic River. Surrounding the canyon are granitic spires and formations—an ideal place for recreation, rock climbing rafting, hiking, fishing, and more. The rock here is ancient, grumpy and crumbly, but among the chossy rock there are some phenomenal climbing areas.

The area has drawn climbers since at least the 1960s. Now there are more than 1,200 climbing routes and boulder problems in the area, stretching up the canyon and closer to Fort Collins. Popular climbing areas in the canyon include The Palace, Gray Rock, and The Narrows. Many of these require crossing the river. Where many other Front Range canyons were carved by creeks, Poudre Canyon was carved by a wider river, meaning it's harder to get across, particularly in late spring and early summer, when water flows are high.

The Narrows boasts some 200 roped climbs and another 100 or so boulder problems in a short stretch of the canyon. The highest concentration and widest variety of classic roped climbs is in the Twilight Area.

Climbing type: Trad, sport, multi-pitch, bouldering
Difficulty: 5.8–5.13d
Rock type: Granitic
Best seasons: Fall, winter, spring
Land status: Primarily Roosevelt National Forest
Maps: USGS Rustic; National Geographic Trails Illustrated #112: Poudre River, Cameron Pass
Nearest town: Fort Collins
Camping, fees, and permits: None
Contact: Canyon Lakes Ranger District, 2150 Centre Ave., Bldg. E, Fort Collins 80526; (970) 295-670; fs.usda.gov/recarea/arp/recarea/?recid=36603

Climbers on Supercollider in The Narrows of Poudre Canyon.

An overview of climbing zones at the Twilight Area in The Narrows of Poudre Canyon.

Getting there: From the intersection of US 287 and CO 14 (Poudre Canyon Road), by Ted's Place, head west on CO 14 for 19 miles and look for a pullout. It's a small pullout, but there are additional small pullouts along the river. GPS: N40.67517° W105.42858°

Finding the crag: The Twilight Area is across the Poudre River from the pullout.

The Climb

The Twilight Area is a large climbing area with four smaller zones. To access it you have to wade across the Poudre River. If the water is more than 2 feet deep, crossing is inadvisable, since it's near stout, Class V rapids. If the river's too high, consider climbing Eden Wall by the parking area, which has some excellent climbs like East of Eden (5.9, trad) and Forbidden Fruit (5.12a, sport). Most people access the Twilight Area by crossing just upstream of the Class V White Line rapid, near river mile 103. The crags—Twilight Wall, Upper Midlife Wall, Sunnyvale, and Wild Wall—are easily recognizable across the river.

Twilight Wall is the closest; Upper Midlife Wall is a fun slabby area just left of Twilight. Sunnyvale and Wild Wall are up and left of Twilight Wall. Sunnyvale is a

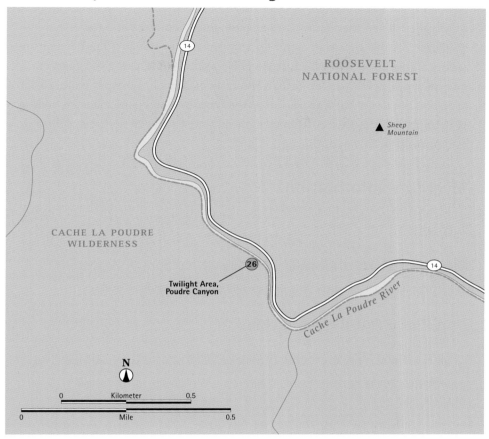

crag with routes as tall as 90 feet. Wild Wall, to the right before turning to access Sunnyvale, is a tough, overhanging crag with 5.12 and 5.13 routes.

Best Routes

Wild and Scenic (5.12d, sport): The rightmost route on Wild Wall. Use long slings to climb over three bolts on 5.8 rock. At the base of the wall, find a 2-bolt anchor to use as a belay. The climb starts with a leaning traverse. Look for big jugs on the left. Pull up into an arch feature to find small holds on the crux. Reaching the chains requires a long reach to a jug. **Descent:** Lower off the rings.

Little Richard Sporter (5.8, trad), 2 pitches: On Upper Midlife Wall, this route starts on the first three bolts of Over the Hillary. **Pitch 1:** Climb the lower part of Over the Hillary, then follow an underclinging hand crack and traverse to the left. Reach a small dihedral; climb up and traverse to the left. Find a slanting crack in a small headwall, which could make a good belay, using the giant crack as an anchor. **Pitch 2:** The route zigzags up the headwall to top out on an easier crack. You can easily build an anchor at the top. There is a good anchor-building opportunity on top. **Descent:** From the top, find a ridge to the west; follow it, then downclimb to the south.

Adventure Information

Outfitters

JAX Outdoor Gear. 1200 N College Ave., Fort Collins; (970) 221-0544; jaxgoods.com

REI Fort Collins. 4025 S College Ave., Fort Collins; (970) 223-0123; rei.com

Great Pre- or Post-Adventure Spots

The Mishawaka. 13714 Poudre Canyon Rd., Bellvue; (888) 843-6474; themishawaka.com

CooperSmith's Pub & Brewing. #5 Old Town Square, Fort Collins; (970) 498-0483; coopersmithspub.com

McClellan's Brewing Co. 1035 S Taft Hill Rd., Fort Collins; (970) 568-8473; mcclellansbrewingcompany.com

Odell Brewing. 800 E Lincoln Ave., Fort Collins; (970) 498-9070; odellbrewing.com

Climb 27 Shelf Road: Cactus Cliff

Shelf Road, originally built in the 1860s, was once a road to riches. From Cañon City, the toll road charged a horse and rider 30 cents and a stagecoach $1.75 to travel along Fourmile Creek to Cripple Creek, a well-known gold mine site. Today the dirt road is free, allowing people to seek different types of riches, experiential ones. The 13-mile dirt road still connects to Cripple Creek, and people still make the trip, but along the way there are opportunities for all sorts of outdoor activities, from hiking and mountain biking to fishing and camping—and of course rock climbing.

Seeing Cactus Cliff and the sprawling rocky, hardscrabble hills, mountains, and valleys behind it is, even from a distance, overwhelming. Cliff bands of 500-million-year-old limestone and Ordovician rock shine in full-day sunlight, a glowing mecca for climbers everywhere. With more than 1,100 routes tucked into the valley and canyon walls in about 1.5 square miles, it's no wonder Shelf Road is an internationally renowned climbing area. Most of the routes on the well-pocketed and featured limestone are single-pitch sport climbs ranging from 5.5 to 5.14a. The majority are rated 5.10a or higher.

The area was first developed in the late 1970s and early 1980s by local climbers. Dale Goddard set some of the region's earliest sport routes in 1986, like the classic 5.12c Line of Strength on the Dark Side wall. Goddard was introduced to sport climbing in France and Germany during a semester overseas. Soon, other local climbers, including Bob D'Antonio, Rich Aschert, Dave Dangle, and Daryl Roth, began setting bolts and anchors on cliffs in the so-called French style, from the top down.

The limestone and dolostone (dolomite) rocks that make up the features of Shelf Road come from the Ordovician period, when Colorado was under a vast ocean. The rocks, which vary in color from light gray or tan to black, are the remnants of an ancient coral reef turned into hard, erosion-resistant rock. Some fossil remains of the coral are still found in the rock, in features that look like honeycombs.

Located close to Cañon City, the weather along Shelf Road is known for being mild throughout the year, making it one of the best places to climb in the chillier months. Cactus Cliff gets southern and southwestern sunlight, making it ideal for climbing on cold days, but it gets boiling hot on summer days. Across Cactus Cliff is the Dark Side, another classic climbing wall that's north-facing, making it a more ideal spot for summer climbing.

On land managed by the Bureau of Land Management (BLM), access to the area is free, but camping at one of the two campgrounds—Sand Gulch and The Bank—is not. Sand Gulch Campground has sixteen campsites, including one group campsite.

Looking to the southeast across Cactus Cliff.

Thanks to the latest expansion, completed in 2019, The Bank Campground, now has thirty-three campsites, including group campsites. The BLM and the Pikes Peak Climbers Alliance funded the recent expansion, which added twenty of the campsites and tripled the size of the parking area.

The campgrounds and parking lot have vault toilets (there's also one on Shelf Road), but there is no water, and the intermittent stream at the bottom of the canyon is usually dry by mid-spring. The campsites have tent pads, picnic tables, and fire rings or pits. Bring your own wood for fires, as cutting down trees for wood is prohibited.

Climbing type: Primarily single-pitch sport climbing
Difficulty: 5.5 to 5.14a/b
Rock type: Limestone
Best seasons: Fall, winter, spring
Land status: BLM
Maps: USGS: Cripple Creek South; National Geographic Trails Illustrated #137: Pikes Peak, Cañon City
Nearest town: Cañon City

Camping, fees, and permits: No fees for day use; campsite fees payable at kiosk (campsites available on a first-come, first-served basis)

Contact: BLM Royal Gorge Field Office, 3028 E Main St., Cañon City 81212; (719) 269-8500; blm.gov/visit/search-details/16855/2

Special considerations: There are a number of prisons near Cañon City, including Colorado's SuperMax prison. Although there haven't been many prison breaks, it's not the best idea to pick up hitchhikers near the city.

Getting there: From the intersection of US 50 and Fourmile Lane, at the eastern side of Cañon City, stay on US 50 for 0.8 mile. Turn right on Dozier Avenue and take the roundabout to the first exit, staying on Dozier heading north. In 1.5 miles turn right on Filed Avenue. In 2.2 miles turn right on Red Canyon Road (CO 9) and continue for 5.8 miles. Turn left onto Garden Park Road and stay on it for 3.2 miles. Turn left at the sign for The Bank Campground and Cripple Creek and continue 1.4 miles to the parking area. GPS: N38.62957° W105.22825°

Finding the crag: From the climbing signs at The Bank day-access parking lot, head right and find an access trail to the right in 400 feet. At 800 feet cross a dirt 4X4 road and continue through the forest. Shortly after, turn right at a trail junction to Cactus Cliff. Stay on the trail as it crosses the intermittent creek bed and meanders through the forest. At a little over 0.4 mile, turn left onto the dirt Shelf Road. At 0.6 mile turn right off Shelf Road to reach the "Cactus Cliff" sign. Access to the 1,460-foot-long crag begins here. GPS: N38.63267° / W105.22379°

The Climb

More than 1,400 feet long and with more than 150 routes, Cactus Cliff is the largest, most popular climbing area at Shelf Road. There are a few easy routes on this crag, but the majority are rated 5.10 and above. The easiest is the short 5.5 Alexi's Climb; the hardest is the 5.14a/b Flight of the Phoenix. There are spectacular routes throughout. Access to Cactus Cliff was ensured in 1998 when the Access Fund purchased the cliff from a private owner. The Access Fund then ceded ownership to BLM, which now manages it. The Rocky Mountain Field Institute and the Access Fund still maintain access to the area. More recently they, along with an AmeriCorps group, helped improve the trail to Cactus Cliff.

This is a truly fantastic site. As climbers rest or top out and look west, they're greeted with a ridge of mountains in the distance, including Crestone Peak, some

Shelf Road: Cactus Cliff

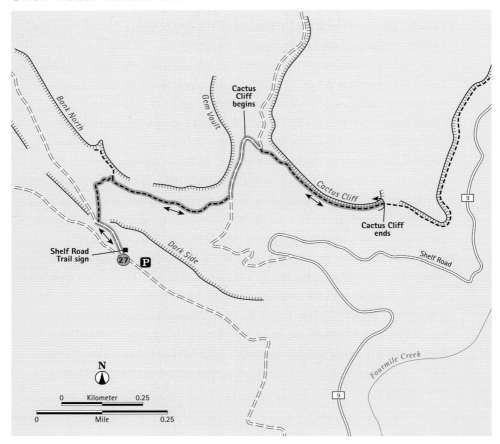

50 miles to the southwest. Between the cliffs and the mountains in the distance is an ocean of peaks and valleys—waves of Colorado's geologic past frozen in time.

Best Routes

Lats Don't Have Feelings (5.11.d, sport), 8 bolts: About halfway across the prow of Cactus Cliff, find a pocket of reddish rock. On the right side, find a route that leads straight up small pockets on a seam. A great, tough climb.

The French Are Here (5.12c, sport), 10 bolts: On an outcropping of the rock face, climb the bulge to the right. Pull with the left side and gaston on the right

A broad view of Cactus Cliff. Lats Don't Have Feelings is just right of the red streak.

for some moves. The crux is the bulge. Beyond that, the route requires sustained 5.11 moves.

Oscar de la Cholla (5.9, sport), 7 bolts: A great, easier climb for Shelf Road. Start with an easy face climb, then follow the bolts on the left side of the crack. Climbing up, the crack narrows, but find holds on the face. A good rest spot is around the fourth bolt on a ledge.

Adventure Information

Outfitters

Red Canyon Cycles/The Bean Pedaler. 410 Main St., Cañon City; (719) 285-8169; redcanyon cycles.com

Mountain Chalet. 15 N Nevada Ave., Colorado Springs; (719) 633-0732; mtnchalet.com

REI Colorado Springs. 1376 E Woodmen Rd., Colorado Springs; (719) 260-1455; rei.com

Great Pre- or Post-Adventure Spots

World's End Brewing Co. 401 Main St., Canon City; (719) 315-2663; worldsendbrewingco .com

The Winery at Holy Cross Abbey. 3011 E US 50, Cañon City; (719) 276-5191; abbeywinery .com

Manitou Brewing Co. 725 Manitou Ave., Manitou Springs; (719) 282-7709; manitoubrewing .com

Penny Arcade. 900 Manitou Ave., Manitou Springs; (719) 685-9815; facebook.com/ manitouspringspennyarcade

CYCLING ADVENTURES

The hills and mountains along Colorado's Front Range provide endless opportunities for road as well as mountain bikers and gravel grinders. Many of the hiking areas in this book, like Mount Falcon, Walker Ranch, Staunton State Park, and Horsetooth Reservoir, also offer fun mountain biking opportunities, but there are also many incredibly fun purpose-built trails in the region, places like Centennial Cone Park and the incredibly fun network of trails built by the volunteers of the Salida Mountain Trails volunteers. Most of trail building has focused on mountain biking, but there are plenty of opportunities for road cycling and gravel grinding as well. These include the 71-mile High Line Trail throughout Denver and the ambitious, 65-miles Peaks to Plains Trail, which will wind through the Clear Creek Canyon, connecting Denver to Idaho Springs away from the interstate and the narrow road that snakes through the canyon, while

Biking through aspen groves.

climbing thousands of feet. Unfortunately that project isn't complete yet. In the meantime mountain roads—though scary as cars whiz by—provide plenty of leg-busting fun and there's almost no more picturesque, famous ride than up the undulating curves of Lookout Mountain, where motorists expect and respect the myriad road bikes they'll encounter every day of the year.

Mountain Bike 28 Centennial Cone Park Loop

Opened to the public in 2006, this close-to-the-city mountain biking getaway offers fun singletrack with a backcountry feel. Rolling across open shrubby meadows and grasslands, it features some fun, rocky descents and climbs. It enters into small patches of forest, all while circling one central peak. The park is populated with elk, mule deer, and bighorn sheep, as well as their natural predators, mountain lions.

Note: The multiuse park and trails are relegated to bikers or hikers and equestrians on weekend days; check the schedule before adventuring out.

Start: Mayhem Gulch Trailhead

Distance: 16.4-mile loop

Riding time: 2.5–3.5 hours

Difficulty: Intermediate; mainly singletrack on varying up-and-down terrain

Elevation gain: About 2,350 feet

Trail surface: Dirt

Best seasons: Late spring through late fall

Other trail users: Hikers, equestrians, class 1 E-bikes. On weekends access for bikers and other users alternates. Bikers have access on even-numbered weekend days.

Canine compatibility: Leashed dogs permitted

Land status: Jefferson County Open Space

Camping, fees, and permits: Free parking

Schedule: Open one hour before sunrise to one hour after sunset. On weekends, bikers allowed only on even-numbered days. Closed to bikers and hikers during hunting season (Dec 1–Jan 31).

Trail contact: Jefferson County Open Space; (303) 271-5925; jeffco.us/open-space

Maps: USGS Saw Pass, Black Hawk; National Geographic Trails Illustrated #100: Boulder/Golden

Special considerations: Elk Range Trail and the interior of the park are closed Feb 1–mid-June to protect elk during their calving season. This park is usually pretty dry, but after rains and snowmelt, it can get pretty soupy and muddy, particularly in the more shaded areas.

Finding the trailhead: From the intersection of US 6 and CO-93, head west on US 6. Continue for 9.5 miles. The parking area is on the right side of the

road (32447 US 6). There is a vault toilet at the trailhead. GPS: N39.73721° /
W105.37110°

The Ride

Perhaps this adventure should be called the Centennial Carousel Loop, since it goes up and down as it circles the park's singular feature: the titular 8,679-foot Centennial Cone. Or perhaps it could be called Sheep's Carousel Loop, which was the peak's name until it was officially changed in 1912 because there were two other peaks called Sheep Mountain. It was renamed Centennial Cone for Centennial Ranch, a nearby ranch at the time.

This is one of the more modern parks in the Jefferson County Open Space. The state started acquiring the land in 1995 and made the last purchase in 2006, the year the park opened to users. Most of the park consists of mixed foothill shrubland, providing good forage for elk, mule deer, bighorn sheep, and black bear. An adventure through the park will also take you through other types of vegetation, including Douglas fir forest, montane grasslands, and ponderosa pine and juniper woodlands; county managers observe that the park has a better than average diversity of native plants.

Still, human presence abounds throughout the park. You're more likely to see domestic cows than wildlife, even though a herd of hundreds of elk migrate through the park and there are elk calving grounds here. The large number of elk in the area is also the reason for the hunting season. Deer hunting is also allowed in the area. The park is the only Jefferson County Park that has a seasonal closure for hunting.

The park remains open while elk are calving, but Elk Range Trail and the interior of the park are off-limits. If you want to ride the park then, you can do an out-and-back trip or perhaps loop around on country roads outside the park.

The high percentage of native wildlife and plants in the area is interesting, because there's evidence that humans have used the area for thousands of years. In fact, one of the trails, Travois, is named for a type of sledge used by Native Americans to carry goods. When Jefferson County conducted an archaeological survey of the park, they uncovered five prehistoric Native American fire hearths, fragments of projectile points, and more dating back to around AD 1,000 to 1500. A local named Carla Swan Coleman told the county she'd heard about sunrise and evening farewell ceremonies at the park held by the Arapaho or Cheyenne. She

The Evening Sun Loop at Centennial Cone Park.

also told of a legend that Native Americans sealed off a huge underground jeweled cave on the park to hide its treasure.

Though some Euro-Americans might have tried mining on the land, it was homesteaded in the late 1880s. A site in the park called "The Plantation" was believed to be settled by a family of freed slaves in the late 1880s or early 1900s. The site includes the remnants of a stone root cellar, a three-sided barn made of logs, and other structures that are unidentified. This area is on the northeast side of Centennial Cone.

As described, this adventure follows a clockwise loop, taking you over the hardest climb of the day first. The initial few miles are on an old dirt road, making it easy for people to pass and to converse with buddies. But as the route reached Travois Trail it becomes flowy singletrack. The more technical part of the trail comes after it passes the Evening Sun Trail and is considered the best singletrack in the area. As the trail reaches high points, look for views down into Clear Creek Canyon to the left (south). There's a long, fun descent down to Elk Creek and then a somewhat tough ascent with tight switchbacks to get out of it. After that it's a mainly easy, undulating ride with beautiful views all around till you're back at the parking lot.

Miles and Directions

0.0 Start by climbing up the Mayhem Gulch Trail, weaving back and forth on switchbacks and gaining 550 feet, head mostly west.

1.5 Take the Juniper Trail to the left at its junction with the Mayhem Gulch Trail.

2.3 At the junction of the Travois and Juniper Trails, head left (north) on Travois Trail.

2.6 The Travois Trail joins the Elk Range Trail. Continue straight (northeast) on the Elk Range Trail as it levels out and passes through a working farm (be wary of roaming livestock!). Heading left on Elk Range leads to a parking lot on the west side of the park with toilets.

3.2 The trail takes a sharp right and heads east before gradually arcing northeast.

3.9 Pass a trail that leads to Centennial Cone. Shortly after, reach the high point of the day.

5.7 At the northern side of the park, turn right, back onto the Travois Trail. This is also the north side access parking lot, with access to toilets. Begin a mile-long descent.

6.3 Pass a junction for the Evening Sun Loop Trail and continue as the trail zags around the east side of a small peak and starts heading more southerly.

6.9 Pass the second junction with the Evening Sun Loop Trail and begin a short ascent as the trail gets a bit more difficult.

7.6 Reach another small high point then descend a number of switchbacks, the start of a 2.4-mile descent.

9.0 The trail begins heading east.

10.0 Reach the low point of the loop and begin a 1.9-mile, 720-foot climb after crossing Elk Creek on a bridge.

11.8 Reach a final high point and begin descending back to the trailhead over a series of smaller hills.

14.0 At the junction of the Mayhem Gulch and Travois Trails, turn left (south) onto the Mayhem Gulch Trail.

14.9 Turn left at the junction of the Mayhem Gulch and Juniper Trails to make the final descent out, returning to the trailhead.

16.4 Arrive back at the trailhead.

Centennial Cone Park Loop

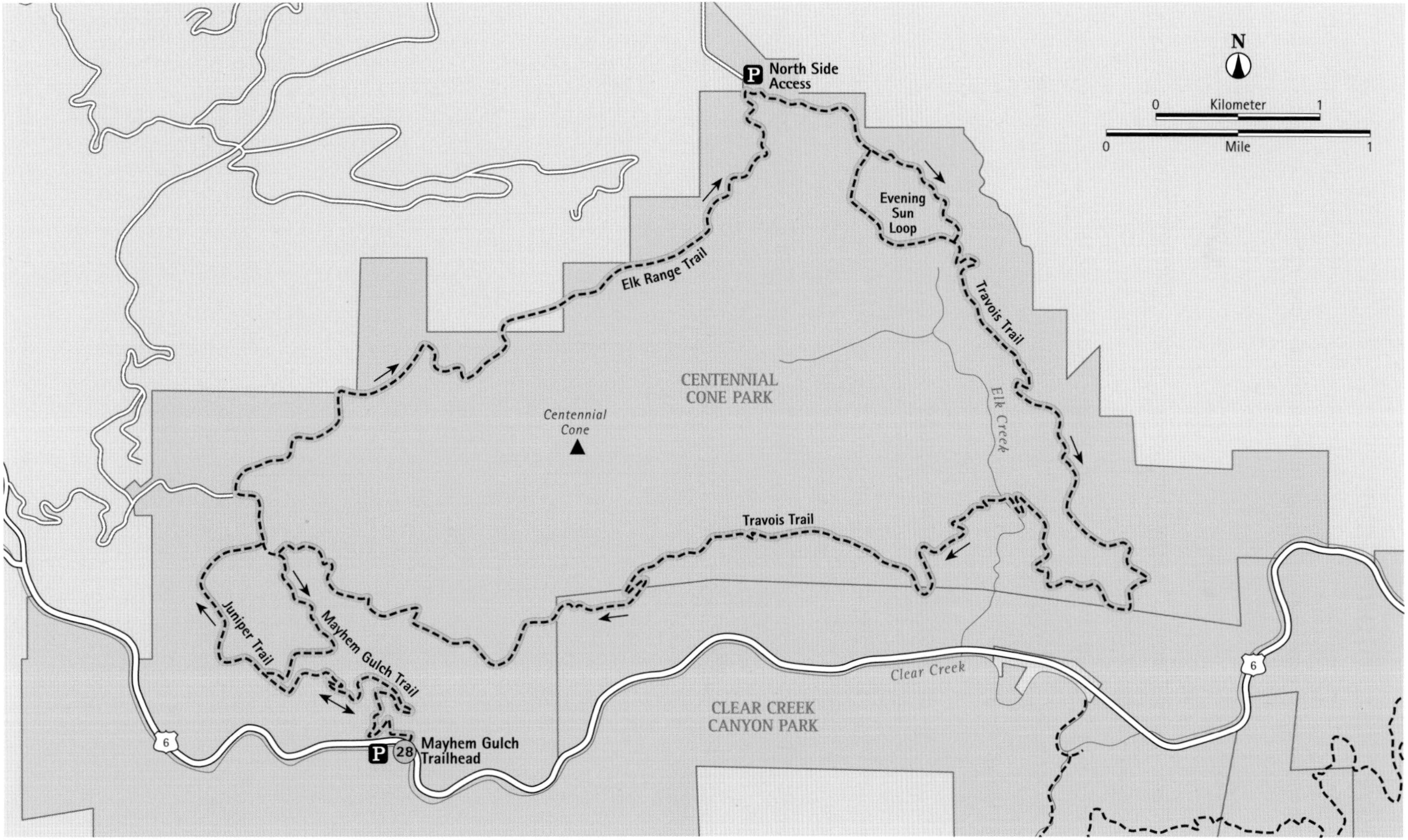

N

Kilometer
0   1
Mile
0   1

North Side Access

Evening Sun Loop

Travois Trail

Elk Creek

Elk Range Trail

CENTENNIAL CONE PARK

Centennial Cone

Travois Trail

Clear Creek

CLEAR CREEK CANYON PARK

Mayhem Gulch Trail

Mayhem Gulch Trailhead

28

Juniper Trail

6

Adventure Information

Centennial Cone Park. www.jeffco.us/1192/Centennial-Cone-Park

Outfitters

Bentgate Mountaineering. 1313 Washington Ave., Golden; (303) 271-9382; bentgate.com. Open Sun–Fri; closed Sat.

Golden Bike Shop. 722 Washington Ave., Golden; (303) 278-6545; goldenbikeshop.com

Vital Outdoors. 1224 Washington Ave., Golden; (303) 215-1644; vitaloutdoors.com

REI Denver Flagship. 1416 Platte St., Denver; (303) 756-3100; rei.com

Great Pre- or Post-Adventure Spots

Woody's Wood Fired Pizza. 1305 Washington Ave., Golden; (303) 277-0443; woodysgolden .com

Barrels & Bottles Brewery. 600 12th St., Unit 180, Golden; (720) 328-3643; barrelsbottles .com

Tributary Food Hall & Drinkery. 701 12th St., Golden; (303) 856-7225; tributarygolden.com

Mountain Bike 29 Doe Creek Loop

This awesome mountain bike adventure takes you through grassy meadows and aspen stands and offers some tough climbing on varying terrain. As it climbs it offers gorgeous views of Lake Granby and into the coniferous forests on the western side of Rocky Mountain National Park. Of course, as with any good mountain bike ride, it culminates in a fun, fast singletrack ride over some rocky terrain and dumps back out into the meadow filled with wildflowers in summer and early fall.

> **Start:** Doe Creek Trailhead, Arapaho National Recreation Area
>
> **Distance:** 6.8 miles out and back, with an opportunity to add small loops
>
> **Riding time:** About 2 hours
>
> **Difficulty:** Intermediate, with some tough climbs on good, well-marked trails
>
> **Elevation gain:** 1,050 feet
>
> **Trail surface:** Dirt and rock
>
> **Best seasons:** Year-round
>
> **Other trail users:** Hikers, equestrians, campers
>
> **Canine compatibility:** Leashed dogs permitted
>
> **Land status:** Arapahoe National Forest
>
> **Camping, fees, and permits:** Recreation pass or daily fee required; camping permits required June 1–Sept 15
>
> **Schedule:** Open 24/7
>
> **Trail contact:** Sulphur Ranger District, 9 Ten Mile Dr., Granby 80446; (970) 887-4100; fs.usda.gov/recarea/arp/recarea/?recid=28658
>
> **Finding the trailhead:** From the intersection of US 40 and US 34 in Granby, take US 34 northeast toward Grand Lake for 5.4 miles. Turn right onto CR 6 and continue for 5.4 miles to the parking area, on the right, just after Kamloop Cove. GPS: N40.13048° / W105.84458°

The Ride

There are over 1,000 miles of mountain biking trails in Grand County. Winter Park alone has claimed the title "Mountain Bike Capital USA," with more than 600 miles of mountain bike trails, including the Trestle Bike Park with lift-serviced rides and more. But there's an insane plethora of options throughout the county, and you don't need to go to a resort to find some of the best trails in the area.

Two of Chris Olivier's favorites are the Doe Creek and Strawberry Creek trail systems. Olivier is the owner of Two Pines Supply in Granby—an outdoors outfitter that also rents equipment, such as mountain bikes.

"When I'm on either of these, I hardly ever see a person," he says. "I know tons of locals who don't know Doe Creek is even a thing. The other interesting part about this, and I've talked to a few mapmakers about it, is that they don't show this trail at all, or they just show one single trail. There's actually a whole other loop, a mile-and-a-half loop, that's not on any map. I think that for mountain biking, Doe Creek is the cooler trail. It has a lot of cool features." He adds, "Doe Creek is not on a lot of maps—not fully. It's very limited as far as what's on any of the maps."

Indeed, there are many signed spurs off the main Doe Creek Trail (9.3) that rejoin it. Thankfully, from the top of the Doe Creek Trail system, they all lead north, back to the parking area. So there are plenty of opportunities for some extra side trips in the area.

Despite traveling through some stands of dead lodgepole pines, the trail is gorgeous. It starts near aspens and quickly opens up into a beautiful, double-track meadow after a short, easy climb. As the adventure continues, it switches to singletrack trail, first climbing through aspens then, as it climbs higher, into lodgepole and ponderosa pine forests.

Toward the end of the Doe Creek climb, the trail steepens significantly, gaining almost 400 feet of elevation in 0.5 mile on steep, tight switchbacks. "You just shoot up," Olivier says.

If you're just doing the Doe Creek Trail system at 1.7 miles, you can keep following the trail as it loops back down. "It's only a 4-mile-ish loop, but it gives you a good workout because it's steady climbing out from the parking and then you have nothing but grins all the way coming down," Olivier gushes.

Or you can keep riding, connecting with the Strawberry Creek trails by continuing on Doe Creek Trail. You can also easily extend the adventure by connecting with the Strawberry Creek Trail at 3.4 miles. Returning via the same route, you can still take the offshoot to the left for a different trail at 5.8 miles and a fun return downhill on some slightly technical, rocky terrain.

Miles and Directions

0.0   Start at the Doe Creek Trailhead. Head southeast on the Doe Creek Trail (9.3) and ride through a forested area.

0.3   Enter a small meadow.

0.4   Turn right at the trail junction with Trail 9.4 to stay on the Doe Creek Trail; reenter forest.

0.5   At the junction with Trail 9.7, stay on the Doe Creek Trail

0.6   Cross into Arapaho National Forest and enter another meadow.

0.8   At the next junction, with Trail 9.4, continue straight, toward the southeastern side of the meadow. Follow the trail as it reenters forest, heading south.

1.3   The trail begins making small switchbacks as it begins to climb.

1.7   As the trail reaches a high point and another junction with Trail 9.7, continue straight on the Doe Creek Trail to Strawberry Creek.

2.3   The trail joins Doe Creek as it heads east and begins climbing again.

2.7   The trail turns right again, heading mainly south as the climb steepens.

2.9   Reach the high point of the trail as it switches back and begins a descent to Strawberry Creek.

Doe Creek Loop

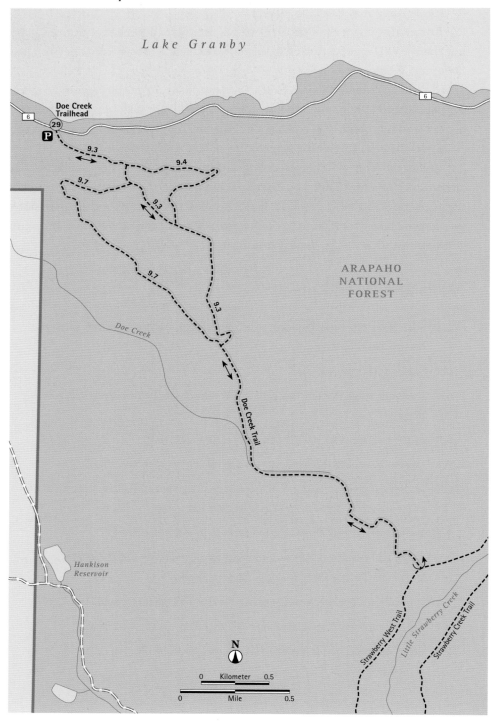

Atop a hill on Doe Creek Trail.

3.4 Reach the Strawberry Creek (9.2) trail junction. Return via the same route. (Option: Play around on some of the other trails in the area; both 9.7 and 9.4 are fun side trips on the way back to the trailhead.)

6.8 Arrive back at the trailhead.

Adventure Information

Outfitters

Two Pines Supply. 150 E Agate Ave., Granby; (970) 363-4054; twopinessupply.com

Great Pre- or Post-Adventure Spots

Never Summer Brewing Co. 62 E Agate Ave., Granby; (970) 887-0333; neversummerbrewing co.com

Fraser River Beer Company. 218 Eisenhower Dr., Fraser; (720) 352-1874; fraserriverbeerco .com

Maverick's Grille. 15 E Agate Ave., Granby; (970) 887-9000; mavericksgrille.com

Mountain Bike 30 Cottonwood Loop in the Arkansas Hills

This awesome mountain biking experience starts with a long uphill slog, but every single turn, jump, and technical move on 7 miles of singletrack descent makes the climb absolutely worth it! The Cottonwood Loop is part of the bigger Arkansas Hills trail network in Salida, and there are some fun side trips or alternative ways to complete this loop, depending on your skill level. The trail system is also notable because it offers some near-year-round riding with little snow.

Start: F Street lot

Distance: 15.4-mile loop

Riding time: About 4.5 hours

Difficulty: Tough mountain biking ride

Elevation gain: 2,500-plus feet

Trail surface: Road and singletrack on dirt and rock

Best seasons: Late spring through late fall; closed Dec 15–Mar 15

Other trail users: Hikers

Canine compatibility: Leashed dogs permitted

Land status: San Isabel National Forest, BLM

Camping, fees, and permits: None

Schedule: Open 24/7, except for seasonal trail closures

Nearest town: Salida

Trail contact: San Isabel National Forest Salida Ranger District, 5575 Cleora Rd., Salida 81201; (719) 539-3591; fs.usda.gov/detail/psicc/about-forest/districts/?cid=fsm9_032697

Maps: USGS Salida East; National Geographic Trails Illustrated #130: Salida, St. Elmo, Shavano Peak; Salida Mountain Trails, Arkansas Hills Trail System

Special considerations: This trail is in an arid part of the state with lots of cactus and little water, especially as summer winds on. With cacti and other sharp things on the trail, it's best to use tubeless tires and carry spare inner tubes or patch kits.

Finding the trailhead: From the intersection of US 285 and US 50, head east on US 50 for 4 miles. Turn left onto F Street. In 1.2 miles cross over the Arkansas River and look for parking on the left (228 N F St.). GPS: N38.53755° / W105.98848°

The Ride

Mountain biking in this Arkansas River town had taken off by the late 1980s, with one local cyclist calling it the Telluride of mountain biking as early as 1988. Locals like "Cactus" Jack Chivvis and bike builders Mike Rust and Don McLung were already riding some trails hidden behind the white "S" on Tenderfoot Hill that's visible almost anywhere in town. So maybe the "S" stood for hiding a badly kept secret.

When the Bureau of Land Management started inventorying its lands and the trails on them near Salida in 2004, a passionate, dedicated volunteer group, Salida Mountain Trails, arose to discuss access to trails on the land. Since then they've navigated the complexities of state, federal, and local politics; developed proposals for a network of sustainable mountain biking trails in the region; built them; and continue to maintain them.

Colin Meehan takes a turn on the Cottonwood Trail.

Salida Mountain Trails broke ground on their first trail on BLM land, the Backbone, in November 2008. The organization called it the foundation for the "stacked-loop" system of trails they submitted in their proposal for the Arkansas Hills Trail System. The stacked-loop system keeps the easier trails closer to the front of Tenderfoot Hill and the town, while many of the more difficult sections of hiking and biking trails are farther away. Since then the organization has built 23 miles of sustainable mountain biking trails in the area. Primarily they're in the Arkansas Hills Trail System and Methodist Mountain System.

Most recently the organization is working to resurrect one of the first trails in the area, the Sunset Trail, which Cactus Jack named. The new trail will use some accessible parts of the original trail—other parts are on private property—and incorporate them into more sustainable trail building. Cactus Jack named the forthcoming trail "Rusty Lung," for the bike-building partners. Sadly, McLung was murdered in 2009 and his remains weren't found until 2016. The perpetrator, who was already in jail for another crime, was found guilty in 2017. That sad story aside, the new trail will add to an outstanding network of fun, exciting trails and stand as a fitting tribute to the pioneering mountain bike builder, who was inducted into the Mountain Bike Hall of Fame in 1991.

The Cottonwood Loop is the farthest extension of the Arkansas Hills Trail System. It offers an impressive range of singletrack terrain and flow-driven riding as it courses into multiple drainages in relatively remote, arid land. As described, the route takes you up the Ute Trail (CR 175) to the trailhead, but you can opt to start the climb on mountain bike trails from the base of Tenderfoot Hill, eventually taking the Backbone Trail to connect with the Ute Trail as it becomes a well-maintained dirt road.

From the trailhead at the top of the Ute Trail (6.9 miles), trail riding starts with a 2.7-mile stretch on the Beasway Trail, carving through a scrubby coniferous forest with some mild elevation gains and moderate drops. The ride continues to undulate for the first 3.0 miles of trail. Shortly after crossing FS 173, an old 4X4 road, and starting the Rumba Trail section, it's almost all downhill, starting with two switchbacks at 10.0 miles into the ride. From here the trail drops into a drainage.

Shortly after reaching the Cottonwood Trail and drainage, the ride becomes more challenging, dropping over a series of small, rocky ledges known as the "Waterfalls." Some may have to dismount here.

As the trail comes closer to the north side of Tenderfoot, more trail options arise. Advanced mountain bikers may want to extend the ride by climbing the

The trail flows effortlessly through the twisted trees.

technical Unkle Nazty section of trail that splits off from Cottonwood at 13.6 miles, for instance. The last stretch of Cottonwood is mellower, however, and offers plenty of other options to return to the parking lot. This tour turns right onto the Backbone Trail to traverse the face of Tenderfoot then turns left onto the Sand Dunes Trail for a fun end to the day.

With little snow falling on the area and its south-facing slopes, the Arkansas Hills Trail System is one to consider for winter rides. Even though the Beasway Trail is closed in the winter to protect wildlife, other trails in the network are still ridable, and you can still make this loop by taking FS 181 to FS 173 and starting at the Rumba Trail.

Miles and Directions

0.0   Start at the parking lot and take the dirt road to the right (east); follow the road as it turns left and crosses the train tracks. Take a left onto CR 177, heading northwest.

1.1   Turn right onto the Ute Trail (CR 175) and Hillside Drive. Heading north, continue on this road for about 5 miles as it climbs 1,900 feet.

Cottonwood Loop in the Arkansas Hills

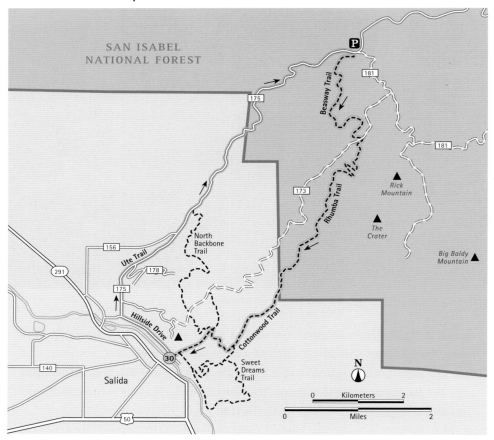

2.6 The road crosses into BLM land, just before an intersection with Pinon Hills Drive (CR 156), and turns into well-graded dirt road.

3.0 Pass the North Backbone Trail to the right, which leads back toward Salida.

5.2 The road turns right in a more northeasterly direction.

6.9 At the junction with CR 181, turn right into a parking lot with a trail kiosk. Find the Cottonwood Trailhead on the south side of the lot, and start riding south on the 2.7-mile Beasway Trail as it enters a coniferous forest and climbs an additional 100 feet.

7.5 Reach the high point for the day at 8,930 feet; begin an easy descent.

8.5 Descend through a series of switchbacks.

8.8 The trail makes a sharp right turn, heading almost due south as it comes close to CR 173, a dirt road.

9.3 Cross CR 173 and begin the next segment, the 2.2-mile Rhumba Trail, as it begins climbing some short switchbacks up a 200-foot hill over the next 0.8 mile.

10.0 Reach the high point on the Rhumba Trail and begin descending on larger switchbacks. The rest of the loop is almost entirely downhill.

10.7 From here to the next section, the Rhumba Trail travels along an intermittent stream in a drainage gully, crossing it numerous times.

11.3 Enter Cottonwood Gulch, a normally dry riverbed. Here the trail becomes the 3.4-mile Cottonwood segment, the most technical of the day.

11.4 Begin descending the "Waterfalls" section of the trail, with technical, rocky features. From here the trail weaves across both sides of the gulch and sometimes straight through the riverbed.

13.6 Pass the junction with Unkle Nazty—a short, very hard trail—and continue on the Cottonwood Trail.

14.0 Reach the junction with the Backbone Trail and take Backbone to the right as it snakes back and forth to the Sand Dunes Trail.

14.7 Turn left on the Sand Dunes Trail to return to the trailhead.

15.4 Cross the train tracks and arrive back at the trailhead.

Adventure Information

Arkansas Hills trail map. salidamountaintrails.org/wp-content/uploads/Arkansas-Hills -Trail-Map-OVERVIEW-Web-v1.jpg

Organizations

Salida Mountain Trails. salidamountaintrails.org

Outfitters

Salida Mountain Sports. 110 North F St., Salida; (719) 539-4400; salidamountainsports .com

Subculture Cyclery. 129 North G St., Salida; (719) 539-5329; subculturecyclery.com

Great Pre- or Post-Adventure Spots

Boathouse Cantina. 228 North F St., Salida; (719) 539-5004; boathousesalida.com. The cantina adds a 1 percent donation to bills (you can opt out) to support Salida Mountain Trails and other local educational and outdoors organizations.

Soulcraft Brewing. 248 W Rainbow Blvd., Salida; (719) 539-5428; soulcraftbeer.com

Moonlight Pizza & Brewpub. 242 F St., Salida; (719) 539-4277; moonlightpizza.biz

Road Bike 31 Lookout Mountain

The pillar-to-post climb of the Lariat Trail Scenic Mountain Drive is one of the most revered and iconic road bike climbs on the Front Range. It's no wonder that, with sweeping views of Golden, North and South Table Mountains, and Denver beyond, almost every recent road bike race in the region includes this stretch of road. This leg-busting, switchbacking climb is well worth the grind, if only to hear the purr of whirring freewheel on the rocketing descent.

Start: Beverly Heights Park lot

Distance: 9.6 miles out and back

Riding time: 1–2 hours

Difficulty: A short but difficult road climb with a steady climb

Elevation gain: 1,400 feet

Trail surface: Road

Best seasons: Year-round (Winter trips will require warmer gear.)

Other users: Cars, motorcycles, mountain bikers

Canine compatibility: Technically yes, but tearing down a mountain at 30+ miles an hour says no.

Land status: Jefferson County Open Space

Camping, fees, and permits: None

Schedule: Road open 24/7; no parking on the road after dark

Nearest town: Golden

Trail contact: Jefferson County Open Space; (303) 271-5925; jeffco.us/open-space

Maps: USGS Golden; National Geographic Trails Illustrated #100: Boulder/Golden

Finding the trailhead: From the roundabout at the junction of US 6 and 19th Street, head west on 19th Street toward Lookout Mountain. In 0.4 mile, shortly after 19th Street turns left, turn left into a parking lot. There is a porta-potty in the lot. GPS: N39.74182° / W105.22828°

The Ride

The "pillar" part of the climb is when most people start timing their ascent: the two stone pillars built in 1917 to start the Lariat Trail Scenic Mountain Drive. The "post" is where they stop timing: the signpost for Buffalo Bill's grave, 4.8 miles and nearly 1,400 feet higher than when they started.

Bikers crossing paths on Lookout Mountain.

The Lariat Trail Scenic Mountain Drive was built by William "Cement Bill" Williams, the second most-famous Bill on the mountain. Cement Bill wanted to attract tourists to Golden and planned a road from the city to the summit of Lookout Mountain. At the same time, Denver wanted to attract more people to its new Denver Mountain Parks system. Williams started building a 2-foot-wide trail in 1910, but the project stalled because of a lack of funding. When funding opened up for the project in 1913, he built an auto road to the summit of Lookout Mountain in three months.

In 1917, over some legal disputes, Denver ultimately forced Cement Bill to sell the plot of the other famous Lookout Mountain Bill, William F. "Buffalo Bill" Cody, to the city. Denver used it as part of the larger Lariat Loop connecting residents and tourists with its mountain parks, passing Lookout Mountain, Bergen Park, Bear Creek Canyon Park, and Red Rocks, among others, in a 40-mile loop. Considered one of the first historic byways in the country, it was added to the National Register of Historic Places in 1976.

As the climb switchbacks up the side of Mount Zion, it passes under the giant white "M" that presides over Golden. This monument was created around 1908 by students at the Colorado School of Mines. The "M" was first lit at night in 1932 and remains lit to this day. From here the road continues its climb, making some final switchbacks before spiraling around to the top of Lookout Mountain and the (supposed) final resting place of Buffalo Bill. The end of this climb and a good place for a rest as well.

Legend has it that when Buffalo Bill—Wyoming's most famous adopted son—died in the winter of 1917, some Wyomingites came down to Colorado and replaced his corpse with a vagrant's. According to the legend, they buried him in Cody, the town the famous showman founded. To tamp down those rumors, the family had an open-casket funeral attended by thousands of mourners. In a further attempt to prevent any tampering with his grave, he was buried in a bronze casket sealed in a tamper-proof case, which was in turn enclosed in concrete and iron. Still, his niece insisted he wanted to be buried in Wyoming; in response, his foster son, Johnny Baker, reburied Buffalo Bill under tons of concrete.

Reflecting on all this after making the long climb, cycling masochists can still make this or other epic road bike loops from Buffalo Bill's grave, continuing on the Lariat Loop. However, they have to use larger roads like I-70 and Evergreen

Bikers climbing the sinuous road up to Lookout Mountain.

Lookout Mountain

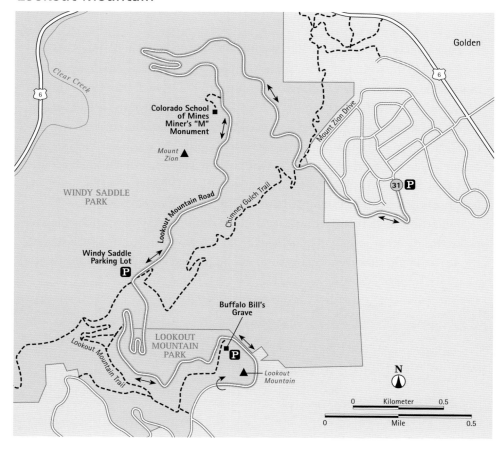

Parkway to connect the Lariat Loop. Those ready for food and libation celebrations can return via the same route—wind whistling through their helmets as hubs clack away furiously, a knowing smile on their face as they see others making the arduous climb.

Miles and Directions

0.0 Start from the parking lot and turn left onto Lookout Mountain Road to begin the long, challenging climb to the top.

0.7 The road has one short downslope section here.

1.5 Reach a series of tight switchbacks.

2.3   Pass the Colorado School of Mines "M" monument, on the west side of the road.

2.5   Pass the peak of Mount Zion, also to the west.

3.1   Reach the Windy Saddle Park parking lot, which has toilets.

3.4   Begin a final series of switchbacks.

4.7   Turn right to enter Lookout Mountain Park and ride toward Buffalo Bill's grave. This area has picnic benches, toilets, and a store.

4.8   Reach Buffalo Bill's grave. Return via the same route.

9.6   Arrive back at the parking lot.

Adventure Information

Outfitters

Bentgate Mountaineering. 1313 Washington Ave., Golden; (303) 271-9382; bentgate.com. Open Sun–Fri; closed Sat.

Golden Bike Shop. 722 Washington Ave., Golden; (303) 278-6545; goldenbikeshop.com

Vital Outdoors. 1224 Washington Ave., Golden; (303) 215-1644; vitaloutdoors.com

REI Denver Flagship. 1416 Platte St., Denver; (303) 756-3100; rei.com

Great Pre- or Post-Adventure Spots

Woody's Wood Fired Pizza. 1305 Washington Ave., Golden; (303) 277-0443; woodysgolden .com

Barrels & Bottles Brewery. 600 12th St., Unit 180, Golden; (720) 328-3643; barrelsbottles .com

Tributary Food Hall & Drinkery. 701 12th St., Golden; (303) 856-7225; tributarygolden.com

PADDLING ADVENTURES

For a state so arid, there's a surprising amount of water in Colorado. It's home to major reservoirs, rivers, creeks, and streams. Its high-mountain rivers feed the plains states to the east; to the west its rivers feed states from Texas and Nevada to California. As a major headwaters state with significant elevation, Colorado has some of the best whitewater in the country. These are the best places to get a taste of all the wet fun the Centennial State has to offer.

A climber on a Tyrolean traverse cross above rafters in Clear Creek Canyon at East Colfax.

Whitewater 32 Clear Creek Canyon

Clear Creek, with floatable water starting near Lawson and ending in Golden, offers the closest whitewater to Denver and Boulder, with an impressive assortment of frothy rapid-fire rapids. Fed by snowmelt, the creek churns through narrow valleys before carving into Clear Creek Canyon. As it enters the canyon, it offers one of the greatest successions of rapids in the state.

Length: 4.0 miles

Paddling time: 2.5–3.5 hours

Difficulty: Class IV–V whitewater

Rapids: Numerous Class IV and some Class V rapids; few eddies

Average gradient: 198 feet per mile

Optimal flow: 350–900 cfs

Flow gauge: Clear Creek at Golden

Water source: Free-flowing snowmelt

Best seasons: June through late July. High snow years offer a longer season, earlier in spring and later in summer.

Land status: Clear Creek County

Fees: Required for some access

Nearest town: Idaho Springs, Golden

Maps: USGS Squaw Pass; National Geographic Trails Illustrated #100: Boulder, Golden; Clear Creek Rapids map, available online at co.clear-creek.co.us/DocumentCenter/View/98/ClearCreekRaftingMap

Craft: Kayaks, inflatable kayaks, rafts

Camping, fees, and permits: No fees, no camping; no parking after dark

Waterway contact: Clear Creek County Tourism Bureau, 2060 Miner St., Idaho Springs 80452; (303) 567-4382; clearcreekcounty.org. Liquid Descent, 1896 Stanley Rd., Idaho Springs 80452; (970) 372-2870; coloradorafting.com.

Put-in (Kermit's Access): From the intersection of US 6 and CO-93, head west on US 6 and drive 12 miles into the canyon. Turn left at the light and continue 2.8 miles; just past the gravel pit there is a pullout across from a restaurant (as of 2020 called Two Bears), about 0.5 mile west of mile marker 258. Also accessible via I-70, but if dropping a takeout vehicle off farther downstream, US 6 offers the best access. GPS: N39.74583° / W105.43813°

Takeout: There is a flatwater takeout at mile marker 260.5, on the south side of US 6. GPS: N39.74398° / W105.39674°

Overview

There is an abundance of whitewater available on Clear Creek. The creek flows more than 20 miles from Lawson to Golden, with whitewater parks bookending the rapids in both towns.

This paddle covers only the 3.6-mile section between Kermit's Access and the pullout at mile marker 360.5—an area Alan Baldo, owner of Liquid Descent, says "is certainly the most continuous stretch of Class IV in the state. There's great Class IV all around the state, but with a lot of them you ride a great rapid and then you've got to paddle 2 miles of flatwater, then you run a rapid and you got another mile of paddling. There is zero flatwater in this section. You're always in [at least] Class II whitewater, so it's magical."

There is tougher water on Clear Creek in a section called Black Rock, with Class V rapids that approach Class VI at higher flow levels.

MULTI-ADVENTURE DAYS

Have you ever dreamed of a day where you wake up for sunrise, downhill on a mountain bike, hike to the put-in at the river, hop into a whitewater raft, and climb out of the canyon to catch the last echoes of sunset? We have. In developing this book, it was gratifying to realize that some of the best areas for adventures in Colorado were extremely close to other great adventure spots, albeit in a different capacity. In some cases, like Clear Creek Canyon and Horsetooth Reservoir, you could find the best types of multiple adventures in that spot.

So of course we had to try it. Taking advantage of an incredible snow season in spring 2019, a group of friends got together for the first Super Fun Adventure Day. We kicked off the day on skis and snowboards at Arapahoe Basin in the morning, headed into Idaho Springs to whitewater raft with Liquid Descents in Clear Creek Canyon, and finished the day climbing in Clear Creek Canyon. To say the least, it was a magical day, and we can't wait to take on new multiday adventures.

With a little planning, it's something you can do too. You can start easy, combining a hike with a mountain bike ride or a rock climb—sometimes you have to do that to get to the crag anyway. But depending on weather conditions and your crew's ability level, you could take down some massively wild adventure days. Imagine backcountry skiing on Mount Shavano's famous couloir—the Angel of Shavano—ripping on bikes into Salida or Villa Grove to put into the Arkansas River in pack rafts or kayaks, stopping at an eddy to trad climb some little-known areas in Browns Canyon.

Or perhaps climbing Horsetooth Mountain in the morning to catch the sunrise over the eastern plains, then canoeing or kayaking across the reservoir to rock climb at Duncan Ridge. End the day racing road or mountain bikes down the eastern side of the reservoir and relishing those after-sunset celebrations.

The point is, there's an endless combination of excellent adventures to be had in a day in Colorado, and choosing them can be fun. Sure beats a birthday party at a roller rink or a pool hall—just sayin'. Most of the limitations are surmountable too. If you or some members of the party don't have the gear needed for one of the adventures, check with local outfitters. Most outfitters in this book have rental programs for some or all of the gear needed. They can also point you to others that offer equipment they can't. Likewise, guide companies can offer equipment rentals and guided tours as well. Their tours can be as easy or as difficult as you want.

Finally, while it's great to have everyone in on all the fun, don't push it. If someone can only make the whitewater or mountain-bike portion of the day, that's fine. Worst-case scenario, they'll have to wait or catch up. Heck, you could even make it an adventure relay day!

The Paddling

As this is a creek fed by snowmelt, expect chilly water, especially if paddling early in the season. Wet suits and splash jackets are recommended through late June.

This nearly 4-mile section of river has ten rapids in quick succession, leaving little time to rest between each. Almost immediately, the fun starts with Upper Beaver Falls and Lower Beaver Falls, back-to-back Class IV rapids. "Those are two about 8-foot drops that start it off with a bang," Baldo says.

The next major rapid is Tricky Dick, a Class III–IV rapid just after mile marker 258, which runs for about 500 feet as the creek turns right. After that the creek

Sarah's first rafting trip was on some pretty big water in Clear Creek, and she had a blast!

hits a 1,400-foot stretch of calmer water before encountering the Class III–IV Guide Ejector rapid.

"Guide Ejector is the first rapid in a long succession. It goes Guide Ejector and then Double Knife, which is my favorite rapid in the stretch," Baldo says. This is also a popular rock-climbing area called East Colfax, and there is a Tyrolean traverse across the creek here.

"Double Knife leads right into Purgatory, which leads right into the Road to Hell, which leads right into Hells Corner, which goes into T2 then into Dog Ball. It just keeps going," Baldo explains. "That section is over a mile long of Class IV. So it's really continuous, super fun!"

After that intense section, there's a short break in rapids. But it quickly picks back up, dropping into another Class III–IV rapid, Horrendous Left Turn. The creek snakes around another oxbow into the Class IV Corkscrew and oxbows again just before the Class III Whew! From here the creek hooks right into calmer water—a good spot for a pullout.

Clear Creek Canyon Whitewater

Kermit's Access Put-In

32

6

Upper Beaver Falls Class IV

Lower Beaver Falls

Highway Access

70

40

182

182

258

Tricky Dick- Class III–IV

Clear Creek

259

6

Guide Ejector- Class III–IV

Hells Corner- Class III–IV

Creekside Playin' Hooky start

Terminator- Class IV

Tunnel 6 Access

Double Knife- Class IV–V

The Safari climbing crag

Other Critters climbing crag

The Doghouse climbing crag

P

Clear Creek Tunnel 5

Horrendous Left Turn- Class III–IV

Whew!- Class III

Terminator- Class IV

260

Mile 260.5 Takeout

119

60

6

CLEAR CREEK CANYON PARK

N

Kilometer 0   0.5

Mile 0   0.5

Adventure Information

Outfitters

Bentgate Mountaineering. 1313 Washington Ave., Golden; (303) 271-9382; bentgate.com. Open Sun–Fri; closed Sat.

Wilderness Exchange. 2401 15th St., Ste. 100, Denver; (303) 964-0708; wildernessx.com

Vital Outdoors. 1224 Washington Ave., Golden; (303) 215-1644; vitaloutdoors.com

REI Denver Flagship. 1416 Platte St., Denver; (303) 756-3100; rei.com

Great Pre- or Post-Adventure Spots

Woody's Wood Fired Pizza. 1305 Washington Ave., Golden; (303) 277-0443; woodysgolden .com

Barrels & Bottles Brewery. 600 12th St., Unit 180, Golden; (720) 328-3643; barrelsbottles .com

Westbound & Down Brewing Company. 1617 Miner St., Idaho Springs; (720) 502-3121; westboundanddown.com

Tommyknocker Brewery & Pub. 1401 Miner St., Idaho Springs; (303) 567-4419; tommy knocker.com

Whitewater 33 Poudre Canyon

The Cache La Poudre River in Poudre Canyon is Colorado's only nationally designated "Wild and Scenic River." Fueled by snowmelt in the Rockies, the river has cut a mighty canyon in northern Colorado, exposing bedrock up to 1.5 billion years old. The river runs roughly 40 miles through much of Roosevelt National Forest's northern reaches and into Fort Collins and eventually Greeley. Along the way it offers incredible whitewater experiences to paddlers; it's also a wild playground for climbing, hiking, biking, and other experiences.

Length: 10.2 miles

Paddling time: 5–6 hours

Difficulty: Class II–IV

Rapids: Numerous Class II–Class IV+ rapids. Some parts may be too shallow in early spring or late summer, but others will still be in. Portaging is easy, with good access to the riverbanks and CO 14.

Average gradient: 63 feet per mile

Optimum flow: 600–3,000 cfs

Flow gauge: Cache La Poudre River at Fort Collins, Hewlett Gulch Bridge

Water source: Free-flowing snowmelt

Best seasons: Late Apr through early Aug; potential for whitewater into Sept in high-snow years

Land status: Primarily Roosevelt National Forest

Fees: None

Nearest town: Fort Collins

Maps: USGS Rustic; National Geographic Trails Illustrated #112: Poudre River, Cameron Pass

Craft: Kayaks, rafts, whitewater canoes, inflatable kayaks, paddleboards

Camping, fees, and permits: None

Waterway contact: Canyon Lakes Ranger District, 2150 Centre Ave., Bldg. E, Fort Collins 80526; (970) 295-6700; fs.usda.gov/recarea/arp/recarea/?recid=36603

Put-in (Steven's Gulch Access): From the intersection of US 287 and CO 14 (Poudre Canyon Road), by Ted's Place, head west on CO 14 for 16.8 miles. The put-in is on the right. GPS: N40.68288° / W105.40084°

Takeout (The Bridges): From the intersection of US 287 and CO 14 (Poudre Canyon Road), by Ted's Place, head west on CO 14 for 7.1 miles. The takeout is on the right. GPS: N40.69703° / W105.26473°

Overview

This adventure takes you into 10 miles of tough, fun rapids and exciting corners leading into some blind rapids, starting above the canyon's famed Mishawka Amphitheatre. The amphitheater is a century-old venue that's seen the likes of Leo Kottke, Arlo Guthrie, Joan Baez, George Clinton, and the Colorado Symphony Orchestra play on the riverside stage. The amphitheater is still operating today, and paddlers can stop for a bite mid-run or after a long day on the rapids for a burger and a drink, assuming the restaurant is open and there's not a show.

Legend has it that Poudre Canyon and the Cache La Poudre River were named by fur traders. During a multiday winter storm around 1825—some say 1836—a group of French-Canadian trappers with William Ashley's fur trading company were hunkered down. Following the storm, the trappers lightened their load before crossing the river by hiding extra supplies in a pit. Much of it was gunpowder. Hence the river was named "Cache la poudre" or "the hiding place of the

Low water by the Mishawaka along the Cache La Poudre River.

powder" in English. Presumably they found it, but that detail is lost to history while the name endures.

Today the river's rapids are explosive, approaching Class V in high-water conditions in an awe-inspiring environment—if you have time to look for it between dropping into the next rapid. When you do, you'll find an ancient canyon teaming with Colorado wildlife. Along the river you'll see subalpine fir, Douglas fir, spruce, and pines throughout the canyon. Closer to the river you'll find willows, wildflowers, and other marshy plants. The canyon is also prime habitat for deer and bighorn sheep; elk and moose are known to be nearby as well.

Unfortunately, forest fires have taken their toll on the canyon, like 2012's massive 85,000-acre, lighting-cased High Park Fire. This adventure travels through some of that damage, and you can see where fire licked the river shores and sometimes leaped across it.

There are numerous picnic sites and campgrounds along the Cache La Poudre River for multiday adventures. Similarly, there are plenty of options for put-ins and takeouts. The Narrows, a 3.5-mile section above this one, has Class V rapids for expert whitewater runners. Below this adventure, there is another, easier section of rapids known as the Filter Plant, but you'd have to portage to reach it from this section.

The river is suitable for kayakers, rafters, inflatables, and whitewater canoes with experienced paddlers. Standup paddleboards are also used on some but not all sections here.

The Paddling

As a river fed by snowmelt, and in a canyon largely running west to east with a lot of shade throughout the day, the Cache La Poudre is cold in spring. Wet suits and splash jackets are recommended early and even later in the season.

Launching into the river at Steven's Gulch around river mile marker 105, this adventure is front-loaded with the toughest rapid in this first stretch. The first 0.5 mile is easy paddling, as is the first rapid, Stove Prairie, by the Stove Prairie campsite. It's a Class II–III rapid to get some good practice on.

Just before reaching mile marker 106, launch into another warm-up rapid, the Class II–III Prelude Rapid. Shortly after that the river elbows to the north and launches into the Class III–IV Three Rocks Rapid (also known as Split Rock Rapid), the first challenge of the day, but it has a good middle line in most water.

As it continues, the Poudre takes serpentine turns over easy whitewater; the river oxbows around the Crystal Wall on the right and turns right into the Crystal Rapid, a Class III rapid that ends with a short pinch point and quickly leads into another Class III, Crystal Wall Rapid. There's a fun spot called the U.S.S.— (Ultimate Squirt Spot) here. After another elbow in the river, it hits the Class III+ Rip Rock Rapid.

The next challenge is Mishawaka Falls, a Class IV rapid, at mile marker 108. Mishawaka Falls is worthy of scouting; you'll find a good spot on the right side to check it out. Make it and choose to break at the Mish—at just about 4 miles in, it's a good break point—or keep on going.

Just after passing the Mishawaka, the river gets a little easier as it encounters the Class III Guide Hole. Stay right, as the left side is shallower and has trees. If you just ate at the Mish, rejoice. You've got a little over a mile traveling over fast-flowing water with a couple of whitecaps before Claire's Rock Rapid, a Class III rapid about 0.5 mile from mile marker 110. Shortly after Claire's the river looks like it branches into two as takes a sharp right turn. Stay on the right branch. The other branch curves around a small island.

Enjoy another relatively quiet section of water, passing through a couple small islands and reach a fun, Class III rapid called Dr. Suckhole. It's right by the Poudre Park picnic area and takeout.

The next section passes through Poudre Park on a mile stretch of relatively straight river. Be careful of bridges and their supports in this area. Also be respectful of the town's quiet zone.

After mile marker 112, things start to pick up. The river turns left as it's bisected by another small island. The right is wider but has bigger boulders. The wave chain of the aptly named Double Bridges Rapid, a Class III, starts here.

Travel under another bridge and head into the beastly Class III–IV Cardiac Corner as the river oxbows. It's easy enough to run, but has scared some paddlers. The river begins another snake curve before the Pineview Falls Rapid, a Class IV–V rapid. There's a takeout just before the rapid, but it makes for an exciting run with some tough holes.

Shortly after mile marker 113, encounter the Class III Greyrock Bridge rapids and pass under the bridge. Continue on fast-moving water and reach the next rapid, Killer Bridge Rapid, a Class III that can suck paddlers uncomfortably close to abutments.

Poudre Canyon Whitewater

ROOSEVELT
NATIONAL FOREST

Greyrock Mountain ▲

Red Mountain ▲

Greyrock Bridge Rapids
Class III

Killer Bridge Rapids
Class III

Red House Hole Rapid
Class III

Bridges Takeout

Greyrock Trailhead

Bridges Put-In

Pineview Falls

Pineview Rapid
Class IV-V

Pineview Takeout

Double Bridges Rapid
Class III

Cardiac Corner Rapid
Class III-IV

Hewlett Gulch Trailhead

Poudre Park

Fire Station

Poudre Park Picnic Area and Takeout

Dr. Suckhole Rapid
Class III

Claire's Rock Rapid
Class III

Young Gulch Trailhead

Ansel Watrous Campground

Dead Deer Put-In

Mishawaka Amphitheatre

Mishawaka Falls
Class III-V+

Three Hocks Rapid
Class III-IV

Three Rocks Rapid
Class III-IV

Rip Rock Rapid
Class III+

Guide Hole Rapid
Class III

Crystal Rapid
Class III+

Crystal Wall Put-In

Prelude Rapid
Class II-III

Stove Prairie Rapid
Class II-III

Stevens Gulch Picnic Area and Put-In

Stove Prairie Campground

N

Kilometers

Miles

105 106 107 108 109 110 111 112 113 114

14 33 27

The next and last rapid of the day is Red House Hole (Class III), denoted by the red house on the left of the river. Pass under a bridge and, just after, make another sharp bend to the right. The pullout is on the right at 10.2 miles.

Adventure Information

Outfitters

JAX Outdoor Gear. 1200 N College Ave., Fort Collins; (970) 221-0544; jaxgoods.com

REI Fort Collins. 4025 S College Ave., Fort Collins; (970) 223-0123; rei.com

Great Pre- or Post-Adventure Spots

The Mishawaka. 13714 Poudre Canyon Rd., Bellvue; (888) 843-6474; themishawaka.com

CooperSmith's Pub & Brewing. #5 Old Town Square, Fort Collins; (970) 498-0483; coopersmithspub.com

McClellan's Brewing Co. 1035 S Taft Hill Rd., Fort Collins; (970) 568-8473; mcclellansbrewingcompany.com

Odell Brewing. 800 E Lincoln Ave., Fort Collins; (970) 498-9070; odellbrewing.com

Whitewater 34 Browns Canyon

The Arkansas River is one of the most popular whitewater destinations in Colorado, if not the country. From its headwaters near Leadville to Cañon City, the river drops more than 4,600 feet over 120 miles, providing awesome outdoor recreation activities, from world-class whitewater to world-class fishing. In this area it flows through multiple picturesque mountain towns, including Buena Vista, Salida, and Cañon City, at times offering awe-inspiring views of the Sawatch Range and Collegiate Peaks—the highest concentration of mountains over 14,000 feet in the contiguous United States—as well as carving through remote mountain canyons.

Length: 8.0 miles

Paddling time: 4–6 hours

Difficulty: Class III–IV whitewater; family-friendly, especially with teens

Rapids: Class II–Class IV rapids; possibility for easily avoided wood strainers

Average gradient: 39 feet per mile

Optimum flow: 1,200–3,000 cfs

Flow gauge: Arkansas River near Nathrop

Water source: Snowmelt; controlled flows through late July

Best seasons: Late May through early Aug; potential for whitewater into Sept in high-snow years

Land status: Managed by Colorado Parks & Wildlife, USDA Forest Service, and Bureau of Land Management

Fees: Required for some access points and campsites

Maps: USGS Buena Vista East, Nathrop; National Geographic #2303: Arkansas River, Leadville to Salida; Arkansas Headwaters Recreation Map

Craft: Kayaks, inflatable kayaks, rafts

Waterway contact: Arkansas Headwaters Recreation Area, 307 W Sackett Ave., Salida 81201; (719) 539-7289; cpw.state.co.us/placestogo/parks/ArkansasHead watersRecreationArea/Pages/Camping.aspx. The Adventure Company, 12847 US 24/285, Buena Vista 81211; (800) 497-7238; theadventurecompany.com

Put-in (Ruby Mountain river access): From the intersection of US 24 and US 285, travel south 1 mile on US 285 and turn right onto CR 301. In 2.8 miles turn left onto CR-300. Stay on CR 300 for 2.4 miles to reach the put-in parking lot. GPS: N38.75241° / W106.07084°

Takeout (Hecla Junction): From the intersection of US 24 and US 285, head south on US 285 for 13 miles. Turn left on CO 194 and stay on the dirt road for 2.4 miles to the takeout parking lot. GPS: N38.65196° / W106.05151°

Overview

The most popular whitewater segments of the Arkansas River start north of Buena Vista, kicked off with the Pine Creek section featuring stout Class IV and Class V rapids. From this paddler's heaven of a start, rapids are found through-out the next 100 or so miles, with some milder Class III- and Class II-dominant sections in between. These milder sections of the river are bookended by another tough section called the Royal Gorge, where narrow canyon walls rise 1,000 feet above the shore and paddlers can see what was the world's highest bridge until it was surpassed in 2001.

This adventure covers the Browns Canyon section of the Arkansas, a stretch of the river that takes paddlers away from the humanity and into one of the United States' newest national monuments—where there are ample bird- and nature-watching opportunities in between Class III and sometimes Class IV rapids.

For multiday adventures, there are numerous campgrounds along the Arkansas River. There are paid sites and primitive backcountry sites available on a first-come, first-served basis. Both Salida and Buena Vista have free whitewater parks for kayakers and standup paddleboarders.

The Paddling

The Arkansas River makes for exciting paddling from May and into August. Years with higher than average snowfall or rainier than usual springs and summers can extend the season into Labor Day. Fed by snowmelt, this river is cold in spring; wet suits and splash jackets are recommended early in the season and into June. As summer wanes into fall, if the flow is still high in late August or early September, consider wearing insulating layers.

This stretch of river covers some of the most fun Class III and Class IV rapids in the state. There are plenty of put-in and takeout opportunities, but this adventure describes the 8.0 miles from the start the of the canyon to Hecla Junction, which offers some sustained rapids and flumes followed by long eddies, allowing

Epic views await in Browns Canyon.

paddlers time to absorb the beauty of the canyon, spot wildlife like bighorn sheep, martens—if you can spot the little varmints—falcons, and eagles.

Browns Canyon is a popular route. If possible, avoid it during summer weekends; it's much less crowded on weekdays.

From the Ruby Mountain River Access, start above river mile marker 41, the float begins on easy water, providing ample chance to practice commands and strokes before hitting the rapids about 2 miles in. Around mile marker 43, hills begin to approach the river shore on the left side (northeast), while the right side remains relatively low, the shore banked with willow and marsh-loving flowers. In about 0.5 mile, hills begin popping up on the right side as well, entering the canyon.

The rapids start with aptly named Canyon Doors, a Class III rapid that starts by mile marker 44. It's a good play spot for kayakers as long as the flow is lower than about 3,000 cubic feet per second. That rapid leads into Pinball Rapid, which ranges from Class IV, depending on the level of the river.

After Pinball Rapid there's a period of good moving water without whitewater. A sandbar (hidden in high water) on the left side usually appears slightly before Browns Creek feeds into the river at 4.0 miles in. There are camping spots on both sides of the river here. This is also a good spot to prepare for one of the biggest rapids of the day: Zoom Flume, which approaches Class III in difficulty. It's 400 feet of fun, choppy water with some decent-size obstacles worth scouting if you haven't been on the river before. This eddies out at Zoom Flume beach shortly after mile marker 45. From here easily navigate some rocks on easy rapids for 0.5 mile before reaching the Class III Squeeze Play, which requires navigation through a series of large boulders.

Enjoy a short, slower section, then look river left to find the Class III Hemorrhoid Rock.

The next challenge is Big Drop Rapid, a Class III rapid at mile marker 46. There are campsites immediately after the rapid. Enjoy the next 0.25 mile of easy water and prepare for Staircase Rapid, another bumpy Class III ride before a good flatter section of water in the canyon.

The next rapid, Widowmaker, is another fun Class III rapid at mile marker 47. From here until the pullout at Hecla Junction, the rapids become a little easier. The last Class III rapid is Raft Ripper, at 7.1 miles in, quickly followed by Graveyard (Class II) at mile marker 48. The last significant rapid in the section is the Class II Last Chance. The Hecla Junction pullout is about 900 feet downriver, on the right.

Adventure Information

Salida Water Park (webcam). coloradowebcam.net/camera/
salida-colorado-steam-plant-theater-arkansas-river-down-river

Buena Vista Water Park (webcam). coloradowebcam.net/camera/
buena-vista-webcam-arkansas-river-surf-hotel-chateau-colorado

Organizations

Arkansas River Outfitters Association. arkansasriveroutfitters.org

Outfitters

Salida Mountain Sports. 110 N F St., Salida; (719) 539-4400; salidamountainsports.com

CKS Main Street. 327 E Main St., Buena Vista; (719) 395-9206; cksmainstreet.com/
retail-store

Browns Canyon Whitewater

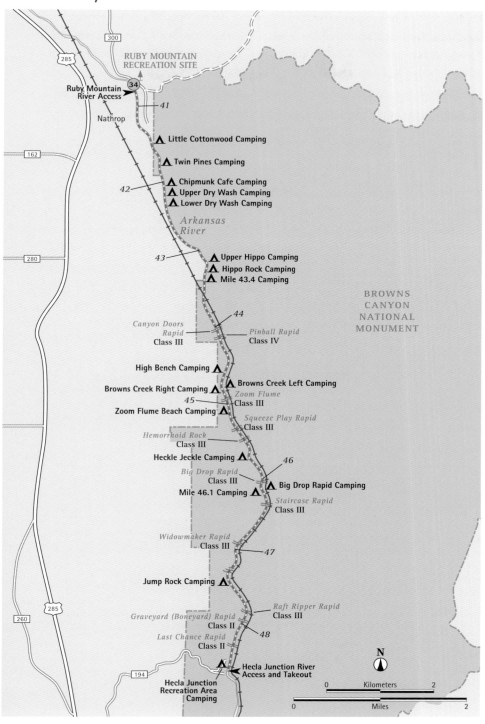

RUBY MOUNTAIN
RECREATION SITE

Ruby Mountain
River Access

Nathrop

41

▲ Little Cottonwood Camping

▲ Twin Pines Camping

▲ Chipmunk Cafe Camping
42
▲ Upper Dry Wash Camping
▲ Lower Dry Wash Camping

*Arkansas
River*

43
▲ Upper Hippo Camping
▲ Hippo Rock Camping
▲ Mile 43.4 Camping

BROWNS
CANYON
NATIONAL
MONUMENT

44

*Canyon Doors
Rapid*
Class III

Pinball Rapid
Class IV

High Bench Camping ▲

Browns Creek Right Camping ▲ ▲ Browns Creek Left Camping
45   *Zoom Flume*
Zoom Flume Beach Camping ▲   Class III

Squeeze Play Rapid
Class III

Hemorrhoid Rock
Class III

Heckle Jeckle Camping ▲   *46*

Big Drop Rapid
Class III   ▲ Big Drop Rapid Camping
Mile 46.1 Camping ▲

Staircase Rapid
Class III

Widowmaker Rapid
Class III   *47*

Jump Rock Camping ▲

Raft Ripper Rapid
Class III
Graveyard (Boneyard) Rapid
Class II
Last Chance Rapid   *48*
Class II

N

▲ Hecla Junction River
Access and Takeout
Hecla Junction
Recreation Area
Camping

0   Kilometers   2

0   Miles   2

Great Pre- or Post-Adventure Spots

Boathouse Cantina. 228 North F St., Salida; (719) 539-5004; boathousesalida.com. The cantina adds a 1 percent donation to bills (you can opt out) to support Salida Mountain Trails and other local educational and outdoors organizations.

Eddyline Restaurant. 926 S Main St., Buena Vista; (719) 966-6000; eddylinerestaurant.com

Soulcraft Brewing Co. 248 W Rainbow Blvd., Salida; (719) 539-5428; soulcraftbeer.com

Moonlight Pizza & Brewpub. 242 F St., Salida; (719) 539-4277; moonlightpizza.biz

Flatwater 35 Fun at Chatfield Reservoir

Adventures at Chatfield State Park and Reservoir aren't necessarily like other adventures in this book. This is a family-friendly park with access to a large lake for swimming and other flatwater activities. Whether it's yoga on a paddleboard or racing on it, canoeing, or kayaking along the shores, you can't find a more gorgeous location close to Denver, abutting the Dakota Hogback and foothills for a plethora of recreational activities. For a fun day of canoeing, kayaking, or standup paddleboarding, you can make a complete loop around the lake.

Length: 8.6 miles

Paddling time: 5–6 hours

Other users: Swimmers, windsurfers, paddleboaters, standup paddleboarders, sailboarders, boaters, equestrians, hikers, campers, bikers, anglers, picnickers, hot air balloons, nature watchers. Winter uses include ice fishing, snowshoeing, ice skating, cross-country skiing, and ice-surfing.

Best seasons: Year-round

Schedule: 5 a.m.–10 p.m.

Fees: Daily and overnight fees, payable at gate; overnight access for anglers and boaters

Maps: USGS Littleton; National Geographic Trails Illustrated #135: Deckers, Rampart Range; Chatfield State Park trail use map

Craft: Canoes, kayaks, paddleboards, inflatable kayaks, rafts, drift boat dories

Waterway contact: Chatfield State Park, 11500 N Roxborough Park Rd., Littleton 80125; (303) 791-7275; cpw.state.co.us/placestogo/parks/Chatfield/Pages/default.aspx. For onsite rentals, check out Colorado Water Sports; (303) 697-7433; coloradowatersports.com.

Getting there: From the intersection of Wadsworth Boulevard (CO 121) and CO 470, head south on Wadsworth. In 1.1 miles turn left into the park at the traffic light; there is a sign for the park. After paying the entrance fee, follow the road through the entrance kiosk and turn right onto Perimeter Road. Turn left into the parking lot. There are restrooms at the beach; to the right there are equipment rentals for standup paddleboards, kayaks, pedalboats, and more. GPS: N39.54287° W105.08316°

Overview

Currently, Chatfield Lake is 1,500 acres, but since 2017 efforts have been under way to expand it, raising the level by 12 feet and expanding its surface area. At maximum levels, the lake can have a surface area of 4,822 acres. The lake is surrounded by 5,831-acre Chatfield State Park. Chatfield is a relatively new state park, inaugurated in 1975, although Euro-Americans first arrived in the area looking for gold in 1858. Isaac Chatfield, a Union Army lieutenant, bought land at the confluence of the South Platte River and Plum Creek in 1870, prior to Colorado's founding as a state. He farmed the land until 1879, leaving the legacy of his name. Chatfield Lake is formed from the confluence of the South Platte and Plum Creek as well as Deer Creek and others that feed into the area.

Over time the area kept flooding, causing damage in Denver. Significant floods occurred in 1933, 1935, and 1942. Perhaps the biggest was in 1965, when floodwaters wiped out homes, businesses, and bridges in Denver. After that flood, the decision was made by state and federal authorities to build Chatfield Dam as flood control. The US Army Corps of Engineers made quick work of the project, starting in 1967. Work on the recreational area began in 1973, and the park opened two years later, in 1975.

Today the park has numerous amenities, including 197 campsites with electricity, access to flush toilets, hot showers, and more. It also offers ADA-compliant access. The lake has wild areas and motorized boating areas, allowing for a wide variety of activities.

The Paddling

For the best views from a watercraft, head north and east from the swim beach. Follow the shoreline, allowing room for people fishing on the shore, and complete the circuit. Depending on the height of the lake at the time, your paddle might be longer or shorter. By going clockwise around the lake and heading east near the dam, you get fantastic views of the hogbacks and mountains to the west. It's also a fantastic opportunity to look for wildlife, such as some of the more than 200 bird species that call the park home, among them eagles, falcons, and blue herons.

At roughly 3.6 miles into the paddle, Plum Creek drains into the lake. If the level's high enough, you can paddle upstream for a ways and then return to the

Paddling on Chatfield Reservoir at sunset.

lake. If just doing the loop, at 4.6 miles you come to the Chatfield Marina, where motorized boats enter the lake. Be aware of them as you paddle through the area. Shortly after the marina, you'll pass the campgrounds as you head south, facing the Rockies.

At 6.7 miles there's another opportunity to paddle up the creek, literally. You can choose to paddle up the South Platte. Otherwise, continue south, facing the mountains. Follow the shoreline as it makes a U-turn and heads back to the swimming beach, completing the circuit in roughly 8.6 miles.

Adventure Information

Outfitters

Bentgate Mountaineering. 1313 Washington Ave., Golden; (303) 271-9382; bentgate.com. Open Sun–Fri; closed Sat.

Wilderness Exchange. 2401 15th St., Ste. 100, Denver; (303) 964-0708; wildernessx.com

REI Lakewood. 5375 S Wadsworth Blvd., Lakewood; (303) 932-0600; rei.com

Flatwater Fun at Chatfield Reservoir

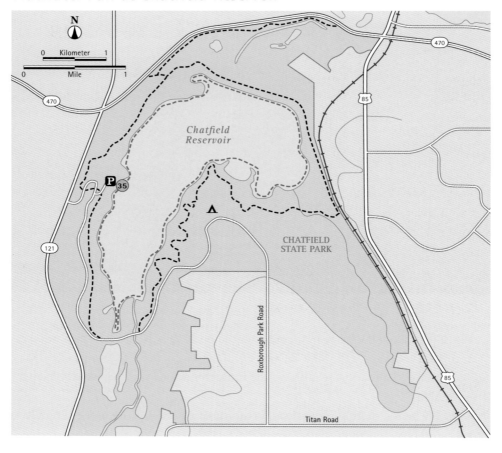

Great Pre- or Post-Adventure Spots

Green Mountain Beer Company. 2585 S Lewis Way, Lakewood; (303) 986-0201; green mountainbeercompany.com

Lariat Lodge Brewing Co. 12684 W Indore Place, Littleton; (303) 979-0797; lariatlodge brewing.com

The Flying Pig Burger Co. 5935 S Zang St., Littleton; (720) 726-4544; flyingpigburgerco .com

Appendix A: Adventure Clubs, Organizations, and Resources

Action Committee for Eldorado (ACE)
PO Box 337, Eldorado Springs 80225
(720) 785-3676
aceeldo.org

The AdAmAn Club
392 Cobblestone Dr., Colorado
Springs 80906
adaman.org

The American Alpine Club
710 10th St., Ste. 100, Golden 80401
(303) 384-0110
americanalpineclub.org

American Mountaineering Center
710 10th St., Ste. 200, Golden 80401
(303) 996-2760
americanmountaineeringcenter.org

American Whitewater
PO Box 1540, Cullowhee, NC 28723
(828) 586-1930

Colorado Fourteeners Initiative
710 10th St., Ste. 220, Golden 80401
(303) 278-7650
14ers.org

Colorado Mountain Club
710 10th St., Ste. 200, Golden 80401
(303) 279-3080
cmc.org

Colorado Search and Rescue Association (CSAR)
1312 17th St., #558, Denver CO
80202
(720) 507-6905
coloradosarboard.org

Colorado Trail Foundation
710 10th St., Ste. 210, Golden 80401
(303) 384-3729
coloradotrail.org

Colorado Whitewater
455 Sherman St., Ste. 300, Denver
80203
coloradowhitewater.org

Colorado Wildlife Federation
1410 Grant St., Ste. C-313, Denver
80203
(303) 987-0400, ext. 1
coloradowildlife.org

Conservation Colorado
1536 Wynkoop St., 5C, Denver 80202
(303) 333-7846
conservationco.org

Continental Divide Trail Coalition
710 10th St., Ste. 200, Golden 80401
(303) 996-2759
continentaldividetrail.org

Environment Colorado
1536 Wynkoop St., #400, Denver
80202
(303) 573-3871
environmentcolorado.org

Friends of Castlewood Canyon State Park
PO Box 403, Franktown 80116
(303) 688-5242
castlewoodfriends.org

Friends of Cheyenne Mountain State Park
410 JL Ranch Heights, Colorado
Springs 80926
friendsofcmsp.org

Friends of Colorado State Parks
PO Box 11623, Denver 80211
(303) 905-9880
friendsofcoloradostateparks.com

Friends of Larimer County Parks and Open Lands
1800 S CR 31, Loveland 80537
(970) 679-4570
larimer.org/friends

Friends of Mount Evans & Lost Creek Wilderness
PO Box 3431, Evergreen 80439
(303) 670-3853
fomelc.org

Friends of the Eagles Nest Wilderness
PO Box 4504, Frisco 80443
(970) 468-5400
fenw.org

High Country Conservation Advocates
PO Box 1066, Crested Butte 81224
(970) 349-7104
hccacb.org

Leave No Trace Center for Outdoor Ethics
PO Box 997, Boulder 80306
(303) 442-8222
lnt.org

The Nature Conservancy, Colorado Chapter
2424 Spruce St., Boulder 80302
(303) 444-2950
tnc.org

The Rocky Mountain Field Institute
815 S 25th St., #101, Colorado
Springs 80904
(719) 471-7736
rmfi.org

Rocky Mountain Wild
1536 Wynkoop St., Ste. 900, Denver
80202
(303) 546-0214
rockymountainwild.org

Salida Mountain Trails
PO Box 612, Salida, CO 81201
salidamountaintrails.org

Sierra Club, Rocky Mountain Chapter
1536 Wynkoop St., Ste. 200, Denver
80202
(303) 861-8819
rmc.sierraclub.org

Volunteers for Outdoor Colorado
600 S Marion Pkwy., Denver 80209
(303) 715-1010
voc.org

Appendix B: Further Reading

Arps, Louisa Ward, and Elinor Eppich Kingery. *High Country Names: Rocky Mountain National Park and the Indian Peaks.* Boulder, CO: Johnson Books, 1994.

Borneman, Marlene, and James Ells. *Rocky Mountain Wildflowers.* Golden, CO: The Colorado Mountain Club Press, 2018.

Buchholtz, C. W. *Rocky Mountain National Park: A History.* Niwot: University Press of Colorado, 1983.

Bueler, William. *Roof of the Rockies: A History of Colorado Mountaineering.* Golden, CO: The Colorado Mountain Club Press, 2000.

Capps, Kevin. *Climbing Clear Creek,* 3rd ed. Boulder, CO: Fixed Pin Press, 2020.

The Colorado Trail Foundation. *The Colorado Trail*, 9th ed. Golden, CO: The Colorado Mountain Club Press, 2017.

Gaug, Maryann, and Sandy Heise. *Hiking Colorado*, 4th ed. Guilford, CT: FalconGuides, 2016.

Gilliland, Mary Ellen. *Summit: A Gold Rush History of Summit County, Colorado.* Silverthorne, CO: Alpenrose Press, 2006.

Green, Stewart. *Best Climbs Denver and Boulder*, 2nd ed. Guilford, CT: FalconGuides, 2019.

Heise, Sandy, and Maryann Gaug. *Best Hikes Near Denver and Boulder*, 2nd ed. Guilford, CT: FalconGuides, 2017.

Hopkins, Ralph, and Lindy Birkel. *Hiking Colorado's Geology.* Seattle, WA: The Mountaineers, 2009.

Jacobs, Randy, and Robert Ormes. *Guide to the Colorado Mountains*, 10th ed. Golden, CO: The Colorado Mountain Club Press, 2003.

Kassar, Chris. *Best Wildflower Hikes Colorado.* Guilford, CT: FalconGuides, 2017.

Lichter, Justin. *Trail-Tested: A Thru-Hiker's Guide to Ultralight Hiking and Backpacking.* Guilford, CT: FalconGuides, 2013.

Meehan, Chris. *Climbing Colorado's Fourteeners: From the Easiest Hikes to the Hardest Climbs.* Guilford, CT: FalconGuides, 2016.

Roach, Gerry. *Colorado's Fourteeners: From Hikes to Climbs*, 3rd ed. Golden, CO: Fulcrum Publishing, 2011.

Robertson, Jan, Jay Fell, David Hite, Chris Case, and Walt Borneman. *100 Years Up High: Colorado Mountains and Mountaineers.* Golden, CO: The Colorado Mountain Club Press, 2011.

About the Author

Chris Meehan grew up in the shadows of the Appalachians, where he cultivated a love of the outdoors. Although he doesn't remember it, he must have heard Horace Greeley's clarion call floating on the wind a hundred years later and unwittingly responded to "Go west young man, and grow up with the country," as Colorado has become his home. He's an author of multiple FalconGuides, *Climbing Colorado's Fourteeners*, and a freelance writer who contributes to *Backpacker*, *Elevation Outdoors*, *Westword*, *5280*, and *Sun & Wind Energy* and has worked with *National Geographic*, among other national and international publications. A former mountain guide, he has taken children as young as 12 and people in their 70s to the top of Colorado's fourteeners. He enjoys sharing adventures with friends, young and old alike, is always hungry to get outdoors, and probably talks too much about what he has learned and is learning along the trail.